D1010541

the next republic

the next republic

the rise of a new radical majority

d. d. guttenplan

seven stories press
new york * london * oakland

A SEVEN STORIES PRESS FIRST EDITION

Seven Stories Press
140 Watts Street
New York, NY 10013
sevenstories.com

College professors and high school and middle school teachers may order free examination copies of Seven Stories Press titles. To order, visit www.sevenstories.com or send a fax on school letterhead to (212) 226-1411.

Library of Congress Cataloging in Publication Data has been applied for.

ISBN 978-1-60980-856-3 (hardcover)
ISBN 978-1-60980-857-0 (ebook)

Printed in the USA.

9 8 7 6 5 4 3 2 1

IN MEMORY OF MY PARENTS,
Jacqueline and Mitchell Guttenplan,
and in the hope that their grandchildren's generation
might find something useful in these pages

CONTENTS

INTRODUCTION

In Search of the Lost Republic

America our nation has been beaten by strangers who have turned our language inside out who have taken the clean words our fathers spoke and made them slimy and foul . . .

America our nation has been beaten by strangers who have bought the laws and fenced off the meadows and cut down the woods for pulp and turned our pleasant cities into slums and sweated the wealth out of our people.

—John Dos Passos, *The Big Money*

As he was leaving Independence Hall one morning in 1789, Benjamin Franklin was accosted by a Philadelphia woman wanting to know what kind of government he and his fellow delegates had devised. The deliberations of the Constitutional Convention had been held in secret, and all kinds of wild rumors were beginning to circulate. "Well, Doctor, what have we got," Elizabeth Powel is said to have demanded, "a republic or a monarchy?" Franklin's reply was brisk: "A republic, Madam—if you can keep it." From its earliest days, the survival of our republic has always been in doubt.

Can we keep it? For many of us that uncertainty became painfully salient on the morning of November 9, 2016. I'd spent the previous fifteen months covering the election for the *Nation*, beginning with the Republican National Committee summer meeting in Cleveland in August 2015, where Sean Spicer boasted to me about how much the party had spent recruiting and training volunteers—and where, after the first Republican debate, I'd written that Donald Trump's "unpredictability—his manifest inability to respect the norms of party, civility, or any institution or structure not bearing the Trump name, preferably in gilded letters—makes him the campaign equivalent of crack cocaine." Though I didn't think any of the other occupants of the Republican clown car could beat Trump, I assumed the RNC would find some other way to stop him.

Over the months that followed I attended Trump rallies in half a dozen states, from Florida to New Hampshire—where I spent the last night of the campaign at a Trump rally in Manchester—yet I was as surprised as anyone else on election night. How could a country that twice sent Barack Obama to the White House do such a thing?

There are plenty of other books that try to answer that question. This one is doing something else. Because while I'd been watching Donald Trump out of the corner of my eye, fascinated by the reinvention of a man whose first brush with bankruptcy I'd covered as a writer at the *Village Voice* and *New York Newsday* in the 1980s, my main focus was elsewhere. Assuming that the campaign would be boring, I'd told my editors I wanted to concentrate not on the candidates, but on the voters, volunteers, activists, and movements that make up the political ground on which elections are fought. I was wrong about the campaign, which turned out to be anything but boring. But I was right in thinking that there was a deeper story to be found far from the lights and the cameras.

Our politics was broken. Walt Whitman had the good fortune to hear America singing. I heard a country screaming—at itself, at shadows, at enemies domestic and foreign. "Lock Her Up!" "Build the Wall!" But I also heard something else, a quieter sound underneath all the shouting, a collective gasp of recognition and amazement. I'd heard it most clearly in a high school gym back in February 2016—on the night Bernie Sanders won the New Hampshire primary. Sanders himself was elated, reminding his supporters that when he'd begun campaigning "we had no campaign organization and we had no money. And we were taking on the most powerful political organization in the United States of America."

Only it wasn't Sanders I was listening to. It was the audience—a mix of old radicals and young activists, tie-dyed grandmothers from California and the Carolinas celebrating with thick-waisted older men in union windbreakers and college students in blue "Feel the Bern" T-shirts. Could Bernie go all the way? That magical night, with Nevada and Michigan still ahead of us, anything seemed possible. But what I remember even more vividly than that moment of wild hope was the sensation of looking across the packed gym and being astonished at how many of us there were—and realizing that everyone else was just as surprised. (Though it being New Hampshire, and a Sanders rally, the crowd was overwhelmingly white.)

For decades the media had been relentlessly reminding us just how far outside the mainstream we were. In a country where Ronald Reagan and Lee Atwater made "liberal" a badge of dishonor, a label to be shunned, where did that leave those of us further left? Since the fall of the Berlin Wall nobody bothered calling us "communists" anymore, but to call yourself a socialist, as Sanders had done, was an invitation to derision. We'd watched in dismay as the bankers deregulated by Bill Clinton crashed the economy—only to be bailed out by Barack Obama, while millions of ordinary Americans lost their homes and their savings. We'd seen George W. Bush's National Security Agency spy on millions of Americans—and Barack Obama's Justice Department try to lock up the whistleblowers. We'd witnessed the War on Terror give way to the war against Iraq, and heard the cries to bomb Damascus and Tehran. So when Bernie stood up and said "Enough is enough," we were ready to stand with him.

But we weren't prepared for what happened next. Grown used to our own marginality, we weren't prepared to discover that there were literally millions of us, in every state and every region of the country. It must be said that Bernie wasn't prepared either. A campaign that began somewhere between a quixotic gesture and a protest movement came close enough to winning the nomination to scare the hell out of the Democratic Party establishment—which hadn't exactly kept its thumbs off the scale during the primaries. Socialism is no longer toxic—indeed, polls show that, among younger Americans, most think it sounds like a pretty good idea.

And yet here we are, with Donald Trump in the White House, Republicans in control of both houses of Congress, and Neil Gorsuch on the Supreme Court. Beyond the immediate damage to the economy, Trump's tax cut gives Republicans a rationale for shrinking an already overburdened state even further—the moment the Democrats return to power. The Italian philosopher Antonio Gramsci warned that while the old order "is dying and the new cannot be born . . . a great variety of morbid symptoms appear." The headlines—and Trump's Twitter account—provide new examples on a daily basis. Yet there are also many signs of rebirth. And not a moment too soon.

For all Trump's noisy—and contradictory—promises of action on gun control and immigration reform and health care, that blank check to the party's big donors may be the Republicans' sole legislative achievement. But his administration's rollback of federal regulations protecting consumers, the environment, and American workers is likely to be equally damaging, while his quiet reshaping of the federal judiciary in favor of economic privilege and social reaction may last for decades to come. With Trump and Mike Pence in the White House, and a conservative majority on the court, decisions that once seemed like settled law—gay marriage, legal abortion, the right to join a union, indeed, the very right to citizenship itself for all born inside this country—may now come under attack. These are all fights we cannot afford to lose. Nor can we allow ourselves to spend the next two years solely on defense, devoting all our efforts to maintaining a status quo that—Hillary Clinton's blithe assurances to the contrary—already wasn't working for most Americans.

And so, despite the temptation to mourn, we have to organize. Because if we can't rely on the president, or the Congress, or the courts, we have no choice but to rely on one another. Not just for comfort, but for survival—and resistance. There are some in immediate peril, who need our help, our energy, and our solidarity. There are others—many, many others—who are already fighting, but who may not see how their battle fits into a bigger picture.

Which is where this book comes in. Not as a prescription or exhortation. And not, I trust, as mere wishful thinking. Ever since Election Day, I've tried to adopt "no more wishful thinking" as my own political mantra. All the same, in my reporting on where the energy and purpose and genuinely radical ambition revealed by the Sanders campaign might be going, I've found ample grounds not just for hope, but for optimism. The United States may be a continental power, and a global empire, but it is not an island, isolated from the currents of world politics. You don't have to be a historical determinist, or an orthodox Marxist—I am neither—to see a surge of majoritarian revolt spreading across the globe from the "pink tide" in Latin America to the democratic ferment that sparked the Arab Spring to the rise of Syriza in Greece and Podemos in Spain.

Not all of these challenges to power will succeed. The Arab Spring liberated Tunisia and electrified the Middle East, but its brief flowering in Egypt provoked a brutal reaction, as did the challenge to Bashir Al-Assad's regime in Syria, while even the tentative shoots it put forth in the Gulf states were quickly suppressed. Nor is it only medieval theocracies that cling to power. The European Union's refusal to allow Greece to depart from the cruel austerity demanded by the continent's central bankers and private bondholders may have involved fewer troops, but neoliberalism showed itself just as willing to impose misery and submission as any dictatorship. It is still too early to say how far Jeremy Corbyn's challenge to the British version of austerity will take the Labour Party. His Momentum supporters, however, have given this global phenomenon what may be its simplest expression in their slogan "For the many, not the few."

In trying to map out how we in the US might, as they say in New England, "get there from here," I've been guided by two principles. The first is to stay close to the grass roots. The movements for social, racial, economic, and environmental justice in the United States have produced some genuinely prophetic voices: not just Bernie Sanders, but Naomi Klein, the Reverend William Barber, Elizabeth Warren, Bill McKibben and May Boeve, Michelle Alexander. Their vision informs many of the people profiled in these pages, but I wanted to introduce readers to people whose names are still unfamiliar, but whose work is every bit as important.

The other principle is that history is essential—not just the first draft of history provided by journalism, but the awareness of possibility, indeed precedent, that only history can provide. I wanted to break through the imposed collective amnesia that lets Americans forget what we have accomplished together in the past—the audacity that let a colony defy the most powerful nation on earth, the courage and solidarity that defeated racial slavery, the democratic confidence that took on fascism in Europe and began the work of building economic security at home. As you will discover, each of these earlier achievements—these lost republics—was only partially successful. If we are to complete the work, or even to advance it, we need to remind ourselves both of what we once accomplished—and of the reasons why previous efforts fell short.

The word "republic" itself has a long and complicated political history. Its roots are Latin, from *res publica*—"public thing, or matter"—and it is perhaps best rendered into English simply as "commonwealth." But it is also the name of Plato's most famous work—the original Greek title, Πολιτεία, from the word Πολις, or "city-state," can be translated variously as "polity" or "the state" or "citizenship—purporting to describe the ideal state, and deeply critical of Athenian democracy. Elitist and democratic strains of republicanism have coexisted uneasily ever since. Franklin and the other Founding Fathers derived their understanding of the term partly from English history: a republic was what you got when you dispensed with the king. But as educated men of their times they'd also read Gibbon's *History of the Decline and Fall of the Roman Empire*, and were acutely aware of the fragility of republican governments, their susceptibility to corruption and decay—especially when faced with the temptations of empire.

As Eric Foner points out, it was Tom Paine's *Common Sense* that "transformed the terms of political debate," giving the word its currency as an American virtue. So in using "republic" to mean a time when Americans felt not only that their government was legitimately elected, but that it genuinely belonged to them, reflecting their interests and responding to their aspirations, rather than being the tool or mechanism by which a particular class or section exercises power, I am not so much adding my own gloss as selecting among the many uses. Besides, I see little need, or prospect, of improving upon Abraham Lincoln (a small as well as capital-R republican) when he spoke simply of "government of the people, by the people, for the people."

Like socialism, that still sounds like a good idea to me. But in the pages that follow, discerning readers will detect sympathy for another ideal, almost equally discredited, namely populism. By which I mean both the historical American movements that comprised the nineteenth-century Populist revolt, and a contemporary sympathy for movements that are frankly majoritarian, trusting in democracy rather than the discovery of correct doctrine. To an extent this may be a matter of temperament. Though I was often frightened and appalled by the things I saw and heard at Trump rallies, Hillary Clinton's description of his voters as a "basket of deplorables"—and her media cheerleaders' eagerness to double down on that contempt—still strikes me as both personally despicable and politically dangerous. Whatever else it is, populism has always represented a political and cultural revolt of the people against the elites—and in that fight I know which side I'm on.

There is a serious strategic point to be made here as well. While the Right might prefer aristocracy, or a plutocracy in which the business of America really is business, we on the left can't just dismiss the people—no matter how much they may disappoint us. Petulance is not politics. There is simply no alternative—no shortcut, as Jane McAlevey says—to the hard work of assembling a majority coalition. To attempt anything else, says McAlevey, would be to "surrender the most important and only weapon that ordinary people have ever had, which is large numbers."

In the pages that follow you'll meet the components of that coalition, starting with McAlevey herself and the work she has been doing in winning strikes and organizing unions under the most difficult conditions. Labor of course is an essential part of any radical majority. But then so are the rural organizing and environmental politics represented by Jane Kleeb in Nebraska, the big city movement politics and immigrant organizing at the center of Carlos Ramirez Rosa's work in Chicago, the fight over the future of the Democratic Party being waged by Waleed Shahid and Corbin Trent (and Jane Kleeb), the struggle for economic independence and radical racial justice behind Chokwe Antar Lumumba's administration in Jackson, Mississippi, and the critique of corporate power (and the danger it represents to our democracy) articulated so powerfully by Zephyr Teachout.

As the historical chapters remind us, excluding or ignoring any one of these fights has been a recipe for failure in the past. (To take just one example, Franklin Roosevelt's New Deal coalition collapsed in part because of its reliance on Southern Democrats committed to maintaining white supremacy.) We are at a crossroads. Though nearly three million more Americans voted for Hillary Clinton than for Donald Trump, many of us did so despite believing that American politics was broken, and with no real enthusiasm for the "four more years" her campaign seemed to offer. Being against Donald Trump wasn't enough to win the election, and though it happily was sufficient motivation to drive millions of women—and their male allies—onto the streets to protest his inauguration, mere opposition won't bring us to the next republic either.

Opposition remains crucial. As Jim Hightower, the ten-gallon-hatted godfather of Texas populism (and chair of that state's chapter of Our Revolution), told me, "It's not enough to be for the farmer. You gotta be against these bastards who are trying to run over the farmer!"[2] But as Naomi Klein points out, "No is not enough. We also need to lay out our Yes." Because it is the sum of those yesses, marching together, working together, striking together and voting together, that will bring us—together—to the next republic. Welcome to the fight.

CHAPTER ONE

Jane McAlevey—Winning Under Conditions of Extreme Adversity

There once was a union maid, she never was afraid
Of goons and ginks and company finks and the deputy sheriffs who made the raid.
—"Union Maid" by Woody Guthrie

My notes from that evening don't say whether labor organizer and author Jane McAlevey actually used the phrase "Not so fast!" But the whole tenor of her argument was one of skepticism, and caution, as she pulled apart what she called "the myth of demography as destiny." It is July 2016—the week of the Democratic Convention—and we are sitting in a Mexican restaurant in Center City Philadelphia eating *nopales* and arguing. Buoyed by the ecstatic reception given to Bernie Sanders's prime-time speech earlier in the week—and, no doubt, by the margaritas we'd ordered—I'm waxing optimistic about Hillary Clinton's upcoming victory in November. With the Democratic Party platform essentially drafted by the Sanders campaign, and with Clinton herself now able to turn her formidable organization toward an all-out fight with Donald Trump, and given the Democrats' widening demographic advantage among the Rising American Electorate of women, millennials, and people of color, surely progressives can stop worrying about the election, and start focusing on how best to push the next Clinton administration to the left?

"She hasn't sealed the deal," says McAlevey. Sure, Clinton had finally come out against the Trans-Pacific Partnership—a huge issue for labor, and therefore a big deal for McAlevey, a veteran union organizer. Though Clinton had been endorsed by labor leaders—not just the national AFL-CIO, but everyone from Steelworkers and Teamsters to the American Federation of Teachers—McAlevey wasn't convinced rank-and-file union members really bought her change of heart. And when it came to the suburban women the Democrats were clearly targeting during the convention—and who were supposed to be sufficiently repelled by both the tone and the substance of the Republican campaign to make their overwhelming support for Clinton in November merely a matter of getting out the vote—McAlevey was emphatic. "I've been in the state for months working for PASNAP [the Pennsylvania Association of Staff Nurses and Allied Professionals, an independent union representing hospital workers], which means I spend a lot of my time listening to women, and talking politics, and she hasn't sealed the deal with suburban women. I don't think she's going to win Pennsylvania." For a reporter on the campaign trail, those last few months of the 2016 election were like watching a train wreck. Even though it all seemed to be happening in slow motion, there was nothing I could do about it. But unlike a lot of other horrified bystanders, I couldn't say I hadn't been warned.

Spend any time with McAlevey and you will hear a lot about winning. "Those of us who still win hard strikes . . ." Explaining why Democrats were wrong to take the Rust Belt for granted: "In Wisconsin, we couldn't win over the union households we needed to get rid of the worst antiunion governor in modern times. In Michigan, the unions put [a measure on the ballot] to enshrine collective bargaining in the Michigan Constitution. In the heartland of the United Auto Workers, we couldn't win over most union households to vote for collective bargaining." Or why she thinks Ralph Nader–

style consumer advocacy, however well intentioned, is a futile tactic: "Because it can't win any serious fight. It can only win small gains."

McAlevey has been in one serious fight after another for the past three decades. Her first arrest, at age nineteen, came during a campaign, ultimately successful, to force the State University of New York to divest its financial interests in South Africa. A few dozen arrests later she's led strikes by janitors in Stamford, Connecticut; built houses and schools in Nicaragua; fought for environmental justice in Central America; run a project on the dangers of toxic pollution in poor rural communities in the United States; organized thousands of hospital workers in Nevada—and been pushed out of the Service Employees International Union over her candid criticism of union leaders' cozy relationship with corporate bosses. *Raising Expectations and Raising Hell*, her unsparing account of her success in winning strikes and securing contracts—and her defeat by the union hierarchy—has become an underground bible for a new generation of labor activists. When we met in Philadelphia she was in the middle of a campaign to organize nurses at seven area hospitals—and had just won a series of crucial votes, adding thousands of members at a time when labor unions were supposed to be in terminal decline.

▫ ▫ ▫

"Winning matters a lot to me. *A lot.* It comes from the old man. My father's attitude was you don't run a left campaign against the Democratic Party just to run it, you fuckin' run it to win." A decorated fighter pilot in World War II, John Francis McAlevey was born in Brooklyn to a family with deep union roots. "My father's father was in the boilermaker's union. My uncle, Dan McVarish, was the head of the Brooklyn building trades." Returning home after the war McAlevey's father finished his degree at Manhattan College and then, thanks to the GI Bill, enrolled at Columbia Law School. But his was not a conventional corporate career.

"My father came home from the war a pacifist. He and my mother were both involved with Dorothy Day and the *Catholic Worker.*" Though today she is little known outside Catholic circles, Day's journey from hard-boiled reporter to Greenwich Village bohemian to missionary to America's forgotten men and women once inspired a generation. At the height of the Great Depression—long before Oscar Romero, liberation theology, or the notion of a "preferential option for the poor"—Day and her collaborator, Peter Maurin, forged a synthesis of radical politics and Catholic social teaching, founding the newspaper *Catholic Worker* and a string of "houses of hospitality" whose inhabitants continue to live among, and minister to, the poor in 216 communities across the United States and in 33 overseas locations from Argentina to Uganda.

John McAlevey was going to be a civil rights lawyer. "He and my mother were living in Shanks Village"—a former army camp in Rockland County that had been turned into low-income housing for veterans and their families. Rent was thirty-two dollars a month. As the youngest of seven, Jane McAlevey is a little hazy on some of the details. "I grew up without a television. By the time I came along my father had a good narrative about it, which was that TVs were just idiot boxes. Much later my older siblings told me he'd made that up to not feel badly that we couldn't afford to replace the only TV that we had—that broke before I was born."

Jane McAlevey was born in Sloatsburg, where her parents had bought a tumbledown farmhouse and some land—and her father had become "an accidental politician. He was new to the area, and the local Democratic Party probably thought, 'He has the right profile: World War II vet, fighter pilot, bunch of kids.' My mom had been in the WAVES [Women's Naval Reserve]. So they asked him if they could put his name on the ballot for village mayor. No Democrat had won for a hundred years. But it was the Kennedy sweep and he won." After two terms, he ran for supervisor of the Town of Ramapo, a commuter town on the west side of the Hudson River just north of the New Jersey state line. The campaign bumper sticker shows little Jane, blonde and barefoot, in her father's arms next to the slogan "Ramapo: A Nice Place to Live."[3]

"I was basically a prop for my father's campaigns," she says. "We had a very complicated family relationship, but he was an amazing political mentor." During his four terms as supervisor, John McAlevey built parks, public swimming pools, and a municipal golf course; established the Ramapo Housing Authority to build public housing for elderly and low-income tenants; instituted a development easement program to preserve open space on privately owned land; and pioneered the first "controlled growth" law, requiring developers to provide schools, sanitation, utilities, and other infrastructure before building—rather than expecting the town to pick up the cost of growth. The town's approach was upheld by the New York State Supreme Court in a 1972 decision, *Ramapo v. Golden*,[4] that is still considered a landmark in planning law.

Her father's positions were not always popular. "I got called names at school. But the idea that you can build public housing and invite black people into the suburbs, and that developers had to pay, were cornerstones of my youth, and they've never gone away." She has nothing but fond memories, however, from another of her father's causes.

"I grew up on picket lines. In '68 and '69 black workers walked out at the Ford plant in Mahwah [New Jersey]. The factory was just over the border from us, and a lot of the workers lived in our town. My father famously said he'd put any of the striking workers who lived in Ramapo on the town payroll so they could get health care and hold out."

But if McAlevey credits her father for her obsession with winning, memories of her mother are all about loss. "Actually I only have one memory of my mother. She's sitting in a big leather chair in our old farmhouse kitchen. I didn't understand any of it, I mean, she was already dying. But there was a huge black La-Z-Boy moved into the kitchen because she couldn't really walk around very much. I was like two and a half or three years old. She was sitting in it and I jumped on the arm, fell off, and screamed. I split my tongue in half. I don't remember the whole moment, but I remember that I got lots of popsicles. My big brothers, many of them, all wanted the grape ones—that was the best flavor. And I remember her yelling I got the grape popsicles. That's literally the only memory I have of my mother."

During World War II Hazel Hansen McAlevey had been a Link Trainer instructor, teaching instrument flying at Corpus Christie Naval Air Station in Texas. Born in the Swedish-speaking part of Finland, she was, according to her obituary, "fluent in Swedish and a perfectionist in English."[5] Though Hazel McAlevey didn't actually die until shortly after Jane's fifth birthday, she disappeared from her daughter's life much earlier. "She functionally left home when I was three. The idea was that babies—toddlers—shouldn't see a dying person. So she got taken away to slowly die of cancer."

McAlevey says she was raised by her siblings, with a little help from "*Moster* [the Swedish word for "aunt"] Hannah and *Moster* Lottie," her mother's sisters, "who pretty much only spoke Swedish. When I was a little girl, they would give me *crème de menthe* in Brooklyn.

"I was out in the woods all the time. I was a super-serious tom-girl with a bunch of boys who were teaching me how to be a tom-girl and my sister Catherine was sort of raising us. She did her best. She was twelve when my mom died."

Emotionally "my father was just . . . completely absent." Unable to talk to his daughter about her mother's death, he gave her a pony instead. "Yeah. I got a pony to distract me from my mother dying. Who had a Shetland pony when they were three years old?" Afterward "my father married several times trying to find someone who would take care of all these kids"; his third and final wife, a second-grade teacher, "was an activist in the teacher's union. They were endorsing my father." By the time McAlevey left home at sixteen she'd acquired two Jewish stepbrothers, and an impressive command of Yiddish curses.

"I wound up going to SUNY Buffalo, because I could afford it. I waited tables and worked as a maid, and then every holiday and vacation I went to my sister Bri [Birgitta]. She lived in something called the Harlem River Women's Collective, a mostly black radical lesbian collective that my blonde sister found herself in. It was a crazy-great house of women who taught me amazing things about race and gender."

Meanwhile, back at school, the newly elected governor, Mario Cuomo, had just proposed a whopping tuition increase. As McAlevey tells it, "I organized a bus to go to Albany to protest, and then I became student body president and then I dropped out of school. We ran a radical left slate against the jocks—the athletes—and the Greeks [fraternities and sororities]. I told them, 'You have to run a whole slate,' because that's what the old man always did. We had a campaign plan, we worked the student buses between the campuses. We door-knocked every dorm like three times. We swept every office."

Besides stopping the tuition increase, McAlevey and her friends protested against Ronald Reagan's Star Wars program, instituted a radical lecture series, sent money to aid the Sandinistas in Nicaragua, and campaigned hard for divestment. After a year she became president of the Student Association of the State University, which gave her a seat on the SUNY board of trustees. "I went to the trustees meeting in Albany. I wore this very bulky outfit and I had chains and padlocks [under my clothes] and a swipe card for the back door. After they voted against divestment, I said I was going to the bathroom, slowly clinking out of the room, and I went downstairs, and opened up a back door and let all the students in." The students then barricaded themselves in the university finance office. Arrested and convicted of criminal trespass, McAlevey was offered the chance to pay a fine if she'd promise not to demonstrate for a year. She refused, and served ten days in Albany County jail, where she was subject to daily body cavity searches.[6] "It was an organizing tool, so we made it as big as we could make it, and by the time I got out of jail" the trustees voted to divest. "It was the largest single anti-apartheid divestiture in the US up till that time, and we won. Winning mattered—not winning like a Stalinist, but winning to teach people: Can we have the confidence to win?"

▫ ▫ ▫

Instead of finishing her degree, McAlevey went to Central America, first to Guatemala to learn Spanish, then on a construction brigade in Nicaragua, and then doing "Witness for Peace work"—shadowing local activists to deter violence, "which was terrifying"—with Architects and Planners in Support of Nicaragua. Eventually she realized her place, and her work, was back in the US. "I came home, broke." The search for a truly useful skill took her to northern Vermont, where she spent nine months working on an organic farm.

And then one day she got a phone call. "It was Josh Karliner, who at the time was the founder of something called the Environmental Project on Central America, EPOCA, part of the Earth Island Institute, which had been started by David Brower, who'd been at the Sierra Club and founded Friends of the Earth. He said, 'We understand you speak Spanish, you've lived in Latin America and you're familiar with integrated pest management organic farming and you know how to organize?' So I moved to San Francisco and began to work for the environmental movement full-time. That was my first paid job."

She enjoyed the work. And felt useful. "I was traveling in Latin America a lot. And I was learning a lot. Josh left, so I had to learn how to talk to donors. We got into the nexus of war and trade and military policy and the environment. But I really thought that the people I was working with were middle-class and white—they were the best of the global environmental movement at the time, but that is what they were—and I found it very stifling. Even though by actual measures—because I believe in actual measures—we were doing good stuff."

In 1988, EPOCA held a conference in Managua on international development and the environment. "EPOCA suggested to David Brower that we should have a delegation of poor people from the United States who are fighting toxic contamination. We should bring a delegation from the United States to explain to the rest of the quote-unquote Third World that we have a Third World, that we have a South in the North, right here."

Which is how she found herself working at the Highlander Center, the legendary training school and cultural center founded by Myles Horton in Monteagle, Tennessee, in 1932. It was Horton's wife, Zilphia, the center's musical director, who'd adapted the civil rights anthem "We Shall Overcome" from a gospel hymn sung by striking tobacco workers—and then taught it to Pete Seeger. A generation later young civil rights activists—Martin Luther King Jr., Rosa Parks, Ralph Abernathy, John Lewis, Ella Baker, and most of the leadership of the Student Nonviolent Coordinating Committee that attended Septima Clark's workshops at Highlander—picked up the tune.

"Myles Horton had just died, and John Gaventa was the head. Highlander sent down a delegation of poor whites and African Americans to our conference, and just before we left [Nicaragua] Gaventa said to me, 'So you're gonna move to Tennessee? You're gonna start a program on globalization at Highlander and teach southern factory workers that it isn't Mexicans stealing their jobs, it's corporations.'

"I said, 'You're smoking crack.' And within a year I was in the hills of Tennessee. He won. When I got there they didn't have any place to put me, so they created an office for me in the library." Which also housed the Highlander archives, kept in a sealed, climate-controlled room—the only respite from the searing summer heat. Where, gradually, McAlevey discovered that this place she knew only through its role in the civil rights movement actually had its origin in the labor struggles of the 1930s.

"White liberals obsess about the civil rights movement in ways that irritate me. Ask them about labor or unions and they talk about corruption, self-dealing . . . I hate the way we reify the civil rights movement and trash the labor movement as nothing but a bunch of corrupt thugs." In the archives, McAlevey saw the famous photograph of Rosa Parks at Highlander in the summer of 1955, taken just a few months before Parks refused to give up her seat on a Montgomery, Alabama, city bus. But she also found labor education material from the 1930s and '40s, when Highlander had been the official labor education school for the new Congress of Industrial Organizations (CIO).

"In the Highlander workshops that were going on in the '30s and '40s they were dealing with the same issues" McAlevey found herself facing half a century later: the splintering effect of racism on organizing, a deeply hostile political environment, and the need to connect labor to broader struggles beyond the shop floor. "You had a labor movement, built by socialists and communists, that helped give birth to the civil rights movement. One movement helped give birth to the other." Looking for a way to escape the heat, McAlevey stumbled upon "the through line for the two movements." In the CIO handbooks from the 1930s she also found a way of working—and looking at the world—that was very different from the community organizing model, derived from the writings of Saul Alinsky, that had come to dominate not just the American labor movement but the whole of the American Left.

Alinsky's *Rules for Radicals* (1971) has been required reading for progressives for decades, influencing everyone from Hillary Clinton (who in her Wellesley senior thesis wrote approvingly of Alinsky's view that "radical goals have to be achieved often by non-radical, even 'anti-radical' means")[7] and Barack Obama (who worked as an organizer on the South Side of Chicago, not far from Alinsky's "Back of the Yards" neighborhood) to groups ranging from ACORN and the United Farmworkers to the Tea Party.

In her second book, *No Shortcuts: Organizing for Power in the New Gilded Age*, McAlevey argues that far from providing a useful blueprint, Alinsky's ideas and influence have been an obstacle to change. Though Alinsky did work briefly for the CIO, his focus on local issues and winnable fights—and his determined exclusion of any larger ideology—represented a profound break from the labor organization, many of whose most gifted organizers were committed Communists and Socialists. But what really offends McAlevey, even more than Alinsky's repeated insistence that organizing was a man's job, is the rationale he provided for removing agency and accountability from the organizations he inspired.[8]

"Unlike the left-wing organizers in the CIO," she writes, Alinsky "wanted to defend and protect capitalism." To his funders, Alinsky vowed "to beat the Communists at their own game."[9] Partly by deliberately not connecting his organizing with any larger structural issues. Partly by fostering an elite corps of so-called outside organizers who, like the young Barack Obama, were typically parachuted into communities where they had no organic ties or prior loyalties. But whose role in guiding—or manipulating—the membership was concealed behind a rhetoric of humility, in which the organizer exists merely to do the bidding of "leaders"—indigenous activists who "make all the decisions." In reality, as McAlevey points out, "the organizers in the Alinsky model make a lot of key decisions."[10]

Her relentless deflation of the "hero organizer" has made McAlevey a lot of enemies. As has her trenchant critique of the "corporate campaign," in which, rather than organizing the workers, unions focus their efforts on mobilizing public opinion to inflict damage on a corporate brand, or a company's share price. Her argument that the Fight for $15 campaign to raise the minimum wage, while "a totally worthwhile and noble effort," ultimately "makes workers symbolic actors in their own liberation" is viewed as heretical by many on the left.

McAlevey doesn't care. She isn't interested in accolades. She's interested in winning. "If you want to win, you have to be able to create a significant crisis for the employer. A strike where one worker at a fast food outlet stands outside for the press conference, surrounded by every liberal clergy member in town and a bunch of great activists, is not a strike. It's what I call pretend power. Pretend power—and fooling ourselves with pretend-power gimmicks—has resulted in thirty-seven state houses flipping red and Trump in the White House."

▪ ▪ ▪

What does real power look like? It starts with wall charts. Although she never finished college, McAlevey recently completed a PhD at the City University of New York and was awarded a postdoctoral fellowship by Harvard Law School. She can talk theory when she has to. But she'd much rather show you her methods.

"The charts are about half the size of a big window—they're big! I was trained at 1199 New England in big wall charting. You could talk to ninety-eight percent of the organizers in the so-called labor movement in the United States and they don't know what a big wall chart is. Talk about a skill gap . . . Because all of us who *are* doing it are still winning.

"They start out blank—the workers have to fill them in with the names of everyone in the workplace. When I was working in Philadelphia, on the second day, the young organizers raise their hands. They go, 'You know Jane, hey, since you were in grad school'—like that was the way they could say it—'we have really sophisticated databases we can just print out.' I just looked at them. 'That's so charming. Do you think we didn't have databases in 2008 in Nevada? This is how you're gonna teach the workers how to build a structure. Not build a structure yourself, in your fucking database.' So that's wall charting. I'm obsessed with wall charting."

In Nevada, a state whose right-to-work law makes organizing extremely difficult, McAlevey took a moribund SEIU local from 25 percent dues paying membership to 75 percent—and went on to lead successful strikes resulting in some of the best hospital contracts in the country. Before that, in Stamford, she'd led a combined campaign that organized 4,500 workers, including Haitian taxi drivers, Jamaican health care workers, and Latin American janitors[II]—gaining not only improved pay and conditions, but enough political power to force one of the wealthiest enclaves in the country to cancel the planned demolition of four public housing complexes, instead committing to $15 million worth of improvements, along with a new "inclusionary zoning ordinance." Because although she gets hired by unions, McAlevey's method is fundamentally political, with applications that go far beyond the shop floor or the hospital ward.

So when McAlevey said they needed wall charts, the organizers got wall charts. On the first page, she writes down what she calls "the five core concepts" that underpin all her work:

1. Structure versus Self-Selecting
2. Leaders versus Activists
3. Majorities (of workers) versus Minorities
4. Whole Worker versus Community-Labor Alliances
5. Organizing versus Mobilizing

McAlevey uses the word "structure" a lot—even more than she talks about winning. In this case it means any preexisting institution where people congregate. "Marx said the workplace because he had this theory of class struggle, which is right, but I'm arguing that class struggle plays out in more than just the workplace." Here, too, the influence of the Highlander archives comes through: "From the 1930s to the mid-1960s, we had movements focused on ordinary people in two core structures: the black church and the workplace. Then we shifted to a model where we just talked to ourselves all the time"—the single-issue activism that McAlevey refers to as "self-selecting."

"It's people who are already with us. They already agree that Wall Street's a problem. They already think climate change is a problem.

They already think racism is a problem. They're already standing with Black Lives Matter. It was like an inverse relationship. At the same time progressive movements turned insular, moved to Washington and thought all we had to do was implement a bunch of laws—Medicare, Medicaid, Social Security, the Voting Rights Act, the Clean Air Act—the right wing says, 'Jesus, we have to go build a base,' and literally 'Jesus' because they go out and start building that evangelical conservative base, the National Rifle Association, the Christian Coalition, the Moral Majority, Phyllis Schlafly's Eagle Forum."

McAlevey tells her organizers "we have to spend most of our time talking with—not at, or to—the people who aren't talking to us. That's what separates organizing from activism—or Trotskyism." Where can those people be found? In churches, mosques, or synagogues—but also at PTA meetings, soccer matches, tenants' committees, bowling leagues. "Having a defined structure allows you to assess constantly whether you're building majorities or not. A self-selecting movement where you put up a Facebook post that says, 'Come to the meeting if you want to stop the pipeline'"—everyone who shows up wants to stop the pipeline, so what are you measuring against?

Because the people who respond most enthusiastically to a union—or to any potentially risky political campaign—are "activists." And however wonderful or energetic or enlightened they may be, they are seldom numerous or influential enough to amount to a majority. "In most of the community organizing world now, if someone comes to a meeting twice, you put them on a leadership development track. That's such a ridiculous threshold if you're trying to build to a strike. All you're doing is testing their commitment to the organization."

The only way to build and hold together an effective majority, says McAlevey, is by recognizing that workers already have leaders—and already know who those leaders are. "It's the guy on the assembly line that makes the whole shift hum. Or the nurse who holds the emergency room together. People say to me, 'Do the workers know?' That's how I can tell someone hasn't ever done real organizing. Of course they know!" But if identifying organic leaders is easy, recruiting them—persuading them to stick their necks out—is the organizer's core skill.

Such people, says McAlevey, are seldom found among the activists. "They're always the best workers. So they get what they want. That's why they think they don't need a union. The boss ain't gonna let them go. In a hospital, the doctors and nurses love them. In an auto plant, the line manager loves them. Because they get shit done! You have to find out what are the one, two, or three things they can't get individually from the boss. That they can only get through collective action in the power of a union contract." Which means a lot of awkward, face-to-face conversations. "One of the axioms of good organizing is that every successful organizing conversation makes *both* people in the conversation a little bit uncomfortable."

Sitting with that discomfort, really listening, and then challenging people to take risks—that's half the job. The first goal is to persuade not just a majority, but a supermajority—75 percent of the workers—to sign cards authorizing a union election. "Because we know the boss can shave 20 percent off our margins at any given moment. Think about Trump as the boss . . . In the workplace they use every tactic Trump and Bannon used, turning the working class against itself. Black against white, women against men, Jew against non-Jew. Hate and division and misogyny and racism are the choice weapons in every union-busting fight in this country."

Teaching the workers to fight back effectively—helping them figure out how to shift that power balance—is the other half. "It's almost impossible to win without first analyzing how much power the employer has, as against the kind of power we can potentially build. Because the bosses start with existing power: control of the plant, or the hospital. Often they're exercising massive political control—as we just saw in the election. We only have potential power."

Once again the charts come out. These charts map the employer's power—economic, political, and social. "Who are they connected with? What other businesses? What politicians are they donating money to?" This kind of analysis has been part of the progressive toolbox since C. Wright Mills published *The Power Elite* in 1956. What distinguishes McAlevey's approach is what comes next—an equally detailed mapping, on the same wall charts where they first tracked relationships inside the workplace, of the workers' own social capital: where they pray, where their children attend school, where they live, what sports they play, what community, fraternal, or religious organizations they belong to.

It is her attention to this complex web of identity, affiliation, and agency that McAlevey calls "whole-worker organizing." Instead of seeing the community as an outside entity or a potential ally, it acknowledges that workers are already in the community, and that the artificial wall—which conventional unions treat as an impenetrable barrier—between the workplace and the world only deprives them of the leverage they need to win. Whether it's by picketing the supermarket where they shop, or asking elected officials for letters of support—"They have to be written," McAlevey insists. "How else can you be really sure they've done it?"—or getting parishioners to ask clergy if they can hold a bargaining session in the local church, the goal is for workers to discover and exercise their own power.

Which is what finally distinguishes the organizing work McAlevey does from mobilization. "What's the role of the worker in the actual effort? Are the workers central to their own liberation? Are they central to the strategy to win a change in their workplace and in their communities? For years we've been running campaigns in this country where the workers' voice has not been decisive . . ."

While mobilizing is "an activist-driven approach" that aims to maximize turnout—to the polls, at a march or demonstration—among the like-minded, organizing "is about expanding the base. It isn't just: Can we get some people to a rally? It's: Who are we getting to a rally? It's: Who got them to the rally? And it's: How long can we sustain the rally? That's a really, really fundamental difference." The difference, you might say, between wishful thinking and a structure test.

In 2009, right after she parted company with SEIU, McAlevey found out she carried the BRCA-1 genetic mutation, meaning she was at greatly increased risk of developing the breast cancer that killed her mother and older sister. When a biopsy revealed early stage cancer, she opted for radical surgery.[12] Wishful thinking isn't her thing.

▫ ▫ ▫

If organizing begins with a series of uncomfortable conversations between people who don't agree with each other, it progresses by means of structure tests. "From day one, we tell the workers it's on them. We're gonna coach you—but in most cases we're not even legally allowed into the workplace." Each step of an organizing campaign—from getting a supermajority of union election cards signed, to marching on the boss's office, to voting to authorize a strike, to contract negotiations—is designed both to gradually increase the risk taken, and to constantly test the workers' commitment. "You're building a structure strong enough to win a strike—or a precinct in an election."

No Shortcuts is filled with blow-by-blow accounts of organizing victories (none of them by McAlevey) won under the most difficult conditions imaginable—by unions in right-to-work states, despite constant harassment, and, in the case of the lengthy battle to organize workers at the Smithfield pork processing plant in Tar Heel, North Carolina, against an employer long practiced in turning native-born African American and immigrant Hispanic workers against each another. As her title suggests, progress can be slow—the

Smithfield fight took fifteen years. (Though as McAlevey also points out, thirteen of those years were wasted on campaigns that didn't measure up to her standard of "whole worker organizing." When "a real organizer, Gene Bruskin, was assigned, and he used all the correct methods, they won.")

But as McAlevey also tells workers who ask her help, "If you can do all these steps, you're probably gonna win." Otherwise, "we're gonna say it's really great to know you and we're gonna walk away. If something changes and you actually believe you can get to your majority—supermajority—come back to us."

When they do, the workers learn not to fear strikes, but to see them as the ultimate structure test. "A strike is the most powerful weapon the working class has. It's powerful as a concept, not just a symbolic word. A strike means you are causing and creating a significant crisis for your employer. It means ninety percent or more of the workers walk off the job." A strike isn't just a tactic, it's a manifestation of power—the power of the majority.

"To win the hardest fights—to win a presidential race, to reclaim the United States of America at the state house level, to actually tame global capital—we cannot rely on advocacy and mobilizing. Because they surrender the most important and only weapon that ordinary people have ever had, which is large numbers."

"*Citizens United* and *McCutcheon* [two Supreme Court decisions removing limits on donations to political campaigns] blew the doors on spending. It's going to be impossible for the social-change movement, including unions, to compete in any significant way on dollar-for-dollar spending in future elections. If we can't create a crisis for employers—workplace by workplace and [in whole] sectors of the economy—I don't think we can win right now.

"The civil rights movement couldn't outvote the political establishment in the South because blacks couldn't vote. That was the whole point. It was only when they could create a crisis for corporations and businesses in the South and get the businesses to say,

'We've got to stop this because it's causing economic harm,' that's when they won. It's the only way that we're going to win in the new Gilded Age."

CHAPTER TWO

The Whiskey Republic

On the worst day of his ultimately unsuccessful 2016 bid to win the Democratic nomination for the US Senate from Pennsylvania, John Fetterman took me on a tour of the Mon Valley. Starting out in Braddock, the dying steel town whose mayor Fetterman has been since 2005, we followed the Monongahela River upstream through Clairton, which still has the largest coke plant—and, not coincidentally, the most toxic air quality—in the country.

At six feet eight inches tall, with a goatee, shaved head, and the build, as he says, "of a professional wrestler rather than a professional politician," Fetterman would probably stand out in a crowd even without the tattoos: "15104," Braddock's ZIP code, is inked across his massive right forearm, while his left bears the dates of each of the nine gun deaths that occurred here since he took office. Rolling down the window so I can smell the stink, Fetterman shakes his head: "The thing is, if the coke works goes, I don't know what the folks here have left."

As if in answer we drive through block after block of shuttered storefronts and abandoned houses in McKeesport, stopping briefly to explore the derelict hulk of the First Baptist Church, whose soaring white domed ceiling looks down on a rotting wooden floor strewn with empty bottles, burn-scarred mattresses, and rat droppings. Then we head south to Monessen, another hollowed-out former steel town whose newspaper, the *Valley Independent*, like McKeesport's *Daily News*, was owned by right-wing financier Richard Mellon Scaife, who closed both papers in 2015.

In 2008, when candidate Barack Obama was being hammered for telling the audience at a San Francisco fundraiser that in "some of these small towns in Pennsylvania" the inhabitants, "bitter" about being left behind economically, "cling to guns and religion," Fetterman was one of the few elected officials who defended him (the overwhelming majority of Pennsylvania's Democratic office holders supported Hillary Clinton). So it came as a cruel disappointment when Fetterman learned, just before we set off in his pickup, that instead of remaining neutral in the Democratic senatorial primary, the president was about to endorse one of his opponents.

Not that either of us needed any help in darkening the mood. "No one is talking about places like this," said Fetterman, as we crossed over the river at Charleroi and followed it back to the converted auto showroom in Braddock where Fetterman lives. "I'm so tired of the Democratic Party using the working poor as props," he said angrily, explaining why the candidate Obama had endorsed, Kathleen McGinty, a state official with extensive ties to the oil and gas industries, would never be elected.

At the time I dismissed Fetterman's diatribe against corporate Democrats as sour grapes—a bitter rant from a man who, to my mounting disbelief, also argued that Donald Trump would not only win the nomination, but would likely carry the state of Pennsylvania. "Supporting Trump is a way for older, white Americans to give the whole country the finger for breaking its promises and leaving them behind. I can kind of understand that."

When I came back to see Fetterman a month after the election it was evident that his prescience brought him no joy. McGinty had indeed lost. Hillary Clinton carried Braddock—with its largely African American population—as she had Pittsburgh and the rest of Allegheny County. But in the two other counties we'd driven through back in March—Westmoreland and Washington—Trump piled up a majority of over eighty-one thousand votes in a state where his winning margin was only sixty-eight thousand.

"I was wrong about one thing," Fetterman reminded me, "when I said no politicians ever come to a place like Monessen." On June 28, 2016—when the NBC News poll had Clinton ahead by five points, and the Fox News poll had her up by six—Donald Trump came to Monessen to deliver a speech the *New York Times* described as "an attack on the economic orthodoxy that has dominated the Republican Party since World War II." Sticking for once to his script, in searing language Trump declared that "the legacy of Pennsylvania steelworkers lives in the bridges, railways and skyscrapers that make up our great American landscape. But our workers' loyalty was repaid with betrayal." Quoting George Washington, Alexander Hamilton—and the left-of-center Economic Policy Institute—on the importance of domestic manufacturing, and the disastrous impact of trade deals negotiated during Bill Clinton's presidency, Trump pledged that under his administration "it will be American steel that will fortify Americans' crumbling bridges . . . It will be American steel that rebuilds our inner cities. It will be American hands that remake this country, and it will be American energy—mined from American resources—that powers this country."[13]

Though he did keep his promise to withdraw from the Trans-Pacific Partnership, calling it "a death blow for American manufacturing," most of what Trump said that day in Monessen turned out to be empty rhetoric. But his mere presence, in a region that has long felt abandoned by Washington, was, said Fetterman, a powerful reminder of a time when the eyes of the whole world were on western Pennsylvania.

The decline goes back decades—by 1978, when the movie *The Deer Hunter* used Clairton as a symbol of neglect, the town had already lost nearly half its population. McKeesport saw employment at National Tube fall from ten thousand to a few hundred before US Steel, which owned the plant, shut it down in the 1980s. But in 1947, thirteen years before their more famous television face-off, two Navy veterans newly elected to Congress, John Kennedy and Richard Nixon, came to McKeesport to debate the implications of the Taft-

Hartley Act, with Nixon highlighting the law's anti-Communist provisions while Kennedy warned the measure would "strangle collective bargaining."[14] President Kennedy returned to McKeesport in 1962, telling the crowd that since his generation had been "beneficiaries of the New Deal," it was their responsibility to solve "the problem of how to keep our people at work."[15] But the government couldn't force factory owners to invest in new equipment, and as competition from modern plants in Europe and Asia increased the American steel industry entered its long death spiral.

One of the last two surviving US Steel plants in the Mon Valley, the Edgar Thomson Works, is literally across the street from Fetterman's front door. Built in 1875 to manufacture rails for the Pennsylvania Railroad, Andrew Carnegie's first steel mill survived the 1892 Homestead strike, sale to J. P. Morgan, and even, thanks to a 1992 conversion from rails to continuous casting, the collapse of the American steel industry, currently accounting for more a quarter of US Steel's domestic production.

But the town of Braddock's claim to significance isn't just as a rust-belt relic—a living museum of industrial architecture. The ground now occupied by the Thomson Works was the setting for a conflict that shaped American history. During the summer of 1755, in the second year of the French and Indian War, General Edward Braddock, commander in chief of British forces in North America, moved to seize Fort Duquesne, a French outpost at the point where the Allegheny and Monongahela Rivers meet to form the Ohio. On July 9, 1755, Braddock led some 1,300 troops across the Monongahela where they were met by a combined force of 800 French soldiers and Native American warriors. Despite their superior numbers, the British tactic of attacking in columns left them vulnerable to their opponents, who fired from behind trees on both sides of the road, leading the panicked British regulars to break ranks and run. Attempting to restore discipline Braddock himself was fatally wounded, and it was largely thanks to a detachment of Virginia militia, long accustomed to fighting in the trees, that a total rout was avoided and the survivors were able to stage an orderly retreat. Braddock himself was sufficiently grateful for the Virginians' efforts to bequeath his ceremonial sash to their twenty-three-year-old commander, Colonel George Washington.

Witnessing that defeat did much to strip away any sense of awe or inferiority the young colonial officer might have felt toward the British Army; the campaign also provided Washington, who two years earlier had personally delivered an ultimatum to the commander of the French garrison in Ohio demanding he withdraw in favor of the British, with a reminder of the vast potential of the western region. Virginia's colonial governor, Robert Dinwiddie, had promised each of the militia volunteers a share in two hundred thousand acres of land west of the Ohio River. Although the Crown, reluctant to antagonize the Native American inhabitants, explicitly barred colonial settlement west of the Allegheny Mountains, Washington would appoint himself a leader in the fight for the veterans' promised bounty—while at the same time instructing his own agents to secure title to as much western land as possible.

That, however, was just the prologue. Braddock's claim as a pivot point in American history arises from the events of August 1794, when seven thousand members of various western Pennsylvania militias assembled on the site of that British defeat—known as "Braddock's Field," occupied today by the Thomson Works—in defiance of the new federal government's proposed tax on whiskey. Within a week the Supreme Court certified that the area was in a state of rebellion, a legal formality authorizing President Washington to take command of state militias. With Washington himself at its head, and the tax's author, Alexander Hamilton, riding at his side, a force of nearly thirteen thousand men—comparable in size to the entire Continental Army—rode west from Philadelphia to put down the revolt.

How had it come to this? In the original Public Theater version of his mega-hit musical *Hamilton*, composer Lin-Manuel Miranda depicts the hero as playing second fiddle to his commander in chief, who tells Hamilton "I have a plan, but it's risky," explaining, "We know from rebellions / We're gonna teach 'em / How to stay in line," with Hamilton then urging the rebels, "Pay your fucking taxes!" Their conspiratorial duet, "One Last Ride," was cut—along with any mention of the Pennsylvania revolt—before the show reached Broadway.

Yet it was Hamilton who not only gave the incident the derisory name—the "Whiskey Rebellion"—it still bears, but who consciously, deliberately provoked the rebels in order both to justify a display of federal power and to put the new government firmly on the side of wealthy commercial interests. Hamilton the plucky immigrant may be boffo box office; Hamilton the politician was a considerably more complex historical figure, who, having risked his neck in the revolution, had no patience with those who thought they were fighting not just for liberty from Britain, but for freedom from all arbitrary authority.

▫ ▫ ▫

The roots of the Whiskey Rebellion go back long before the American Revolution, with its radical declaration that "all men are created equal," all the way to the English Civil War of the previous century. Although in England itself the republican government that executed Charles I, and under Oliver Cromwell ruled over a united "Commonwealth of England, Scotland, and Ireland," was followed by the restoration of the monarchy under Charles II, republican ideas retained considerable power. Especially in the North American colonies, many founded by Puritans, Quakers, and other dissenters from the Church of England—some of which even bore the title of "Commonwealth."

By the time of the Hanoverian succession in 1714 the mainstream of British political thought had repressed the memory of popular sovereignty to the point where "republicanism" signified merely a defense of constitutional monarchy.[16] But while few in England would have publicly agreed with the diarist Samuel Pepys's private avowal that "better things were done, and better managed . . . under a commonwealth" than under a king, the Country Party, which stood against the corruptions of the Georgian court during Robert Walpole's long ministry, and more especially the group of writers known as "Commonwealth Men," found avid admirers in the colonies. In Britain John Trenchard and Thomas Gordon, publishers of the weekly *Independent Whig*, remained marginal figures. But according to the historian Bernard Bailyn a copy of their pseudonymous collection *Cato's Letters*, defiantly republican and filled with warnings about how quickly arbitrary power turns to tyranny, could be found in half the private libraries of North America.[17]

If the enlightenment rationalism of John Locke and David Hume, radical Whig thought, and the debates among Cromwell's New Model Army all helped to shape colonial politics, the religious convulsions known as the First Great Awakening were equally important. Between Jonathan Edwards of Massachusetts, with his grisly depiction of the torments awaiting sinners, and George Whitefield, the British revivalist who made seven trips to the colonies between 1738 and 1770, eighteenth-century Americans were steeped in the doctrine of personal salvation and "New Light" Protestantism's disdain for hierarchal authority. Even Benjamin Franklin, who described himself as a "thoroughgoing Deist," got drawn into Whitefield's orbit, publishing the preacher's sermons in his *Pennsylvania Gazette* and donating money to the orphanage Whitefield was building in Georgia. In the decades preceding the revolution "defiance to the highest constituted powers poured from colonial presses and was hurled from half the pulpits in the land . . . Obedience as a principle was only too well known; disobedience as a doctrine was not. It was therefore asserted again and again."[18]

But there is also a third strand to the revolutionary braid—though given far less space in the textbooks—and that is the question of property. Just as England's republican revolution was fertile ground for both Protestant Dissenters and political radicals like John Lilburne, Richard Overton, and Gerrard Winstanley[19] (whose followers, known as True Levellers or Diggers, pulled down the fences used by private landlords, planting crops on land they claimed had been stolen from the people), so the rejection of British rule in the colonies inspired many participants to regard any form of hereditary power—political or economic—with suspicion.

In his *Second Treatise on Civil Government* (1690) Locke had argued both that all property rights begin with a person's ownership of his or her own body, and that any further property rights are only gained through the addition, or "mixing in," of labor. Locke also held that such "appropriation" is only valid if "there is enough, and as good, left in common for others"—a position that found ready acceptance among the settlers of the American frontier. Though it would take another generation before the logical force of Locke's implicit critique of slavery* gained political pertinence, the consequences of his view of the earth as a common inheritance became apparent the moment British authority, and British institutions, were nullified. Primogeniture and entail, for example, the two legal devices by which the British aristocracy consolidated and maintained their lands and fortunes, were abolished by all of the new America states in the decades immediately following the revolution.

Arguing that such arrangements operated to give certain wealthy families "an unequal and undue influence in a republic," the North Carolina legislature said that banning them would "tend to promote that equality of property which is of the spirit and principle of a genuine republic."[20] North Carolina was also the state that had given birth to the Regulators, armed rural irregulars who, a decade before

---

* Less implicitly, Locke famously begins his *Two Treatises of Government* with a defense of slavery—albeit in the context of penal servitude. He also drafted the *Fundamental Constitutions of Carolina*, which gave "every freeman of Carolina . . . absolute power and authority over his negro slaves," and was himself a beneficiary of the British slave trade as a shareholder in the Royal African Company.

Lexington and Concord, banded together to enforce "people's justice" against colonial officials, preventing evictions and the seizure of farms for unpaid taxes. In their petitions the Regulators called for nothing less than an economic revolution, demanding a land bank to provide affordable credit to farmers, provision for taxes to be paid in paper currency, public access to tax records, and land titles granted only to those who improve, or work, the land—not absentee landlords. "Most radically of all, they wanted taxes proportional to wealth."[21] Colonial Governor William Tryon's response was to crush the movement, and hang its leaders.

After the revolution, matters were supposed to be different. In *Leviathan* Thomas Hobbes had argued that only an all-powerful state could restrain the "war of all against all." But the revolutionaries knew from personal experience that wasn't true. "In one colony after another the old political institutions lost their authority and new ones—committees of safety and correspondence, provincial conventions—took power." As Thomas Paine observed, "For upward of two years from the commencement of the American War, and to a longer period in several of the American states, there were no established forms of government. The old governments had been abolished, and the country was too much occupied in defense, to employ its attention in establishing new governments; yet during this interval, order and harmony were preserved as inviolate as in any country in Europe."[22]

How far might this new spirit of equality go? The answer varied considerably. In plantation economies like the Virginia Tidewater, or trading centers such as New York and Boston, the wealthy maintained and even extended their privileges after the revolution. Vermont, admitted to the union in 1791, was the first state to grant universal suffrage to all male inhabitants, regardless of property ownership. But then property ownership in America, where two-thirds of the white colonial population owned land, was already of a different order than in England, where some four hundred families owned a fifth of all the land in the country—and where, even after the 1832 Reform Act, property requirements restricted the franchise to a mere 18 percent of the adult male population.[23] In most American states land was cheap enough, and the property qualification low enough, to allow about 80 percent of the male inhabitants to vote for that state's lower house of the legislature—and thus to be eligible to vote for members of the House of Representatives.[24]

Historians still disagree about the extent to which radical American praxis drew on radical English theory—just as they still differ over whether the American Revolution was a social, as well as a political, revolution. But there is no argument at all about where, during the revolution and immediately afterward, radical ideas about equality were most fully enacted into law. Written under the influence of Thomas Paine's *Common Sense*, the Pennsylvania Constitution of 1776—published in January of that year—was by far the most democratic charter produced by any of the former colonies. Although the draft language proposed by the Committee of Privates arguing that "an enormous Proportion of Property vested in a few individuals is dangerous to the Rights, and destructive of the Common Happiness, of Mankind," and should therefore be discouraged by law, never made it into the Declaration of Rights, the final version did provide for a unicameral legislature, whose members served one-year terms, and the elimination of property qualifications to vote or hold office.

"In the Pennsylvania press of 1776," writes Gordon S. Wood, "the typical Whig outbursts against Tories and Crown were overshadowed by expressions of . . . social hostility. In fact, to judge solely from the literature the Revolution in Pennsylvania had become a class war . . . between the common people and the privileged few."[25] For both the radical artisans of urban Philadelphia and their rural counterparts a prime focus of this hostility was Robert Morris, wealthiest merchant in the state, richest man in the country, leader of the Federalists—and George Washington's Philadelphia landlord.

In 1786, when westerners in the Pennsylvania General Assembly argued that "a democratic government like ours admits of no superiority," Morris scornfully replied, "Is it insisted that there is no distinction of character?" But William Findley, an Irish-born weaver elected from Westmoreland County, held firm, allowing that while the rich might have "more money than their neighbors," in America "no man has a greater claim of special privilege for his £100,000 than I have for my £5."[26] (An echo, whether conscious or not, of the Leveller spokesman Thomas Rainsborough's claim in the Putney Debates that "the poorest he that is in England has a life to live as the greatest he.")

▫ ▫ ▫

So it was no accident at all that, Congress having enacted a much-resented, widely disregarded tax on domestic whiskey production, Alexander Hamilton would apply the full might of the new government to western Pennsylvania. Because if he had only been looking to enforce the law, Hamilton could have turned to western Massachusetts, western Maryland, the frontier areas of Virginia, Georgia, the Carolinas—all hotbeds of resistance to the new tax. Or the entire state of Kentucky, which failed to appoint a single tax collector—probably because prospective candidates were reliably informed the job would be hazardous to their continued health. When a hapless federal prosecutor eventually did bring charges, Kentucky juries consistently refused to convict.[27]

Why was the tax so fiercely resisted? Partly because it was, in the shared language of English Whigs and American revolutionaries, what was known as an "excise" or "internal tax." Unlike customs duties, which raised money by a tariff on imported goods, paid as they came into the country, excise taxes were regarded as both an imposition and an irresistible temptation for corrupt officials. Long before the Stamp Tax and the Townshend Acts stirred passions in the colonies, violent protests by British taxpayers in the 1730s forced Walpole's government to withdraw an excise on salt. A similar fate befell a proposed tax on cider in 1763, with riots in the West Country leading the prime minister, Lord Bute, to resign. "When the Excise Man's Deputy comes," an opposition pamphleteer predicted, "if he likes the poor Man's Wife, he will not like his Account."[28] In 1775 the Continental Congress tried to persuade the people of Quebec to join their revolution by noting that Canadians had been subjected "to the imposition of excise, *the borrower of all free states*, thus wresting your property from you by *the most odious of taxes*."[29] Indeed it was the long history of abuse by British excise collectors that eventually led to the Fourth Amendment to the Constitution.

Mainly though, the tax was hated because of the unique role of whiskey in the frontier economy. Unlike farmers along the seaboard, who had access both to markets and to money, settlers in the interior had great difficulty in selling their crops. The Mississippi belonged to Spain, which refused to allow Americans navigation rights. (The federal government's apparent lack of interest in negotiating a treaty with Spain was a constant source of vexation to westerners—especially when contrasted with the Federalists' obvious eagerness to agree to terms with Britain.) A western farmer might harvest twenty-four bushels of rye, but it would take three animals to haul the grain over the Alleghenies—at a cost far higher than the six dollars he might get when he sold it. Distilled into whiskey, however, that same grain would yield sixteen gallons—which, when split between two kegs, needed only a single animal to reach market, where (freed from worry over spoilage) the farmer might get as much as sixteen dollars.[30]

Of course not all western whiskey went to market. The chronic shortage of hard currency, and the absence of local banks on the frontier, made whiskey an ideal medium of exchange for farmers, artisans, and local merchants. With Americans drinking an average of five gallons a year—more than any European nation at the time—demand, and prices, remained high.[31]

Nor was Hamilton's tax equally applied. Big eastern distillers, located mainly in cities and towns where their production could be more readily monitored, were allowed to pay a nine cents per gallon tax on what they actually distilled. Small producers, or those located in rural areas, were taxed on the capacity of their stills—at a rate that assumed year-round production at full capacity, often amounting to as much as twenty-five cents a gallon. Producers were also offered a discount if they paid their tax in cash—an option not available in the countryside, where cash was scarce. "In every configuration, at every level, Hamilton had designed the law to charge small producers who could least afford it a higher tax . . . Small producers would have to raise prices. Big producers could lower prices, sharply underselling the small distillers, ultimately driving small producers out of business . . . The whiskey tax pushed self-employed farmers and artisans into the factories of their creditors."[32]

For western farmers and mechanics who'd endured long years of fighting—on the most meager rations, their pay often in arrears—the excise on whiskey added insult to injury. Because while the burden of the tax fell chiefly on men like themselves, the funds collected would go to pay off the government's creditors—wealthy merchants like Robert Morris and his friends in New York and Philadelphia. Throughout the war Congress had issued paper money whose value depreciated so rapidly it gave rise to the expression "not worth a Continental." Yet there was no refusing armed procurement officers. Suppliers who complied willingly got chits or IOUs—sometimes from Congress, sometimes from the states. Like the Continental dollar, these chits were considered practically worthless—sold to speculators for pennies on the dollar. Now Hamilton and Morris wanted to exchange all this paper for bonds—at face value—to be paid by the federal government, creating a huge windfall for speculators, or anyone with advance knowledge of the arrangement.

Despite Hamilton's propaganda, the whiskey rebels weren't against taxes, regularly proposing levies on land, or increased tariffs on imported crops, to finance the new government. But Hamilton considered property taxes an extreme measure only justified during wartime. Higher tariffs, he wrote, could not be imposed "without contravening the sense of the body of the merchants." The rebels only refused "what they called unequal taxation, which redistributed wealth to a few holders of federal bonds and kept small farms and businesses commercially paralyzed . . . [F]acing daily anxiety over debt foreclosure and tax imprisonment, [they] feared becoming landless laborers, their businesses bought cheaply by the very men in whose mills and factories they would then be forced to toil."[33]

Such fears were far from groundless. General John Neville, in 1791 the newly appointed revenue inspector for western Pennsylvania, was a commercial farmer whose plantation, Bower Hill, also housed a commercial distillery. For three years Neville tried—and failed—to persuade his neighbors to pay the tax. Those who initially registered found their stills perforated by bullets; after the first few collectors—or even anyone foolish enough to rent office space to a collector—were tarred and feathered, local enforcement efforts were abandoned. In Pennsylvania, as elsewhere throughout the west, liberty poles—tall wooden flagstaffs bearing the legends "Don't Tread on Me," "Equality of Rights—No Excise," and other insurrectionary slogans—began sprouting in a profusion not seen since the summer of '76. In Pennsylvania, as in Maryland, local militias had begun to assemble.

By the summer of 1794 Hamilton had had enough, dispatching US marshal David Lenox to Pennsylvania to serve writs on delinquent taxpayers. On July 15, Lenox, accompanied by Neville, attempted to deliver a writ to William Miller, a farmer in Allegheny County about twelve miles south of Pittsburgh, demanding payment of a ruinous $250 fine for failing to register his still. The summons also required Miller, who was in the middle of harvesting his crops, to travel to Philadelphia to appear in court. A group of Miller's neighbors assembled, firing warning shots to disrupt the proceedings. Lenox escaped to Pittsburgh, but when Neville withdrew, the group followed him to Bower Hill.

The next morning the angry crowd outside Neville's house was bolstered by local militiamen. When they demanded Neville deliver Lenox, whom they mistakenly believed was sheltering inside, Neville ordered them to "stand off" and then fired, fatally wounding Miller's young nephew Oliver. The militia withdrew, but returned the following morning, July 17, with a force of five hundred men, led by James McFarlane, a major in the Pennsylvania militia and, like Neville, a hero of the revolution. Neville also had reinforcements—a small detachment of federal troops under the command of his brother-in-law, Major Abraham Kirkpatrick.

Neville and McFarlane had both endured the hardships of Valley Forge, and fought together at Germantown and Monmouth.[34] But while Neville, a Virginian who'd served in Braddock's failed expedition then moved to the area, bringing his slaves with him, had amassed a ten-thousand-acre estate, McFarlane's prosperity was not of the sort to set him apart from his neighbors, who elected him to his position in the militia. Demanding that Neville resign from his office, McFarlane was informed the general was not home. Both sides then began shooting, until McFarlane, believing he'd seen a white flag, ordered his men to hold their fire. As he stepped from behind cover McFarlane was killed by a shot fired from the house, which his enraged troops then proceeded to burn to the ground, along with Neville's barns, fences, crops, and storehouses. Only the slave quarters and the smokehouse, where the slaves' food was kept, were spared.[35]

It was as a response to these events that the combined western Pennsylvania militias mustered at Braddock's Field two weeks later. And it was in response to that show of force—the rebels were only narrowly diverted from burning Pittsburgh—that Washington and Hamilton led what the locals called their "watermelon army" (owing to the practice of seizing provisions en route) over the Alleghenies.

Militarily the denouement was predictable: by the time the troops reached western Pennsylvania the rebels had already dispersed. Washington, who'd accompanied the army as far as Carlisle, left Hamilton in charge, and on November 13, 1794—known in Pittsburgh lore as "Dreadful Night"—hundreds of men were dragged out of bed and marched at bayonet point through snow-covered streets while their families were told they were going to be hanged. In the end, only a couple of dozen prisoners were taken east; of those, ten were tried for high treason—and only two were convicted and sentenced to be hanged.

Washington pardoned them both, supposedly finding one of the men to be "a simpleton" and the other "insane." But Washington's clemency might also have been influenced by the knowledge that, with federal authority over the West now firmly established, his own vast holdings in the area—amounting to nearly twenty thousand acres in western Pennsylvania alone—had now increased in value by some 50 percent. Washington also set up a still at Mount Vernon, and continued to take a close interest in the management of his western lands by his new agent, Presley Neville—John Neville's son.[36]

The immediate practical consequence of the Whiskey Rebellion was the military occupation of western Pennsylvania, and the apparent confirmation of both federal authority and Alexander Hamilton's influence. Despite his failure to secure a conviction against his archenemy, the Swiss-born Albert Gallatin, who as congressman from western Pennsylvania had opposed the whiskey tax, Hamilton's triumph over his political opponents appeared secure. But while armed resistance had been crushed, the whiskey tax remained a fiscal disappointment, widely disregarded throughout the backcountry until it was finally repealed in 1802—by Treasury Secretary Albert Gallatin.[37]

Politically, however, the reversal of Federalist policies signaled by the election of Thomas Jefferson in 1800 was just the most obvious legacy of the Whiskey Rebellion. Beyond the oscillations of party politics, the rebels' democratic vision of a government not merely in the public interest, nor simply responsive to the popular will, but genuinely of, by, and for the people, would retain its radical appeal long after the rebels—and their persecutors—were in the grave. Far from disappearing, the liberty poles returned to service by the rebels would continue to proliferate—in even greater numbers—to protest the Alien and Sedition Acts passed during John Adams's presidency (aimed, in part, at émigrés like Gallatin).[38]

More significant, in my view, was the dilemma first exposed by the whiskey rebels—namely how to confront the unjust laws and oppressive actions of an elected government. Although not one of the many accounts of the rebellion mention it, the height of the battle over the excise also saw the passage of the first Fugitive Slave Act (1793), which allowed escaped slaves to be hunted down even in states that had abolished slavery—and aimed to compel local authorities to assist in their capture.

At the time, the links between the mythology of white supremacy and the sanctity of private property were far from clear (though the militia at Bower Hill seemed to have noticed the connection). Americans would have to wait another half century—until the publication of Thoreau's *Civil Disobedience* in 1849—before the practice, once so widespread in western Pennsylvania, would be dignified by a theory. In the end it would be Lincoln, not Jefferson, who, by confiscating $2 billion worth of slaves without compensation, took the argument to its logical, radical conclusion.[39] But that would be getting ahead of our story . . .

CHAPTER THREE

Jane Kleeb—The Accidental Environmentalist

Tourists who got up early to beat the crowds on the National Mall on April 22, 2014, might well have thought they'd stumbled onto a mirage—or a movie set. Rising out of the grassy corridor between the National Gallery and the Natural History Museum on one side, and the Smithsonian, the Air and Space Museum, and the Museum of the American Indian on the other, a dozen teepees stood silent in the morning mist. Most were the plain white canvas-and-poles of a thousand Westerns. But one, with a blue stripe circling the base showing fish and ducks swimming in clear water, and a middle section painted with a procession of buffalo, moose, caribou, wolves, and deer, bore the admonition to "Honor the Earth." Another, with the same water/earth/sky motif—green and blue waves under a band of brightly colored horses, with a gigantic turtle gazing upward at the black night sky—also carried the inscriptions "*Oyate Owicakiye Wicasa*" and "*Awe Kooda bilaxpak Kuuxshish*," the names given to President Barack Obama by the Lakota and the Crow nations. (The names mean "Man Who Helps the People" and "One Who Helps People throughout the Land.") A third, striped in sand, black and red, was decorated with a bright red circle with the words "Protect and Reject" in big letters and, in smaller letters, "The Cowboy and Indian Alliance."

As if on cue, a troop of mounted riders, about half of them bareback or on blankets, wearing feathered headdresses, and the rest on western saddles wearing cowboy hats and boots, came riding up Independence Avenue from the Reflecting Pool into the encampment. Later that week, thousands of protesters marched—and rode—past the Capitol demanding the Obama administration block TransCanada from building the 1,200-mile-long Keystone XL pipeline. Among the crowd was a slightly built woman with a pageboy haircut, wearing a denim jacket and black jeans tucked into the top of a pair of cowboy boots. On the front of each boot a blue-gray sandhill crane takes off against a red leather sky. Her mobile phone rang, showing a White House exchange. Rohan Patel, special assistant to the president and senior advisor for climate and energy policy, was on the line. "Well, Jane," he said, "you have our attention."

"Can we come over and meet?" asked Jane Kleeb, head of BOLD Nebraska, and midwife to the Cowboy and Indian Alliance. Seven months later, in the Roosevelt Room, President Obama announced that the State Department had decided the "Keystone XL pipeline would not serve the national interests of the United States. I agree with that decision."

▫ ▫ ▫

If it wasn't for her eating disorder, Jane Kleeb might still be a Republican. Instead, since December 2016 she's been the chair of the Nebraska Democratic Party, as well as serving on the board of Our Revolution, the political group founded to continue the legacy of Bernie Sanders's 2016 presidential campaign. As one of the highest-profile Sanders backers inside the Democratic Party, Kleeb herself has become a target for those with a stake in defending the party's reliance on corporate funding—or the revolving door between Democratic policy makers and K Street lobbying firms. Her position on the Democratic National Committee's twenty-one-member Unity Commission also puts her on the front line in battles over how the party itself should be run.

Yet Kleeb sees herself primarily as an advocate for rural America—the parts that Democrats on both coasts all too often deride as "flyover country."

"I keep hearing Democrats say, 'We need to reach out to rural voters and working class folks.' Number one, we're not animals at a zoo. That's number one. We probably care about a lot of the same things that you care about. We might talk about them in different ways. I might wear boots and you may wear Prada, but we're still putting shoes on. We all have bathrooms. Indoors."

I first met Kleeb in Omaha, in the spring of 2017—the middle of a long season of heartbreaking losses for Democrats, especially in red states like Nebraska. Up on stage in front of six thousand people at the Baxter Arena she seemed tiny, and frail, beginning her speech, as she often does, by describing her own long struggle with anorexia. Afterward, I asked her why she did that.

"Because I'm an organizer. For me, telling stories is how you connect with people. And how you really show folks that our political leaders don't have to be some magical people picked out of the ground. That all of us have stories. And all of us have the ability to lead on these issues and to lead in politics. I never want to hide that part of me."

Kleeb grew up in Plantation, Florida. Her mother was the chair of the Broward County Right to Life Committee. Her father was president of the North Dade Chamber of Commerce. Both were staunch Republicans—as was she. "My dad and my grandmother had a Burger King in Hollywood, Florida. I was draining pickles and cutting tomatoes and onions in the back growing up."

She started dieting in sixth grade. When, aged fifteen, she fainted and was rushed to the emergency room, where she went into cardiac arrest, she weighed just seventy pounds. In her eight years of treatment she saw many women discharged after a week, or a month—whenever their funds ran out. Eventually Kleeb's family insurance coverage reached its benefit cap. She told the crowd in Omaha that she was only able to remain in the treatment that was saving her life thanks to financial support from her grandmother—a circumstance that first led her to question her own Republican roots.

In college, at Stetson University in DeLand, Florida, Kleeb "wasn't really involved in politics. I was very involved in community service. I was raised in a Catholic school, and that's when Clinton started talking about AmeriCorps. That was this other political moment for me: a politician is actually talking about something that I care about. Community service, being connected to my community . . ."

Her first job after graduation was running an AmeriCorps program in Tallahassee. "I was very young. I don't know how I was able to convince them that I should be running it at twenty-one, or whatever I was. We were doing literacy for kids in a one hundred percent African American school in a deep-poverty area of Tallahassee that I lived in. I did that for five years. And there, too, the only way I was able to get parents to the table to help their kids learn to read was by telling my own story."

She then enrolled in a master's degree program at American University and moved to Washington, DC. "I wanted to test out the theory that activism and community service kept me alive, kept me connected to recovery. I did my fieldwork at the same treatment center I had been in."

Kleeb was still a Republican. "This is when the whole Terri Schiavo thing happened. She was in that coma because she had bulimia. So she couldn't get access to mental-health care. But here [Jeb] Bush wasn't funding mental-health care, but wanted to keep her [alive in a coma]. It really pissed me off. And I started to try to get involved in politics."

Two friends from college had formed a political consulting firm whose biggest client was Peter Lewis, chairman of Progressive Insurance and a major donor to liberal causes. One day they invited Kleeb along to a meeting. "They were talking about the youth vote; [how] young people never turn out, so candidates don't talk to them. I was young at the time, and I was like, 'Give me a million dollars and we'll figure it out.' I was always big on issue-based organizing, and they wanted it to be Democratic, so they gave the money to Young Democrats of America and told them: 'Hire Jane.' They said they'd hire me if they got the money. But they also said I'd have to change my registration, because I was still a Republican!"

▫ ▫ ▫

Kleeb's conviction that political activism had saved her own life made her an effective, charismatic organizer. After bottoming out in 1996 and 2000, participation rates for young voters started to rise. The Iraq War doubtless had an effect; while rates for eighteen- to twenty-four-year-old Republicans continued to fall slightly in 2004, rates for young Democrats increased by 6 percent.[40] The trend continued in 2008 with the historic candidacy of Barack Obama.

As executive director of the Young Democrats, Kleeb worked with Rock the Vote, which led to a job with MTV's "Street Team." An encounter at the 2005 Democratic National Committee meeting in Phoenix had more lasting consequences. She heard that a candidate for the House of Representatives from Nebraska wanted to speak to Kleeb's group. "Nebraska? No way," Kleeb later described her response to the *New York Times*. "I'm not helping some Republican fake liberal who just wants to use the youth vote to get out of the primaries." Then she saw the candidate's picture, and decided Scott Kleeb might be worth meeting. "Whatever it takes to get him here."[41] Scott Kleeb wasn't a fake, or a Republican. A fourth-generation Nebraskan who'd been on the bull-riding team at the University of Colorado, and spent his summers working as a ranch hand, Kleeb had written a prize-winning PhD dissertation at Yale on the history of cattle ranching.

Running in the heavily Republican Third District—which had given George W. Bush, who campaigned for his opponent, 75 percent of the vote in 2004—Kleeb lost by ten points. During the campaign he'd asked Jane to help him organize young voters, taking her to see the family homestead in Broken Bow. "I fell in love with the Sandhills way before I fell in love with Scott."[42] The Thanksgiving after the 2006 election she returned to Nebraska to spend the holiday with Scott and his family. Married the following March, they bought a house in Hastings, a town of about twenty-five thousand at the intersection of two railroad lines.

"I always try to remind people that if I had been fighting an oil train rather than a pipeline, I don't think we would have been able to galvanize the unlikely alliance that we did, because so many people have deep connections and strong emotional ties to the railroads. If you drive down NE-2, the Sandhills Byway we call it, you'll see beautiful rolling sand hills, nothing, nothing, nothing, and then you'll see a town similar to Hastings . . . Kool-Aid was invented in Hastings. That's our claim to fame."

With Obama in the White House and committed to health care reform, Kleeb became Nebraska state director of Change That Works. Funded by the Service Employees International Union, the group was intended to mobilize grassroots support in twelve states for what would become the Affordable Care Act. Ben Nelson, Nebraska's lone Democratic senator and a serial defector against his party, was a prime target. Part of what made the group different was that, after years of Democrats writing off rural America, Change That Works built a progressive infrastructure in Arkansas (two votes in the Senate for the ACA), North Dakota (two votes in the Senate for the ACA), and Nebraska.[43] The other thing different about Nebraska was Jane Kleeb.

SEIU officials in Washington repeatedly pushed Kleeb "to be more aggressive with Nelson, but she refused."[44] It wasn't because she was soft—or squeamish. "We used to have these things called 'Wimp Wednesdays,' where we were highlighting conservatives that would be wimpy on issues—which was funny." She just didn't think playing hardball with Nelson would work. Instead she began collecting stories.

"We started recording people in rural Nebraska and in urban Nebraska telling their health care stories, and telling their union organizing stories [remember, the SEIU was paying for this] and we put them up on YouTube. We did this Twenty-Four Hours of Health Care, where we posted a new YouTube video every hour—they're still there, actually.[45] That was the first time where it hit me like a big truck that people in rural Nebraska were actually not that different than people in urban Nebraska. They didn't see themselves in our political leaders, and they desperately needed affordable health care."

"We also collected letters from people all across the state" detailing their own health insurance horror stories, then strung huge clotheslines outside of Nelson's office in Lincoln "and pinned all the letters onto it." Realizing the depth of Nelson's religious faith, Kleeb arranged for a pastor with breast cancer, who had been denied coverage by her insurer, to meet with the senator. Her group also got two dozen religious leaders—including Catholic priests, Protestant pastors, and a rabbi—to sign a letter saying the law would do nothing to change existing prohibitions on federal funding for abortion (which Nelson had cited as a ground for objection). Kleeb's patient, constant pressure paid off when Nelson became the sixtieth, and final, vote in favor of Obamacare.

▫ ▫ ▫

Although it would consume the next four years of her life, the Keystone XL pipeline was not yet on Jane Kleeb's radar. She wanted to keep working in Nebraska "organizing people based on issues, but doing it from a progressive and populist perspective," and with Obamacare on the statute books "I knew the SEIU would be pulling out." So she went to see Dick Holland, an Omaha advertising man who'd been an early investor in his friend Warren Buffet's Berkshire Hathaway company, and who spent the latter half of his life giving away much of the fortune he'd made.

"I said, 'Listen. We just did all this great organizing on health reform. I can't go into the [Democratic] Party because the party is not ready for this level of organizing.' He knew that too." Holland agreed to fund a new group, BOLD Nebraska, that would work on progressive issues across party lines. "We thought we'd start by sticking with health care," pressing for the state to set up an exchange. Three months into the campaign Kleeb "started to get calls from farmers and ranchers because of my husband," who was working at the Morgan Ranch, a family-run operation in the Sandhills raising Herefords and Japanese Wagyu beef cattle.

"They'd say, 'Can you help us? We have no idea what we're doing, but we know we're up against a big oil company.' I wasn't yet connected to any of the national environmental groups. I had no environmental background. I didn't even know who Bill McKibben was.

"I did know that Republicans would be for it, because they love oil pipeline companies," which meant that, in Nebraska, she'd be fighting uphill. Since it was ranchers who'd approached her, "I immediately started organizing landowners." Her first move was to contact John Hansen, longtime president of the Nebraska Farmers Union. "I asked John Hansen if he would come and validate what oil was doing in these small towns. He came with us for the first several community-education sessions . . . [H]e would ask a local rancher or a farmer to give the opening remarks."

At the time, there didn't appear to be much common ground between often-conservative farmers and ranchers and the environmental movement, whose supporters were typically depicted in the media as young, urban, and unkempt. The pipeline itself—a thirty-six-inch steel tube stretching from Hardisty in Alberta, Canada, to Steele City, Nebraska, capable of carrying 830,000 barrels a day of tar sands oil, fracked oil from the Bakken shale in North Dakota, and dilbit (a cocktail of thick, tar-like petroleum thinned with benzene and other chemicals so it flows faster)—was often described as a lifeline freeing US consumers from dependence on oil imported from the Middle East.

TransCanada also claimed the pipeline would create forty-two thousand American jobs, and though the official State Department report estimated there would only be thirty-five permanent jobs, it did estimate that building the pipeline would create an additional 3,900 temporary jobs during two years of construction.[46] Those were more than enough to win the support of the United Association, the pipefitters and plumbers union—and, initially, the backing of Hillary Clinton, who in October 2010 said she was "inclined" to approve the pipeline.* "We're either going to be dependent on dirty oil from the Gulf or dirty oil from Canada," Clinton said. With labor and its traditional allies on one side, and the environmental movement on the other, the Democratic Party was divided—and paralyzed.

That didn't stop Kleeb. "You had some people who felt it was our patriotic duty to help get us off Middle East oil. [And] some people were opposed to it . . . from day one because of eminent domain." (Under eminent domain the state is allowed to take private property for public use. In the case of Keystone XL, opponents argued that building a pipeline for a Canadian company was not a valid public purpose.) "It was a mixed crowd. So we would go and do these community education sessions: PowerPoints, handouts—whatever I could find online. I was learning about the issue as I was teaching, and so were farmers and ranchers, and so we were all teaching each other, which looking back was probably one of the most successful parts of the model because it wasn't like some expert coming in and then leaving.

"We were all literally in it together trying to figure it out. People

* According to OpenSecrets.org, the United Association donated $4,008,894 to the Clinton campaign during the 2016 election cycle. As secretary of state, Clinton had allowed Cardno Entrix, a private consulting firm whose clients included TransCanada, to conduct the department's first environmental impact statement for the pipeline. After repeatedly avoiding the question, Clinton withdrew her support for Keystone in September 2015.

in rural communities have a deep connection to the birds, to the cranes in particular, and they're in a migratory path with the pipeline, and so there were all these reasons why people in rural communities would be against this big pipeline. And then I started to realize that we have to get landowners to say that they are not going to sign contracts—"

It took two years for Kleeb to realize that she needed to organize a landowners' strike. "Now when we're advising other communities, we tell them, 'Day one this is what you need to do.' Still, we do have twenty percent of the pipeline locked up. If we'd started earlier we would have had fifty percent locked up.

"TransCanada had started this group called Landowners for Fairness. They would have landowners sign a contract saying, 'We're going to negotiate the easement terms as a group.' So they were never trying to stop the pipeline. They were just trying to get a better deal for the landowners. I thought, 'Well, that's fundamentally messed up. They are immediately surrendering.' So I started flyering at those meetings in the parking lot, and asked Native Americans to come and drum, and we had people holding signs against the pipeline."

▫ ▫ ▫

The involvement of Native Americans changed the nature of the battle—and the lives of many of those involved. It also meant bridging perhaps the deepest divide in American life. "Faith Spotted Eagle, a member of the Yankton Sioux, asked me to come to a meeting that she was holding where they were going to sign a treaty against the Keystone XL Pipeline. She wanted me and the farmers and ranchers to come up and do a workshop on the Ogallala Aquifer, because obviously water is very important to the Native Americans . . . I had never worked with Native Americans."

A vast underground reservoir, the Ogallala Aquifer holds enough water to cover the entire continental US to the depth of two feet.

Stretching from South Dakota to Texas, its center is right under the state of Nebraska.[47] The source of about 30 percent of the groundwater used for irrigation in American agriculture, if it became depleted or contaminated the Great Plains, bread basket for the country, would quickly become the Great American Desert. The water is very near the surface; in the Sandhills, ranchers typically just dig a hole and the water pours in. TransCanada's original plan took the pipeline through ninety-two miles of the Sandhills, with the pipe often buried in water.[48]

TransCanada itself admitted the pipeline was likely to leak eleven times over its fifty-year lifespan; John Stansbury, who teaches engineering at the University of Nebraska, says the risk was ten times that.[49] In November 2017, another Keystone pipeline in South Dakota leaked 210,000 gallons of oil near the Lake Traverse Indian Reservation.

"I felt sure there would be some hostile feelings, because they are now farming and ranching [land that used to belong to Native Americans], especially up in the Sandhills where you find arrowheads where you're just walking. It is Native American land.

"So, I brought fifteen farmers and ranchers with me, and we went out to the Rosebud Casino, and it was a two-day meeting. At first we were all very nervous. And they organize their meetings differently. It's not like, 'Here is the schedule.' There was no real agenda, and about half a day of just ceremony before anything was discussed. But then they asked us to do our presentation, so I got up and gave this PowerPoint presentation about the Ogallala Aquifer, and then one of the elders asked if the farmers and ranchers would tell their stories.

"They got up one by one. We were all sitting in a circle at this point, and they started telling their stories, and naturally, not prodded or anything, started talking about how they knew that the land that they're now farming and ranching is [the Native Americans'] ancestral home ground, and that they love the land just as much as they know Native Americans do, and that is the common bond between them, that they take care of the land for the next generation, which is a deeply held value of farmers and ranchers, especially in the Sandhills where they're going on seven generations at this point, and have family members lined up to take over the ranch.

"Chief Arvol Looking Horse, who is one of the huge spiritual leaders of the Sioux, was there. He didn't say a word the whole day, and sat there with his arms crossed, just looking down. I was very nervous. So, he stands up and he just looks at everybody and opens his hands, and says, 'Welcome to the tribe.' After that it was easy moving forward, because I'm a fast talker!"

One thing Kleeb says she learned from the experience is that sometimes she needs to slow down. Another is "that I don't have all the answers. That maybe [my] idea is not the best idea." Wincing at the memory, she recalls "some really stupid mistakes. We had to get a permit for those twelve tepees. Part of the agreement with the Parks Police was that we wouldn't have people sleep in them. And I didn't know the deep emotional tie that people have to tepees, and so on one of the calls there was a clear pushback: 'You have no idea what you're doing . . . These are our sacred homes.' And I just did not get it, and was like, 'You can't sleep in them. This is not Occupy Wall Street,' and that was obviously very offensive."

▫ ▫ ▫

Local knowledge—the kind you can only get from attentive, face-to-face listening—is crucial to the way Kleeb works. But that doesn't make her a technophobe. Before it became a movement, BOLD was a website. "I think people assumed, because we were organizing mostly rural folks, that somehow they're not online. They very much are online, and are on Facebook all the time! Maybe Twitter not so much, but definitely Facebook. They go to websites to get information, because their newspapers only come out once a week or once every two weeks. Our BOLD website was critical for sharing long pieces of information. We used Facebook for all those strong actions—like 'Call Senator Heineman,' or 'Write a letter to the editor'—that keep people engaged. We created a very strong visual brand so people felt tied—emotionally tied—to fighting the pipeline."

The Keystone XL pipeline route passes through three states on its way to Steele City, and three more down to the Gulf. Yet the most significant opposition has come in Nebraska. According to Kleeb, that's no accident. "My first conversations in Nebraska were around a tiny, little kitchen table in the ranch house that Scott lived in with other ranchers. And they all described politics in a very populist way. They hated big corporations and they hate big government. That the only people that they can rely on are their neighbors. They would talk about the land in ways that Bill McKibben would talk about the land."

Nebraska was where, on July 4, 1892, the men and women attending the inaugural convention of the Populist Party at the Omaha Coliseum voted to endorse what became known as the Omaha Platform. "We meet," proclaimed the preamble, "in the midst of a nation brought to the verge of moral, political, and material ruin. Corruption dominates the ballot-box, the Legislatures, the Congress, and touches even the ermine of the bench." The party's purpose? "Assembled on the anniversary of the birthday of the nation . . . we seek to restore the government of the Republic to the hands of 'the plain people.'" Many of their demands—women's suffrage, a graduated income tax, secret ballot, the direct election of senators, enforcement of the eight-hour day—though radical at the time, have long since passed into law. Others, like the call to protect "American labor" from exploited foreign competition, remain controversial.

But as Kleeb reminded me, Nebraska still has no private utilities. "Yeah, it's from the Populists. And because eighty years ago, when they were creating public power, our small rural towns didn't have any electricity, and it would have been too expensive—there's no way a private utility would have made money. But it's still against the law. The same thing with public education. We don't allow charter schools in our state."

Nebraska's Populist heritage means that what can seem radical elsewhere is accepted here as just common sense—or at least worth debating. Nebraska remains the only state with a unicameral legislature—another legacy of Populism. Some aspects of the state's distinctive political landscape, though, are less congenial to progressives. While Kleeb insists that rural and urban areas share the same basic concerns, "there's no question they use different words. Rural folks definitely use the word 'community' and 'God' way more than urban people. Here you can't just say that you respect people that are pro-life. You have to deeply understand where they're coming from."

As perhaps the most effective "wedge issue" in electoral politics, differences over abortion and a woman's right to control her own fertility have repeatedly allowed Republicans to attract and hold voters who disagree with them on economics or the environment—especially in rural states. Here again, Kleeb uses her own story to connect, describing herself as "both pro-life and pro-choice."

"I think the vast majority of Americans are both pro-life and pro-choice. We've forced politicians, and sometimes individuals, to say that you're one or the other, and that it's some black-and-white issue. I've had an abortion, and I think it's really difficult to put women and their families—when families are involved in the decision—into this black-and-white position. It's a very personal choice, and I don't think that government should ever restrict women's right to make that choice in their own lives."

"But I also . . . there's no question in my mind that life begins at conception and that that is a precious life, that we should do everything we can when women decide to give birth, to make sure that they have the health care they need."

When Kleeb had Kora [the oldest of her three daughters], "I was a single mom. So I both had an abortion and [then] chose to have a baby as a single mom, [when] I was working full-time and going to graduate school . . . And because family leave is not a great thing in our country, I had to go on WIC [the Special Supplemental Nutrition Program for Women, Infants, and Children] for almost three months because I didn't have the income from my full-time job anymore. Those are the programs that, from a very personal perspective, are why I firmly am in the Democratic column . . . I believe that government is a safety net for families. I sometimes feel that some pro-choice leaders don't talk about those aspects.

"[But] I've never met a woman that's proud she had an abortion. It's not like I'm putting a bumper sticker on my minivan that I had an abortion. And maybe some people in the pro-choice community wish that that was different . . ."

▪ ▪ ▪

When Kleeb was elected chair of the Nebraska Democrats in June 2016, *Esquire* political columnist Charles Pierce called it "a textbook example of how movements outside the formal political process can energize the institutions within the formal political process." Kleeb, he wrote, "will turn out to be a formidable surrogate" for Hillary Clinton[50]—positioning her to push the incoming administration to the left. "I decided to run for party chair because I honestly thought Clinton was going to win, and if the pipeline came back up I'd be in a position with the party where I could be advocating on a high political level and we'd be okay," she told me. Once Keystone XL was finally laid to rest she could turn all her attention to organizing.

It didn't quite work out that way. Donald Trump carried Nebraska by twenty-five points. His victory not only brought the "Black Snake"—as the Native Americans called the pipeline—back from the dead.[51] It also set off a civil war between Clinton Democrats and Sanders supporters that made the task of building an effective opposition even harder. In late January 2018, the party's Unity and

Reform Commission issued a report calling for a 60 percent cut in the number of superdelegates, a transparent vote count in caucus states, same-day registration, and primaries open to independent voters—all key Sanders demands. But the report, itself the result of compromise and negotiations—endorsed by both DNC chair Tom Perez (seen as aligned with the Clinton wing) and vice chair Keith Ellison (a Sanders backer)—has yet to take effect. Meanwhile Kleeb has been struggling to raise the money to pay her own salary.

Asked how the national party could help, she responded, "One, stop screwing our local candidates. Two . . . stop giving lip service to rural and red states and actually give us the resources—both financial and training—that we need. If you're serious about turning around a party, it is a full-time job . . . It is mind-boggling to me that we only have twelve paid [state] chairs. All the rest are either part-time, or full-time volunteers like me. And then you wonder why we're losing elections at the state level . . ."

Not that Kleeb is waiting around. "We're doing these Blue Bench trainings. When we first introduced this and said, 'We're gonna do one in Omaha, one in Lincoln, and one in a rural community,' each time, people thought I was crazy. This next one is: How do you do GOTV [Get Out the Vote]? How do you target? How do you cut walk lists [showing door-to-door canvassers which houses to visit]? How do you even get into the VAN [the party's Voter Activation Network software]? We have this stripped-down training, so we're not locking people in a room for eight hours. It's a three-hour training each time. Forty minutes of concrete nuts and bolts—and then we're out in the field." When 2017 began, Kleeb already had two hundred thousand miles on her minivan.

As for Keystone XL, Trump issued an executive order approving the pipeline within days of his inauguration. Yet Kleeb remains not just optimistic, but confident. In November 2017 the Nebraska Public Service Commission approved a route for the pipeline—only it wasn't the route TransCanada had applied for. That same month a federal judge ruled that a lawsuit against the pipeline brought by BOLD, the Sierra Club, the National Resources Defense Council, and other environmental groups could proceed.

Kleeb explained why, contrary to most press coverage, both decisions were "a win for us, because I'm not sure TransCanada can afford two years . . . In order to get all the other easements they would then need in South Dakota [to follow the route the state approved to connect with an older pipeline] . . . They'd have to go across the border and then come down. They would have to cross tribal land, and there's no way the Rosebud Sioux, for example, are going to give up their land to Keystone."

Time—and the falling price of oil—is on the side of Keystone's opponents. And if it comes to that, Kleeb knows the Cowboy and Indian Alliance is ready to ride again.

CHAPTER FOUR

Carlos Ramirez-Rosa—Chicago Rules

Governing from the Left

They wanted a better life. His father was a teacher. His mother was a teacher, too, but her father—his grandfather—worked in the Mexican coal mines. He also drove a taxi. Once he was so exhausted by working two jobs he fell asleep in a mineshaft deep underground, waking up in the blackness.

When Carlos Ramirez-Rosa was four years old his mother took him from their home on the North Side of Chicago to Springfield, the state capital. "It was a four-and-a-half-hour bus ride. He asked why were we going, and I told him it was to get more money for the schools," his mother told me. "Afterward he asked, 'Where are we going now?' I told him we were going home. He said, 'But we didn't get the money!' Carlos has always had a conscience."

They just wanted a better life. His father grew up in Puerto Rico, in the cradle of that island's independence movement. His mother's family came from Monterrey, in Mexico. Her father, she said, brought them to America so his three daughters "could have a future. Because Mexico is so *machisto*." In Chicago he found work in a steel mill, joined the union, sent his daughters to college. "[My parents] came in at the sweet spot right before neoliberalism, where you still have the state playing a role in lifting people out of poverty. People like my parents—brown folks and black folks—were able to enter good-paying government jobs, institutions of higher education, and benefit from the social safety net and the hand up."

His grandparents lived in Lincoln Park, sharing a single bathroom with another family in a three-story house with five other families. Today that house is a mansion; the neighborhood is now one of the richest in the city. But when his mother's family arrived it was full of immigrants—first-generation immigrants from Latin America and second-generation immigrants from Eastern Europe. The Young Lords Party had just taken over the Armitage Methodist Church around the corner, an early outpost in the losing battle against gentrification.

His immigrant parents wanted a better life. He just wanted to live his own life. "Growing up, I was always taught by my parents to be proud of my Latino identity. [They] would take me to the Mexican Independence Parade, and they would dress me up in a *charro* suit, which is like a mariachi suit. I would wave the Mexican flag." Then in June "they would take me to the Puerto Rican parade, and I would put on traditional Puerto Rican dress and wave a Puerto Rican flag."

It was different when he realized he was gay. "[I grew up] just a few blocks from Boystown [the center of Chicago's LGBTQ community] . . . We'd drive around with my father, may he rest in peace, and he'd be like, 'Oh, look at that faggot there!' Although I knew from a very young age that I was queer, it wasn't until my senior year of high school that I came out to my peers. I still didn't come out to my family.

"I came out to my siblings in my freshman year [of college]. My parents divorced when I was in high school, and I was home for winter break, walking down the stairs, and my mother just stops me and goes, 'Are you gay?' I go, 'Yeah.' She goes, 'You know, I love you no matter what.' That was a good experience."

Only his mother also said, "Don't tell your grandmother. Don't tell anyone else in the family. Just wait until your grandmother dies."

He waited, but in 2015 Carlos Ramirez-Rosa became the city's youngest Alderman—and the first openly gay Latino ever elected to any office in Chicago. "At that point, I had no choice, because my grandma is going to hear about this somewhere. It might as well be from me."

▫ ▫ ▫

Wearing a "Soy Queer Latin@" T-shirt, Anthony Joel Quezada is standing on the corner of Sawyer Avenue and Altgeld Street on a sweltering summer afternoon trying to get his audience to summon up the courage to defy the law. Quezada, a young activist who is on Alderman Ramirez-Rosa's staff, tells the crowd of thirty people gathered in the shade of a community garden in Chicago's rapidly gentrifying Logan Square neighborhood that since Donald Trump became president, the threat of deportation has brought fear to the city's immigrant communities.

The atmosphere may be festive—there are pizzas and watermelon slices spread out on makeshift tables, coolers full of bottled water, and small children playing hide-and-seek among the planters—but the speeches are serious. For Quezada, the issue is personal as well as political. "My father is still an undocumented person," he tells them.

Charles Rosentel, a teacher who lives in the neighborhood, says the issue hits close to home for him, too. Rosenstel teaches world history and coaches the debate team at a charter high school in Hermosa, a few blocks to the west. He talks about one of his students, "the most gifted debater I've ever coached.

"If she wants to go to Harvard, she's got the talent," he says, "but I can't take her to the state championships because she's afraid that if she leaves Chicago, even for a day, the aunt and uncle she lives with—her guardians—might not be there when she gets back."

Several weeks earlier, Rosentel and his wife, also a teacher in Hermosa, attended an Immigration 101 class organized by Quezada's boss, Carlos Ramirez-Rosa. Aimed at educating potential allies, the sessions were held at the same time as a Know Your Rights class for immigrants and their families.

Before Ramirez-Rosa speaks, he stops for a kiss from his mother, Margarita Rosa, who reaches up to adjust his collar. "Carlos has always been for justice," she tells me. When the alderman steps up to the mic, he begins by telling the group, "Today we have chosen to come together and keep each other safe." After the speeches the audience is broken up into teams to leaflet the neighborhood with flyers advising residents what to do if officials from Immigration and Customs Enforcement (ICE) knock on their door. At the same time, he and Quezada ask those who are willing to physically block attempted deportations—and get arrested while doing so—to identify themselves. These people will be trained in nonviolent civil disobedience and organized into a phone tree covering the entire Thirty-Fifth Ward, with the whole campaign directed and funded out of Ramirez-Rosa's office.

As volunteers for arrest step forward, Quezada turns to me. "This is what governing from the left looks like," he says.

▫ ▫ ▫

At a time when the Right seems triumphant at every level of government, from Tea Party–dominated boards of education to reactionary state legislatures to the Republican Congress to the alt-right spectacle provided by the Trump presidency, the very idea of using the machinery of the state for progressive ends can seem like a pipe dream. Protest, certainly. Even, with a little organizational inspiration, resistance. But actual power? Over long decades of opposition, the Left has developed a well-founded skepticism toward power—one that neither the corrupt clientelism of Rahm Emanuel's local administration, nor the periodic election of neoliberal Democrats nationally, has done anything to dispel.

Ramirez-Rosa is a different kind of Democrat—a self-proclaimed Democratic Socialist in the Bernie Sanders mold who sees himself not as a powerbroker but as what he calls "a movement-elected official." Using his district office and staff budget to organize community-defense committees is part of it. So is being the chief sponsor of a bill to reinstate the corporate "head tax" on firms with more than fifty employees, the proceeds of which would go to fund Chicago's cash-strapped public schools. (The city had a similar tax from 1973 to 2014, when Emanuel abolished it.) Ramirez-Rosa's version would also encourage companies to hire from the city's most disadvantaged neighborhoods by making their residents exempt from being counted under the head tax.

He's backed calls by local activists for a Civilian Police Accountability Council, a democratically elected body that would make civilian control over the police more than mere rhetoric. He's also been an important voice for the public financing of elections through a New York City–style small-donor matching system—a potentially transformative reform in a city where the mayor is a master of big-donor fund-raising. And he's introduced a bill to divest city funds from companies involved in the Dakota Access Pipeline. "I'm working on the legislative end and in the community garnering support," he tells me when we sit down in his office. "To me, that is what movement politics looks like."

That connection—between a community-based movement and the elected officials the movement holds to account—is central to his vision. As Ramirez-Rosa says, that kind of politics may be new to Chicago, but "the MAS, Movimiento al Socialismo in Bolivia—I'm not saying that they're perfect, but I think that they've done an amazing job of checking neoliberalism in Bolivia. Their first foray into politics they were in just six percent of municipal seats in the country. Six years later, they went on to win the presidency. I think that that's the direction that we need to be moving towards as the Left.

"Another inspiration is the Movimiento de Pobladores in Chile. These are poor people, working people who are being displaced from their neighborhoods in Chilean cities and began to occupy space. They've run members for office. The member has to subsume their legislative agenda to the community assembly of the *pobladores*, and do things like engaging in direct action and getting arrested. I think that's a model as well. We can even look to something like the Paris Commune. This is an experiment. Working people said we are going to seize power and we're going to govern. There are many examples both contemporary and historical, where we've seen an alternative to the status quo . . ."

▫ ▫ ▫

Though Ramirez-Rosa talks knowledgeably about the "pink tide" of Latin American socialists and can quote Zapatista leader Subcomandante Marcos and Bolivia's Evo Morales, he also cites George Washington Plunkitt as a source of inspiration. Describing the nineteenth-century head of New York's Tammany Hall machine as "a very smart man," he says that too often the Left has failed to think tactically. "The onus is now on movements that are aspiring to gain electoral power to say, 'What are our opportunities and where can we take them?' I'd like to be positioned to play that role for leftist movements, to say, 'Okay, can we now move and take over this seat? Can we take over this administrative office?' Then we can bring the power and the resources that office has to bear on improving people's everyday lives."

Which may explain why, for all his radical commitments, Ramirez-Rosa also pays such close attention to the potholes and zoning issues that are a council member's bread and butter. One of the community's grievances with Ramirez-Rosa's predecessor was his cozy relationship with a local developer. "This guy owns seventy-four million dollars' worth of property in this neighborhood alone," Ramirez-Rosa says. "After the election, he came to me to try to cut a deal. When I turned him down, he went and bought this building. Luckily, I have a four-year lease."

"But the tenants that were on a month to month, he came to

them and said, 'Next month, your rent is going to double—from seven hundred dollars to fourteen hundred dollars.' In the 1990s, the state legislature—at the behest of the real estate industry—passed preemption. Meaning that no municipality anywhere in Illinois can impose any type of rent control or rent stabilization scheme. I share office space with Representative Will Guzzardi. He's filed a bill to overturn that, and I've said that if we can overturn Rent Control Preemption in Springfield, we can have [rent control] in Chicago."

Local issues also offer Ramirez-Rosa an opportunity for organizing through the use of participatory budgeting. "We do a yearlong process with community assemblies.* Each alderman gets $1.3 million to spend. Basically we say, 'What do you want to see built in your community? Do you want the streets resurfaced? Do you want to see new lighting? Do you want to see a soccer field built at a local school?' We have one assembly in every neighborhood in the ward. People brainstorm ideas. We also go to block parties, churches, schools."

The process generates a list of proposals that are put to a vote, and the top winners get funded. "In order to vote, you don't have to be a US citizen," Ramirez-Rosa adds. "You don't have to be a registered voter. You just have to prove that you live in the community—and you have to be at least fourteen years old."

Ramirez-Rosa hopes that participatory budgeting can extend beyond funding neighborhood improvements to give residents democratic control over zoning and development. "What people have told me is that they want Logan Square to remain economically and racially diverse," he says. This resistance to gentrification puts him on a collision course with City Hall.

"I was very explicit that I would be an organizing alderman," Ramirez-Rosa says. "That I would work to build a base of people in my community who will hold me accountable and fight for progres-

---

* See p. 143 for a similar idea adopted by the new administration in Jackson, Mississippi.

sive change—and who, when I pick fights with Rahm Emanuel, will have my back."

Although the current balance of power on the City Council favors the mayor, the progressive coalition that forced him into a runoff in 2015 didn't disappear with the defeat of challenger Jesús "Chuy" García. Indeed, the coalition's efforts in down-ballot races, and in changing the terms of debate, led *Crain's Chicago Business* to proclaim that "Emanuel won the mayor's race, but progressives won the election."

Ramirez-Rosa expects that trend to continue. "I'm a big believer that we can build socialism from below. We need to create these opportunities for working people to hold the reins of power and govern themselves," he says.

▫ ▫ ▫

With his boyish undercut hairstyle and black-rimmed nerd glasses Ramirez-Rosa doesn't look like a typical urban politician. But then most big-city officials shy away from any mention of socialism. Yet it isn't just the way he looks, or talks about politics—or sexuality—that sets Ramirez-Rosa apart. There's also the path he took to elected office. And the alliances he formed along the way.

Growing up in a household with two teachers, "we would talk about school reform" around the family dinner table. "My parents were very critical about what some people today try to pass off as school reform. 'Voucher' and 'charter' were always dirty words in my house."

After attending the Inter-American Magnet School—founded in part through his parents' efforts—Ramirez-Rosa graduated from Whitney Young High, another magnet school. "It's one of the ways the city's elite have been able to separate their own children," he says, adding, "but it also has one of the highest percentages of students eligible for free lunches."

"Whitney Young was actually built a mile west from the Loop, on the site of a factory building that burned down during the 1968 race riots after Martin Luther King's assassination. The school was thirty percent black, thirty percent white, twenty percent Latino, and twenty percent Asian. That was a great experience because it was the first time that I met someone of Muslim descent. It was the first time that one of my classmates was Jewish."

In a city whose diverse population has long sheltered behind—or been shut out by—a patchwork of starkly segregated neighborhoods, the experience was eye-opening. "Chicago geographically is very large. To be able to meet people from all different parts of the city . . ."

One thing he learned was that the economic factors that forced his family out of Lincoln Park were operating throughout the city. "Chicago has been at the forefront of the movement to push poor people out of major urban centers—push them out into the outskirts, into the suburbs, in many ways replicating the *favelas* that surround so many Latin American cities. This began here in the 1970s, before we even had the words for 'gentrification' or 'displacement.' Mayor Daley was calling it 'urban renewal.'

"One of the greatest travesties of the ability of the rich to displace poor people from areas deemed to be desirable is the way it disrupts entire communities. We now know—the research lays out very clearly—how it disconnects people from public transportation and parks. That's what we're seeing right now here in Logan Square."

After high school Ramirez-Rosa enrolled at the University of Illinois in Urbana-Champagne, an experience he describes as "culture shock. I went from a grammar school that was very much a leftist bubble, to a high school that was this very diverse, cosmopolitan setting—to the cornfields. I'm suddenly meeting folks from central and southern Illinois, and the Chicago suburbs. I arrived on campus a year after the most popular fraternity-sorority had thrown a party called Tacos and Tequila where the girls dressed up as if they were pregnant. The men dressed up as if they were 'illegal aliens.' So I got engaged in student activism.

"I was involved doing undergraduate solidarity work with the food and service workers that were represented by SEIU Local 73. Then with the graduate employee union GEO, which is affiliated with the American Federation of Teachers. The GEO actually went on strike, and I organized undergraduates to join them on the picket line. You get to hang out with cool smart graduate students. You get to help them win a fair contract. It's a lot of fun."

After college, Ramirez-Rosa went to work for Luis Gutiérrez, the longtime representative from Illinois's Fourth Congressional District—gerrymandered to combine the largely Puerto Rican neighborhoods on the city's northwest side with Mexican areas south of the Loop into a majority Hispanic district. "I'm young, I'm idealistic, thinking I'm going to go work for this member of the Congressional Progressive Caucus, the national champion of immigration reform."

The experience was eye-opening—and disappointing. "I quickly saw how he and his office were not connected to the grassroots movement led by undocumented people. I saw compromises I did not think were in the best interests of the progressive movement, like his support for Mayor Rahm Emanuel [whom Gutiérrez endorsed in 2015]. In many ways, I lost my belief in electoral politics."

So Ramirez-Rosa began working for the Illinois Coalition for Immigrant and Refugee Rights (ICIRR). "I was running their deportation defense effort. Again, I kept coming up against elected officials who just didn't get it. We were down in Springfield lobbying for a bill that would protect immigrants from deportation and make sure that Illinois wasn't collaborating with ICE. We would run into progressive Democrats from Chicago, many of whom were also Latino, who just didn't understand. I started to think, 'Okay, what would a politician connected to a movement look like?'"

In the summer of 2014, ICIRR sent him on a training run by National People's Action. Now known simply as People's Action, the Chicago-based organization has a long history of using direct action to confront corporate power. But in 2014, the group sensed an electoral opening. "What really pushed me," Ramirez-Rosa says, "was the notion that we had to take risks. They said, 'You know, billionaires don't question themselves.' They never question their ability to govern, to lead—but queer people, people of color, women, they question themselves all the time. Poor people say, 'I'm not smart. I'm not good enough.' We're fed these messages."

▫ ▫ ▫

Ramirez-Rosa may have been a reluctant recruit to electoral politics. But his decision to run for office came at a time when the relationship between political movements and political parties was being radically reimagined—not just in Chicago, or the United States, but throughout the world. Even as Latin America's pink tide began to recede or retrench, the rise of Syriza in Greece and Podemos in Spain seemed to show a new way forward for social democratic politics that had become exhausted by endless accommodations with neoliberalism. And though Syriza would itself become yet another cautionary tale of the risks of assuming political responsibility without genuine political (and economic) agency, the continued flourishing of Podemos—whose more agile activists, though prepared to govern, put less emphasis on parliamentary politics and more on maintaining their connection with the movements that gave birth to the party—suggested that the "Syriza trap" of coming to power only in order to administer a more "humane" version of austerity may not be the inevitable fate of radicals in government. At the same time the remarkable revival of Britain's Labour Party under leader Jeremy Corbyn provided yet another example of what can happen when a populism of the Left is allowed to confront authoritarian austerity.

Despite—or, in many cases, in response to—Mayor Rahm Emanuel's seemingly unbreakable grip on the city's Democratic machine,

Chicago, too, saw a flourishing of movement politics. As in the rest of America, much of the credit is due to Bernie Sanders, whose near-miss campaign for the Democratic nomination almost single-handedly rescued American socialism from the ash heap of history. "Bernie Sanders did more to raise class consciousness by running in one primary than all the socialist papers sold in the last thirty years," Ramirez-Rosa told me. In the wake of the Vermonter's crusade, membership in DSA, the Democratic Socialists of America, went from eight thousand members in 2015 to twenty-five thousand two years later, making it officially the largest Marxist organization in the country.[52]

In Chicago, activists from the National Nurses Union (NNU) got together with the People's Lobby, a membership-based local grassroots organization, to form Reclaim Chicago. Avowedly populist, the aim was to take the city back from developers—and take local political power back from Emanuel's corporate-funded Democratic machine, beginning with the Chicago City Council. The group also played a crucial role in replacing Anita Alvarez, the Cook County state's attorney who bungled the investigation into the police shooting of Laquan McDonald, with Kim Foxx.

"Reclaim Chicago is a model for movement electoral politics," said Michael Lighty, NNU's director of policy. "What Reclaim does is target specific wards where existing community groups have a base, identify people who are angry, disenchanted with politics as usual, and tell them, 'There's something you can do about it.'"

"Bernie Sanders woke a sleeping giant," Amanda Weaver, Reclaim Chicago's executive director, told me. "We can't just keep fighting for our neighborhoods in our neighborhoods." The ability to connect local issues to larger struggles is one thing that sets Reclaim Chicago apart from traditional community organizers.

Another is the ease with which they braid together the personal and the political. When I first heard Weaver speak, she introduced herself as "a survivor of sexual assault, a daughter of low-income parents, and a sister who lost a brother to the opioid epidemic." I asked her why she did that.

"It's important to stand up, say my story, be vulnerable," she replied. "I think if we're fighting for our lives together, we have to know each other. It's important that our relationships are not just transactional."

This idea—that justice isn't just a matter of redistribution of resources, that politics is as much about who we are as what we want, and that the whole enterprise is more than simply a sequence of bargains and tradeoffs—is not new. But it does seem to resonate with particular power among millennial activists. The result is populism—but not as their parents or grandparents, or Europeans worried about the resurgence of the Far Right, understand the term. Instead of a racial or ethnic definition of "the people" that then excludes and demonizes all "others"—the racist original sin that turned America's nineteenth-century agrarian radicals into twentieth-century recruits for the Ku Klux Klan—this populism accepts and embraces racial, ethnic, and gender difference. Inherently "intersectional," it follows the British-Jamaican philosopher Stuart Hall's admonition that in a modern multicultural society only a politics "which works with and through difference, [will be] able to build those forms of solidarity and identification which make common struggle and resistance possible."[53]

To anyone with a sense of history, there is something both ironic and poignant about the revival of radical politics in Chicago—a city known not only for a brutal police riot during the 1968 Democratic National Convention, but also as the home of Saul Alinsky, the legendary organizer whose *Rules for Radicals* is shot through with disdain for electoral politics.

"We realized the limitations of doing Alinsky-style organizing—only picking goals winnable in the short term. That's not a thing we agree with anymore," says Kristi Sanford, another Reclaim Chicago activist. "We believe that you won't be taken seriously if you can't pose an electoral threat, endorse candidates, and take out people who impede you at every turn."

Strategy aside, Sanford says, "people don't always understand what issue organizing is about. People get elections—there's a very clear ladder of engagement with elections."

▫ ▫ ▫

When Ramirez-Rosa decided to run for office he was twenty-six years old. "I had two suits—a wool suit that Mom had bought me when I graduated from high school, and a polyester suit I bought at the Bloomington Coat Factory for four hundred dollars when I was working at Congressman Gutiérrez's office." This was in November, which was fortunate, because campaigning through a Chicago summer in a polyester suit would have been extremely uncomfortable. "I had enough money saved to pay four months' rent." The election was in February.

"I had this notion: What if we created a base of people in the community to hold the elected official accountable? My idea was to bring this experiment to the US. But I looked at my own financial situation and was like, 'I can't self-fund my campaign.' All my closest friends are poor millennials just like me. Many of them with retail jobs. They certainly can't cut big checks to my campaign, and I'm not willing to sell out to corporate interests to see if they'd be willing to fund my campaign."

Still, thanks to People's Action, he felt he had to try. "We're letting the Right and the corporations win if we count ourselves out," he told me. So he turned first to his own family for financial support. "You're going to have to ask a lot of people who you don't even know, so if you can't ask your family and your friends for money, how are you going to do that?" Though his relatives urged him to go to law school instead, once he laid out why he thought he could actually win, they agreed to help. Not just with money.

"My family was helping me knock doors, too. My friends, people in the community were also helping me knock doors. Out of a core group of thirty, we could rely on fifteen people every weekend to come out and help me collect the thousand signatures I needed to get on the ballot."

His opponent, Rey Colón, was a three-term incumbent backed by Chicago Forward, Mayor Rahm Emanuel's super PAC. "When he first ran, he ran as a progressive. People had become disillusioned once he was corrupted by the Daley machine and the status quo. They were looking to replace him." Ramirez-Rosa won two-thirds of the vote.

But it was what came next that marked him as a different kind of politician. "I was very explicit that I would be an organizing alderman. I was elected in February. I didn't take office until May. We spent the next three months connecting with people, writing letters, holding meetings and coffee mornings and saying, 'Hey, remember I knocked on your door in the campaign trail? This is this organization we're going to be starting."

With the $10,000 left in his campaign checking account he started United Neighbors of the Thirty-Fifth Ward. "I hired my field director. I'm working to set up my ward office and setting up this organization, but she was solely focused on setting up the ward organization. We're an autonomous group led by the members of the organization. Membership is based on your involvement. If you're involved at least once a month for the last three months, you have voting rights. We've done things like fight for affordable housing. When a neighboring alderman was facing stiff opposition to building a mixed-use affordable housing development, we went out there to canvass for him."

"We had the largest percentage of the vote for Bernie Sanders on Election Day in any ward in the City of Chicago. We were also one of only two majority-Latino wards to go for Kim Foxx [who beat District Attorney] Anita Alvarez, who covered up Laquan McDonald's murder—to the benefit of Rahm Emanuel. We also delivered the ward to our local state senator Omar Aquino, who was in a very tough fight with an opponent funded by the charter school lobby and one of Chicago's richest families, the Pritzkers."

Mention of the Pritzkers reminds me of Ramirez-Rosa's brief candidacy for lieutenant governor—and the first real test of his integrity. In 2017 J. B. Pritzker, who runs the family firm with his brother Tony, announced his candidacy for the Democratic nomination for governor. That September Daniel Biss, a state senator running as a progressive challenger to Pritzker, asked Ramirez-Rosa, who'd quickly emerged as one of the most charismatic young politicians in the state, to be his running mate. As a Chicago alderman, Ramirez-Rosa doesn't have much to do with Middle East policy. But when his membership of DSA became an issue thanks to the group's support for the Boycott, Divestment, Sanctions (BDS) movement on Israel/Palestine, he refused to disavow a group he'd joined only a few months before.

"Bernie Sanders opened up that door for me," Ramirez-Rosa told the *Chicago Reader*. "I said, if someone could run for president of the United States and say 'I'm a democratic socialist,' then, hell, I can come out of the closet. I've come out of the closet before."[54] Biss dumped him less than a week after recruiting him. Yet far from hurting Ramirez-Rosa, the dispute only served to raise his profile—and spread his reputation for embodying an end to the litmus tests and patronage politics of Chicago's past.

"We're going to build a different kind of power," Ramirez-Rosa vows. And Reclaim Chicago is just the beginning, says Tobita Chow, chair of the People's Lobby. The new movement-backed politics shaking Chicago is a model that Chow wants to see exported as widely as possible: "Because it's not enough to lobby the government, not enough to appeal to the government. It's time for us to *be* the government."

"It's a long game," says Carlos Ramirez-Rosa, a young man in a hurry.

CHAPTER FIVE

When the Republicans Were "Woke"

The Death and Life of the Lincoln Republic

We have used up all our inherited freedom. If we would save our lives, we must fight for them.

—Henry David Thoreau, "Slavery in Massachusetts"

If, as William Faulkner insisted, the high-water mark of the Confederacy can be found partway up the slope of Cemetery Ridge, a low rise a few miles south of Gettysburg, Pennsylvania, just before two o'clock on the afternoon of July 3, 1863—a moment when, speaking for "every Southern boy fourteen years old," Faulkner wrote, "it's all in the balance, it hasn't happened yet," meaning that some fifteen thousand charging Confederates, led by Major General George Pickett, had not yet been flanked and cut to pieces by, among others, two regiments of the Second Vermont Brigade, ending Robert E. Lee's invasion of the North—the fullest flourishing of the Lincoln Republic is harder to specify.

Lincoln himself remains a complex, largely unknowable figure whose brooding dominance over our history still manages to leave room in the popular imagination for everything from the fanciful adventures of *Abraham Lincoln: Vampire Hunter* to controversy over whether the sixteenth president had, as his biographer Carl Sandburg (and many others since) have claimed, a "streak of lavender."[55] Instead we have Lincoln's rhetoric, itself encompassing not only the patient exposition of the Peoria speech and the Cooper Union address (which helped win him the Republican nomination) and the peerless concision of the Gettysburg Address but also the prophetic reckoning—and promised reconciliation—of the second inaugural.

The Lincoln Republic is another thing. Though named for the man who both enunciated its highest ideals and whose calculating response to the exigencies of warfare brought it into being, the Lincoln Republic owed no more—and no less—to Lincoln himself than a child owes to a parent who dies before its birth. The struggles for workers' rights, racial justice, and economic equity in America existed before Abraham Lincoln, and carry on today. But the fusing together of those battles into a great national mobilization enlisting not only millions of Americans, but the vast power of the federal government—though largely forgotten today—is as much Lincoln's legacy as any speech or statue. As we find ourselves, yet again, in a time when the arrogance of wealth seems restrained neither by law nor custom, it may be useful to recall how our ancestors confronted and overcame the dominant oligarchy of their day—and how, at the very moment of victory, they were cheated of their prize.

▫ ▫ ▫

In the decades after the Whiskey Rebellion the questions of who, precisely, were the people, and who had the right to speak in their name, came to dominate American politics. The demise of Hamilton's Federalists and the rise of Jefferson's Democratic-Republicans saw not only a steady widening of the franchise—at least for whites; for free blacks the opposite was true—but the gradual transformation of informal political clubs into organized parties. The increasing influence of the people out-of-doors, climaxing in the election of Andrew Jackson, gave rise in turn to competing visions of the economy and the role of the government, with Jackson's opponents, the Whig Party, favoring high tariffs for the protection of native industry, a national bank (which Jackson shut down), and a program of internal improvements funded by a national debt. The Jacksonians, on the other hand, were for westward expansion (and the removal of Native Americans), suspicious of banks and finance, and inclined to favor the presidency over the legislative branch.

With argument raging over everything from the financing of roads and canals to the price of bread—a meeting called by the Locofocos, a faction of the Democratic Party in New York City, led to a flour riot in February 1837—to states' rights, immigration, and the role of the Catholic Church, neither Whigs nor Democrats were able to fully contain the debate. United in their hatred of Jackson and his works, the Whigs were vulnerable to raids by temperance crusaders and nativists. The Democrats, meanwhile, were riven by faction, with conservative Hunkers and radical Barnburners fighting for control in New York State and over Vice President John C. Calhoun's theory that individual states had the right to "nullify" federal laws, pitting him against President Jackson. Yet amid all this discord, there was one issue both parties agreed was out of bounds.

As has often been noted, the words "slave" and "slavery" do not appear in the Constitution. In this the Framers were merely pioneering what would become common ground for their successors—deferral of the issue. Historians still differ over whether, by incorporating the three-fifths clause, which apportioned congressional representation according to the free population of a state and "three fifths of all other Persons," and a further stipulation that a "Person held to Service or Labour in one State" who escapes into another must be returned (without specifying how this is to be enforced), the Framers were bowing to slaveholders, or merely buying time.[56] Because at the turn of the nineteenth century, the belief that slavery was, as Lincoln would later put it, on "the course of ultimate extinction" was widespread. In Virginia, yields of tobacco kept falling due to depletion of the soil. By 1804, all the northern states had banned slavery; four years later, Congress outlawed the African slave trade.

Though native-born slaves could still be bought and sold throughout the South, the market for their labor was shrinking fast—until the invention of the cotton gin.

Unlike the long staple cotton that grew only on the barrier islands of Georgia and South Carolina, upland or short staple cotton was full of seeds; it could take a slave a whole day to process, or "gin," a single pound. By allowing two slaves to process fifty pounds of cotton a day, Eli Whitney transformed the American economy, turning the Plantation South into an export powerhouse that produced 75 percent of the world's supply of cotton—most of it bound for the mills of Britain or New England.[57] Growing demand fuelled by the Industrial Revolution saw cotton production double every decade between 1800 and 1850, setting off a boom in the price of both land and slaves. With a combined value of some $3.8 billion, slaves were by a considerable measure the largest asset class in the American economy, worth more than the total value of all the buildings and farmland in the South—or, for that matter, *more than all manufacturing and railroads in the entire country*.[58] When James Hammond, the South Carolina planter, told his fellow senators in March 1858 that "Cotton is king" he was not exaggerating.[59] Yet less than five years after he spoke, that kingdom would be in ruins.

▫ ▫ ▫

At first, the only people who objected to slavery were the slaves themselves, and abolitionists, many on religious grounds. Rebellion is as old as slavery, but with most slaves dispersed on plantations, organized resistance was rare—indeed, two of the earliest American examples, Gabriel's rebellion in Richmond, Virginia, in 1800 and Denmark Vesey's revolt in Charleston twenty years later, took place in cities. Both were quickly—and brutally—suppressed. As for the abolitionists, they saw slavery primarily as a moral issue—which of course it was. But however sincere their convictions, or eloquent their denunciations, they had little political influence.

In response to agitation by free blacks, the four New England states quickly abolished slavery,[60] joined by Vermont (which never had it in the first place), Pennsylvania, New York, and New Jersey.* But Kentucky and Tennessee entered the Union as slave states, balancing the total at eight each. From then onward states were typically admitted in pairs, maintaining a balance in the Senate—an arrangement formalized by the Missouri Compromise of 1820, which also barred slavery from any other territory north of latitude 36° 30' in the lands acquired by the Louisiana Purchase. (The Northwest Ordinance of 1787 already banned slavery in the territory west of the Allegheny Mountains and north of the Ohio River. That measure was uncontroversial—partly because southern tobacco planters were happy to avoid competition.) Despite the slaves' misery, white indifference or fear for their fellow citizens—and the prevalence of racial prejudice even among many abolitionists—helped keep the "peculiar institution" off the political agenda.

In his diary, John Quincy Adams describes walking home with John C. Calhoun on the afternoon Congress voted through the Missouri Compromise. "Slavery," the former president believed, was "the great and foul stain upon the North American Union." Calhoun was slavery's most eloquent defender. Earlier in the week he'd told Adams that should slavery be threatened, the South would be prepared to leave the Union and form an alliance with Great Britain.

"I said that would be returning to the colonial state," Adams recalled.

"Yes, pretty much, but it would be forced upon them," Calhoun had replied.

After the vote the two men discussed their differing views of labor, with Adams arguing that the "confounding . . . of servitude and labor was one of the bad effects of slavery," while Calhoun countered

* "Gradual emancipation" laws in Pennsylvania, Rhode Island, and Connecticut meant some slaves remained in bondage for decades. In New Jersey slavery didn't end until the state legislature ratified the Thirteenth Amendment on December 6, 1865.

that on the contrary, having slaves to perform manual labor was "the best guarantee to equality among the whites." Adams was appalled. "The discussion of this Missouri question," he wrote, "has betrayed the secret of their souls." Southerners "fancy themselves more generous and noble-hearted than the plain freemen who labor for subsistence. They look down upon the simplicity of a Yankee's manners, because he has no habits of overbearing . . . and cannot treat negroes like dogs." If the "Union must be dissolved," Adams decided, "slavery is precisely the question upon which it ought to break." Yet the two men parted amicably, since "for the present . . . this contest is laid asleep."[61] Keeping it asleep—excluding the desperate cry of the slave from the political arena—would be the glue that bound America's political class through the next three decades.

What woke them up? The slaves themselves. By continuing to revolt, slaves demolished the myth of "the happy slave," while Nat Turner's Rebellion (1831), the Seminole Rebellion (1835), and above all the example of the Haitian Revolution showed what slaves could do—and would do, if given the means and opportunity. A growing body of allies was becoming increasingly militant. In 1831, William Lloyd Garrison began publishing the *Liberator*, demanding immediate emancipation and vowing to be "as harsh as truth, and as uncompromising as justice . . . urge me not to use moderation in a cause like the present. I am in earnest—I will not equivocate—I will not excuse—I will not retreat a single inch—*and I will be heard!*"

Though three-quarters of the *Liberator*'s subscribers were black, the American Anti-Slavery Society, which Garrison also led, attracted many whites, among them Theodore Weld. In 1834, Weld and a group of students at the Lane Theological Seminary in Cincinnati held a series of debates—participants included both former slaves and the sons of slave owners—culminating in a vote for immediate abolition, and a resolution to help free the 1,500 slaves residing just south of the Ohio River in Kentucky. When the school's board of trustees* moved to ban abolitionist activity on campus, forty of the Lane rebels decamped for the new Oberlin College, making it the first racially integrated undergraduate institution in the country.

Garrison was a revolutionary, who believed, as he said in an oration on July 4, 1837, that American society was built on "slavery and the slave trade." Branding the Constitution a "covenant with death," Garrison and his followers shunned electoral politics.[62] But the influence of abolitionist movement culture soon spread far beyond the bounds of the movement itself. In contrast with other reform movements, which tended to be organized from the top down by a genteel elite who, in Garrison's words, "have little sympathy with the common people," abolitionism had "a *republican* character" welcoming "persons of both sexes, and of all classes and complexions—farmers, mechanics, workingmen, 'niggers,' women, and all."[63]

Garrison's determination to "go for the whole people" wasn't just a figure of speech. Most of the women who signed the feminist Declaration of Sentiments in Seneca Falls, New York, in 1848 got their introduction to politics through the abolitionist movement. Two of them, Elizabeth Cady Stanton, who drafted the declaration, and Lucretia Mott, first met when they were both excluded, because they were women, from the 1840 World Anti-Slavery Convention in London, prompting Garrison, the leader of the American delegation, to sit with the women in the gallery at Freemasons' Hall, where he was joined by Nathaniel Rogers, editor of the New Hampshire abolitionist paper the *Herald of Freedom*.[64]

It was Rogers, with his firsthand knowledge of working conditions in the mill towns along the Merrimac, who, reflecting on abolitionism's failures, concluded they had been addressing the wrong audience. Instead of preaching to the gentry, he wrote, "We got to look to the working people of the North, to sustain and carry on the

* The board's response was endorsed by Lane's president, Lyman Beecher, who lived on campus with his family including his daughter, Harriet, the future author of *Uncle Tom's Cabin*.

Anti-Slavery Movement. The people who work and are disrespected here, and who disrespect labor themselves, and disrespect themselves because they labor—they have got to abolish slavery. And in order to do this, they must be emancipated themselves first."[65]

Rogers's linkage of southern bondsmen and northern workers, whom he called "the slaves of Capital," won him few friends among the wealthy Quakers and northern industrialists who supplied the bulk of the funds—if not the rank and file—for the movement. In the very first issue of the *Liberator*, Garrison himself warned against what he described as an attempt "to inflame the minds of our working classes against the more opulent, and to persuade men that they are contemned and oppressed by a wealthy aristocracy." As Eric Foner points out, while "both abolitionists and labor leaders spoke of the alliance between the Lords of the Loom and the Lords of the Lash—the textile manufacturers of New England and slave owners of the South . . . each drew from it a different conclusion. To the labor movement, factory owner and slave owner were both non-producers who fattened on the fruits of the labor of others; to the abolitionists what was objectionable in the factory owners was precisely their pro-slavery political stance, not their treatment of their employees."[66] Yet as Foner also notes, "the American anti-slavery movement, which began as a moral crusade, eventually found it would have to turn to politics to achieve its goals."[67] To do that, it would need to find a way to make working men and women see they had a stake in the fight.

▫ ▫ ▫

When Abraham Lincoln told the crowd at the Wisconsin State Fair in September 1859 that "labor is prior to, and independent of, capital; that, in fact, capital is the fruit of labor, and could never have existed if labor had not *first* existed—that labor can exist without capital, but that capital could never have existed without labor," he wasn't quoting Karl Marx, whose own variation on the labor theory of value wouldn't appear until his 1865 speech "Value, Price and Profit." (Marx himself was happy to credit "the famous" Ben Franklin for the view that labor was the source and measure of all value.)[68]

Lincoln's use of this "producerist" language was deliberate and self-conscious. It allowed him to appeal to the widest possible audience—as he remarked in Milwaukee, though farmers "are neither better nor worse than any other class . . . [they are, however,] the most numerous class"—while also assembling a coalition which, though perhaps inured to slavery where it existed, had a common interest in opposing the encroachments of slavery's defenders on their own lives. By the 1850s, he had a rich stock of incident and anecdote to draw upon.

The repeated failure to pass the Wilmot Proviso, which would have barred slavery from any territories acquired as a result of the war with Mexico, split the Democratic Party, with Northern Democrats rallying instead to the new Free Soil Party, many of whose leaders, like David Wilmot himself, professed indifference or outright hostility to blacks, but viewed the spread of slavery as a bar to the settlement of white farmers and workers. Their opponents, too, were divided between "Conscience Whigs" and "Cotton Whigs." The Compromise of 1850—brokered by Kentucky Whig Henry Clay and Illinois Democrat Stephen Douglas, which theoretically allowed slavery in the Southwest, and more concretely made the rendition of fugitive slaves a federal responsibility—represented a last, doomed attempt to keep slavery out of politics. Doomed because even as southerners became convinced that unless slavery were free to expand it would ultimately collapse, northerners—and a growing number of non-slave-owning southern whites—had become increasingly conscious of their own peril.

From the very first, slavery had imposed limits on Americans' freedom of debate—through the dominance the three-fifths clause gave to southern strength in the House of Representatives and in presidential elections, and then through an actual "gag rule" forbidding the House from even considering anti-slavery petitions.[69] The murder of Elijah Lovejoy, an Illinois printer, by a pro-slavery mob, and the brutal beating of Charles Sumner on the floor of the Senate showed how far abolitionism's opponents were prepared to go to maintain their power. Numbering fifteen states by 1850, the "Slave Power" balked at tariffs or taxes, saw no need for publicly financed schools or roads, and seemed ever-alert for new lands to conquer, from Kansas to Cuba. The 1854 Kansas-Nebraska Act, forced into law by a Democratic Party that controlled both houses of Congress as well as the White House, set off a bloody battle for Kansas with free-soil settlers subject to repeated violence while the Pierce administration took the pro-slavery side.

In 1856 a new party, the Republicans, finally made slavery into an electoral issue. Turnout in the North reached 83 percent, with supporters of nominee John C. Frémont forming "Wide Awake" clubs and parading through nighttime streets by torchlight chanting "Free Soil, Free Speech, Free Men, Frémont!" Republican rallies frequently mobilized crowds of twenty to fifty thousand, with one in Philadelphia attracting a majority of the city's voting age population.[70] But former president Millard Fillmore, running on the nativist American Party as a "moderate," drew enough votes to give Democrat James Buchanan the presidency. Just two days after administering the oath of office, Chief Justice Roger Taney handed down his decision in the case of Dred Scott, a slave who had been taken by his master into a free state. By a 7–2 majority the court barred Congress from any interference with slavery; Taney also declared that even free blacks were not American citizens, as blacks had "had no rights which the white man was bound to respect." If the 1856 Republican campaign had been a dress rehearsal for revolution, inspiring but ultimately abortive, the Dred Scott decision insured that next time the revolution would not be denied.

▪ ▪ ▪

The Republican Party of 1860 was still a movement party; slavery, at last, was the dominant issue. Yet the nominee was cautious. In his speech at Cooper Union in February he framed the question not as immediate abolition, but simply whether the Constitution prohibited the federal government from controlling the spread of slavery—as the Supreme Court had just ruled. The court, Lincoln declared, had been divided—and was mistaken. As for his critics, who derided "Black Republicans" for promoting not just abolition but social equality, Lincoln preferred ridicule to rebuttal, as he'd done in Springfield three years earlier, lampooning "that counterfeit logic which concludes that, because I do not want a black woman for a *slave* I must necessarily want her for a *wife* . . . In some respects she certainly is not my equal; but in her natural right to eat the bread she earns with her own hands without asking leave of any one else, she is my equal, and the equal of all others."[71]

To overcome entrenched power he saw, and described, not in sectional terms but as a "political dynasty," Lincoln assembled a majoritarian coalition of interests that, from a solidly abolitionist core, embraced not only the New England artisan and the western farmer, but urban immigrants in the Midwest and even female slaves. In Hartford in March 1860 he gave a speech linking the rights of workers to strike with the need to limit slavery—and set off a revival of the Wide Awake clubs that roused a young generation disgusted by the corrupt and compromised politics of the 1850s.[72] That summer William Seward, campaigning in Detroit on behalf of the man who'd beaten him for the Republican nomination, found himself addressing fully a tenth of the city's population at a single rally. "The reason we didn't get an honest President in 1856," Seward told the crowd, "was because the old men of the last generation were not Wide-Awake, and the young men of this generation hadn't got their eyes open. Now the old men are folding their arms and going to sleep, and the young men throughout the land are Wide Awake."[73]

If legions of "woke" activists in the streets wasn't enough *déjà vu*,

Republicans frequently described their opponents in terms that seem remarkably contemporary. "This Slave Power consists," said Charles Francis Adams, "of about three hundred and fifty thousand active men," which in a population of 31.4 million amounted to little more than . . . the top 1 percent. Yet this tiny minority was able to control fifteen states directly, influence the government of five or six more, and through its "numerous friends and dependents" elsewhere, determine the course of the federal government. While reformers argued among themselves, warned Adams, the Slave Power "never relaxes its vigilance over public events."[74]

Though the South threatened to secede if Lincoln won the election, it is a mistake to see the dispute as primarily sectional, and an even bigger mistake to see the Republicans' republican rhetoric—their resentment of the Slave Power's economic as well as political coercion, Lincoln's frequent endorsement of the view that labor creates value, and that labor is entitled to the full value of its products—as a mask for capitalist consolidation. Lincoln himself, who as a not-very-pious Kentucky-born lawyer should, on aggregate data, have been a pro-slavery Democrat, is sufficient warning against easy generalizations.[75] What we can say is that once the South did secede, Lincoln pursued a course that led inexorably to full emancipation—and to greater interference in the rights of property than any administration before or since.

When the war broke out in April 1861, there were only 16,367 men in the whole US Army, including 1,100 officers—of whom about a fifth resigned to join the Confederate States Army. Lincoln's initial call for 75,000 volunteers was easily met, and of the over two million men who eventually fought for the Union the vast majority—more than 94 percent—were volunteers.

In European armies, General Grant wrote in his memoirs, the majority of soldiers "are taken from a class of people who . . . have very little interest in the contest . . . Our armies were composed of men who were able to read, men who knew what they were fighting for."[76] They also knew what they were fighting against. In the same speech in which he'd proclaimed cotton's dominion, South Carolina senator James Hammond laid out his view that "in all social systems there must be a class to do the menial duties, to perform the drudgery of life." This class, said Hammond, "constitutes the very mud-sill of society and of political government." Hammond argued that restricting that role to black slaves guaranteed southern whites were all social equals—making the Confederacy what would later be called a *Herrenvolk* (master race) democracy.

Some whites, North and South, eagerly accepted the "psychological wage"—as W. E. B. Du Bois described it—of racial privilege.[77] Others realized that a society built on the backs of "mud-sills" had little claim to republican virtue. The soldier in the Ninety-Third Illinois who wrote to his parents that he and his two brothers—all farmers' sons—were eager for the "chance to try our *Enfields* on some of their villainous hides and let a little of that *high Blood* out of them, which I think will increase their respect for the *northern mud sills*" was not very unusual.

Nor was Peter Welsh, an Irish-born private in the Twenty-Eighth Massachusetts, who angrily rebuked his wife back in Ireland for questioning his judgment fighting for the "Black Republican" Lincoln administration. "This is the first test of a modern free government in the act of sustaining itself against internal enemys," he wrote in 1863. "[I]f it fail then the hopes of milions fall and the desighns and wishes of all tyrants will suceed the old cry will be sent forth from the aristocrats of europe that such is the comon lot of all republics." Welsh, a carpenter, wrote to his father-in-law that "Irishmen and their descendants have . . . a stake in [this] nation . . . America is Irlands refuge Irlands last hope destroy this republic and her hopes are blasted."[78] After Appomattox, a fifty-one-year-old colonel from New Jersey told his wife that it had been his "privilege to live and take part in the struggle that has decided for all time to come that Republics are not a failure."[79]

One need not agree with the historian Charles A. Beard that slavery "hardly deserved a footnote in the history of the Civil War" to see that the war was also—especially in the minds of the men who fought—a battle to save the republic.[80] Or to recognize how profoundly Lincoln, both by mobilizing the nation to fight, and by acting to end slavery to win that fight, would change the nature of that republic.

▫ ▫ ▫

It was the war, more than the man himself, that gave birth to the Lincoln Republic. At least since his speech in Peoria in 1854, Lincoln had been clear in his view that civic equality was "the sheet anchor of American republicanism." Slavery, he'd said then, was not just wrong, it was "monstrous . . . because it deprives our republican example of its just influence in the world—enables the enemies of free institutions, with plausibility, to taunt us as hypocrites." Yet as he admitted Lincoln saw no way to end actually existing slavery by legislative fiat—a view he repeated in his first inaugural.

Once again it was the slaves themselves that forced the issue, fleeing plantations in their thousands for Union lines, and gradually making the administration realize that they—their bodies, their labor, their eagerness to fight for freedom—were the hinge on which the fortunes of war would swing. In that sense, at least, the Emancipation Proclamation was the Lincoln Republic's founding document. Not just for what it did—which, in practical terms, wasn't all that much, since the writ of the federal government on January 1, 1863, didn't actually run to the states "in rebellion." But for what it promised: when the war was won, the Confederacy's slaves would be "forever free."

As he'd intended, Lincoln's Proclamation put paid to Gladstone's campaign to have Britain recognize the Confederacy. It also meant that abolition in America would follow a very different course than it had in Britain's colonies. When the British abolished slavery in 1833, the government had paid slave owners £20 million in compensation—an enormous sum amounting to 40 percent of the Treasury's annual budget. (Gladstone's father, John, received £106,769 for the 2,508 slaves he owned across nine plantations—the equivalent of about £80 million today.)[81] Before the war even most American abolitionists balked at the cost of "buying out" slavery. With Lincoln's promise, and its fulfillment in the Thirteenth Amendment three years later, the government had simply expropriated and liquidated assets worth nearly *fifty times* the entire $78 million federal budget for 1860.[82] Imposing a total ban on the use of fossil fuels today would be a small step in comparison.*

Other wartime economic measures were almost as significant—and as radical. In order to finance the war the government issued over a billion dollars worth of bonds, many of them sold to investors overseas, and imposed the country's first federal income tax—a flat 3 percent on incomes of over $800 a year—and a property tax. (Since only the top 3 percent of the population earned enough to have to pay it, the income tax was widely popular, but also ineffective; in 1862 the measure was revised to make the tax progressive, with a 3 percent rate on incomes above $600 and 5 percent on incomes over $10,000, and on the income of Americans who lived abroad.) The Legal Tender Act of 1862 allowed the government to issue "fiat currency"—paper money not convertible to gold or silver—printing hundreds of millions of dollars in "greenbacks" to pay for goods and services.

At the same time, the absence of Southern Democratic legislators let the Republican Congress act both on infrastructure projects long favored by former Whigs and the homesteading agenda of the former Free Soil Democrats. The Morrill Tariff not only raised revenue to

* For perspective, the current federal budget is $3.8 trillion. Estimates of the cost of buying out $3.8 billion worth of slaves in today's money range from $44 billion to $6.5 *trillion*—more than the combined market capitalization of the world's ten largest oil companies.

fight the war, but also shielded American industry from European competition; the Homestead Act and the Land-Grant College Act provided free land, public education, and the agricultural development of the West; the Pacific Railroad Act launched a continental railroad that led to the creation of a national market and accelerated the settlement of the frontier.[83]

Although Marx himself* wrote to Lincoln that "the working classes of Europe understood at once . . . that the slaveholders' rebellion was to sound the tocsin for a general holy crusade of property against labor," and that "as the American War of Independence initiated a new era of ascendancy for the middle class, so the American Antislavery War will do for the working classes,"[84] the Republican program fell well short of socialism. J. & W. Seligman (which got its start selling US government bonds in Europe), Lehman Brothers (Alabama cotton brokers who moved to New York City just before the war), Citibank (the underwriter on $50 million in Union war bonds) and the Morgan bank (J. Pierpont Morgan sold defective carbines to the Union army) all grew fat on war profits.[85] John D. Rockefeller, who like many wealthy men paid a substitute $300 to take his place in the army, kept the family's shipping business going on government contracts until his new venture—a Cleveland oil refinery—took off. Philip Armour made millions supplying meat to the Union army. The railroads gorged on 155 million acres of land grants from the public domain.[86]

But for every baby robber baron, there were thousands like the lieutenant in the Second Minnesota who, though bitterly opposed to emancipation, enlisted to save the Union, and by 1863 had come to the view that "Slavery and Aristocracy go hand in hand. An

* A frequent contributor to the *New York Tribune*, and a longtime friend of its editor, Charles A. Dana, Marx had apparently once considered immigrating to Texas. Marx admired the president he described as "Abraham Lincoln, the single-minded son of the working class," and remained in touch with Dana, who during the war became the White House's intermediary with General Grant.

Aristocracy brought on this war—that Aristocracy must be broken up."[87]

Or August Willich. A Prussian immigrant who during the Palatine uprising of 1848 had the young Friedrich Engels as his aide-de-camp, and later led the left opposition to Marx in the Communist League, Willich edited a German-language newspaper in Cincinnati before enlisting in the Union Army. Elected as colonel of the Thirty-Second Indiana Volunteers,* Willich was in command of the regiment at Shiloh where, on the second day, his men began to fire wildly. Riding to the front of his troops he commanded the regimental band to play "La Marseillaise," anthem of all republican movements, and then led his men in a bayonet charge which broke the Confederate line.

Was Willich deluded in believing the Civil War was a revolutionary struggle? His old sectarian adversary didn't think so. "In the Civil War in North America," Marx wrote, "Willich showed that he is more than a visionary."[88] In December 1863 the War Department worried that, just as General Grant was gearing up for a spring offensive, half the volunteer regiments were about to go out of existence. With their three-year enlistments about to expire, none of these men were subject to the draft. Yet 136,000 of these volunteers, who'd seen some of the hardest fighting in the war, re-enlisted. In Georgia, on the front lines of the transformation wrought by the Emancipation Proclamation, whole regiments of Sherman's army signed up en masse.[89]

Those men, too, knew what they were fighting for. So did the thirty-eight-year-old black barber from Philadelphia, who after fighting through the war with the Fifty-Fourth Massachusetts decided that mere freedom was not enough. "If we fight to maintain a Republican Government, we want Republican privileges," he declared. "All we ask is the proper enjoyment of the rights of citizenship."[90]

His view found its strongest expression in a new publication, launched by Radical Republicans, as the most aggressive campaigners

* In most volunteer regiments the men elected their company officers.

for racial justice called themselves, within weeks of the surrender at Appomattox. Declaring the Union victory a triumph of "democratic principles everywhere," the editors of the *Nation* were jubilant: "We utter no idle boast when we say that if the conflict of the ages, the great strife between the few and the many, between privilege and equality, between law and power, between opinion and the sword, was not closed on the day on which Lee threw down his arms, the issue was placed beyond doubt."[91]

▫ ▫ ▫

If it was the war that made the Lincoln Republic possible—necessary, even—it was Reconstruction that made it real. The Confederate army had been defeated, but the passage of "Black Codes" in many Southern states, aimed at keeping freed slaves on the land and obliged to work for their former masters, and race riots in Memphis in 1866 and New Orleans the same year indicated that winning the peace was going to be at least as difficult. Under the Louisiana code, blacks were required to have a labor contract by the tenth of January—and not allowed to leave until the following year. Refusal to work or absence from work was defined as vagrancy, which, upon conviction, meant being rented out as convict labor for private or public projects. South Carolina required blacks to pass an examination and pay a fee ranging from ten dollars to one hundred dollars in order to hold any job other than farm laborer or domestic servant.[92]

For Radical Republicans, who emerged from the 1866 elections dominant in both houses of Congress, such intransigence could only be countered by the active exercise of federal power—and by the complete integration of the freedmen into political and civil life. Thaddeus Stevens, the Pennsylvania congressman who, along with Massachusetts senator Charles Sumner, provided the Radicals' ideological leadership, said in the debate over the Fourteenth Amendment, one of the cornerstones of Reconstruction, that he had been waiting his whole life for "any fortunate chance" to remodel "all our institutions" in such a way as to free them from "every vestige of human oppression, of inequality of rights, of the recognized degradation of the poor, and the superior caste of the rich . . . [N]o distinction would be tolerated in this purified Republic but what arose from merit and conduct."[93]

Radicalism "united the Jacksonian Democratic belief in the unlimited rule of the majority with the Whiggist conception of an active state." If Southern Democrats bitterly resented the changes wrought by the war, and moderate Republicans viewed them as temporary emergency measures—and favored scaling back the state's influence over the economy and private property at the earliest opportunity—"Radicals . . . welcomed" such developments unequivocally.[94]

Like Lenin's quip that Communism was simply rural electrification plus all power to the Soviets, it sometimes seemed that Radical Republicanism was just black suffrage and equal citizenship—which, after the passage of the Fifteenth Amendment, left equal citizenship as the sole ground of contention. Radicals, drawing on free labor ideology, believed that "economic independence, gained through the ownership of real property or the possession of a skill" were the only guarantees of genuine equality.[95] Stephens in particular argued forcefully for confiscation of rebel land and redistribution to the slaves: "No people will ever be republican in spirit and practice where a few own immense manors and the masses are landless. Small independent landholders are the support and guardians of republican liberty."[96] But as the *New York Times*, the voice of Northern plutocracy, warned, "if Congress is to take cognizance of the claims of labor against capital . . . there can be no decent pretense for confining the task to the slave-holder of the South."[97]

Still, so long as the arguments were restricted to the rights of freed blacks, Republicans held firm, winning the presidency in 1868. As commander of Union forces in the West, Ulysses Grant had welcomed black "contrabands" into his camps, paying them for their labor. A supporter of the Reconstruction Acts passed by Radicals over President Andrew Johnson's veto, Grant took office determined that black lives, and votes, would be protected, sending three bills to Congress allowing the president to call out federal troops to enforce voting rights and federal prosecutors to pursue the Ku Klux Klan when state law enforcement failed to act.

Resistance to Radical Reconstruction wasn't confined to the South. Northern investors, many of them former abolitionists, who'd looked forward to the resumption of the cotton boom under wage labor—and enlightened Yankee tutelage—were distressed to discover that, left to their own devices, former slaves didn't want to plant cotton. From the Port Royal experiment on the Carolina coast during the war to the few plantations that were divided and sold to former slaves, "black landowners and renters preferred to farm much in the manner of ante-bellum upcountry white yeomen, concentrating on food crops as a first priority." And while the investors were disappointed, Southern landowners were desperate, since even if only "a few black farmers succeeded economically . . . all the others will be dissatisfied with their wage."[98]

▫ ▫ ▫

The glimpse into the future afforded by the Lincoln Republic was simply too dangerous. What did this future look like? On December 17, 1871, the International Workingmen's Association held a parade in New York City to commemorate the martyrs of the Paris Commune. The front rank—the place of honor—was assigned to the Skidmore Guards, an armed militia of black veterans. The seventy thousand marchers that followed included delegations from the Cuban independence movement (marching under a Cuban flag), an array of trade unions, an Irish band, and both the German-language Section 1 and the English-language Section 12 of the IWA. (Section 12 was led by the feminist campaigner and free-love advocate Victoria Woodhull,* who in 1872 became the first woman to run for president as the nominee of the Equal Rights Party.)[100]

By far the largest cohort, however, were supporters of the eight-hour movement. A goal of social reformers like the utopian Robert Owen, who limited the workday to eight hours in his experimental communities in Scotland and the US, the American eight-hour movement initially struggled to escape the shadow of slavery's more salient horror. Emancipation changed all that, and in 1865 the Eight Hour movement spread rapidly from Boston—where it was immediately endorsed by Wendell Phillips, who'd displaced his mentor William Lloyd Garrison as head of the American Anti-Slavery Society**—to Illinois, where in March 1867 the legislature enacted the country's first eight-hour law. Marx hailed it as "the first fruit of the American Civil War."

Until they marched south, many Union volunteers had never seen a slave. Having risked their lives to end one form of degradation, many came home determined to continue the fight. For such men, the war had been a nightmare, with greenback-fuelled inflation compounding the misery of combat, illness, and privation. Ira Steward, a Boston machinist, spoke for many when he warned that "while we will bear with patient endurance the burden of the public debt, we yet want it to be known that the workingmen of America will in future claim a more equal share in the wealth their industry creates in peace and a more equal participation in the privileges and blessings of those free institutions, defended by their manhood on many a bloody field of battle . . ."[101]

---

* *Woodhull and Claflin's Weekly*, the newspaper Woodhull edited with her sister Tennessee Claflin, published the first English translation of *The Communist Manifesto* in the United States.

** Unlike Garrison, who greeted the passage of the Thirteenth Amendment by declaring "my vocation as an Abolitionist, thank God, is ended," Phillips agreed with Frederick Douglass that without a guarantee of suffrage and redistribution of land to the freedmen, emancipation by itself would prove a hollow promise. Garrison's motion to disband the AASS in the summer of 1865 was rejected by a vote of 118–48, leaving Phillips in charge of the organization.

Making explicit the link between workers' rights and republican principles, a submission to the Massachusetts commission on working hours argued that current arrangements left workers no time "to comply with the public duties which we are having thrust upon us, or for the exercise of any personal gifts or longings for refined pleasures."[102]

Faced with such demands, a group calling themselves Liberal Republicans began to reconsider their allegiance to the priority of labor over capital. Horace White, co-owner of the *Chicago Tribune*, warned: "Capital moves the world and keeps the hammer, the engine and the spindle at work, but it must be handled judiciously, and receive its remuneration, else its motive power ceases and it flies away to countries which appreciate it more highly."[103]

Fear of what might happen if power currently wielded by the "best men" wound up in the hands of workingmen and women even prompted some Republicans to waver in their devotion to the tariff. "Protectionism," warned *Nation* editor E. L. Godkin, "contains the germ of communism; what may be in the hands of the sober, thoughtful capitalist a means of stimulating a useful industry, becomes in the hands of ignorant and fanatical socialists a justification of an equal division of goods."[104]

Though these former Radicals now described themselves as "liberals," and their new views as *laissez-faire*—implying a detached, Olympian attitude to the struggle between capital and labor—Wendell Phillips vowed that so long as the privileges of capital were sheltered by the state, labor would defend itself. "Labor comes up, and says, 'They have shotted their cannon to the lips; they have roughground their swords as in battle; they have adopted every new method; they have invented every dangerous machine; and it is all planted like a great park of artillery against us. They have incorporated wealth; they have hidden behind banks; they have concealed themselves in currency; they have sheltered themselves in taxation; they have passed rules to govern us: and we will improve upon the lesson they have taught us. When they disarm, we will—not before.'"[105]

The eight-hour movement, not racial prejudice alone, was the rock that broke Radical Reconstruction. "Filtered through the ballot-box comes the will of the people, and statesmen bow to it," said Phillips. It was that specter of a mass movement—terrifying even in defeat—that led E. L. Godkin's *Nation*, a journal founded to champion the freedmen's cause, to greet the fall of the Paris Commune with a denunciation of governments led by "trashy whites and ignorant negroes" in the American South.[106] Like the protagonist of Brecht's "The Solution," who suggests "the government . . . dissolve the people / And elect another," Godkin even co-authored a proposal with New York governor Samuel Tilden recommending the vote in large cities be restricted to taxpayers.[107]

If the battles of Reconstruction were too recent to tamper with the franchise—at least on economic grounds—race was another matter. Liberal Republicans joined Democrats in 1872 on a fusion ticket calling for an end to Reconstruction. And though Grant won reelection by a 12 percent margin of the popular vote, and an even wider margin in the Electoral College,* elite support for enforcing black civil rights was exhausted. Reconstruction, declared the *Nation*, was "simply a cover for robbery."[108] When a mob of white Democrats and Confederate veterans murdered 150 freedmen in Colfax, Louisiana, in 1873, the *Nation* depicted the massacre as a battle between a government composed of "ignorant negroes and white rogues" and the more able citizens "who find their civilized and complex society . . . suddenly taken possession of by a large body of people sunk in barbarism." If only Southern blacks would stop clamoring for their rights. "To those who say the negroes cannot trust the whites to govern them," the *Nation* replied: "Where they are forced to trust them, all goes well."[109]

---

* The Liberal Republican-Democrat nominee, Horace Greeley, died before the Electoral College voted; his electors were scattered among four other candidates.

Far more "intersectional" in their thinking than their opponents, the turncoat Radicals abandoned both the freedmen and democracy, replacing republican citizens with economic man. Recognizing the difficulty of convincing a majority not to vote in their own economic interest, they moved first to restrict the scope for intervention—in the economy, by replacing greenbacks with hard currency, and in the workplace, by denying the legitimacy of laws regulating working hours and conditions. By 1873, when Justice Stephen Field wrote his influential dissent in the *Slaughter-House Cases*, the Fourteenth Amendment itself, written to protect the rights of freedmen in the South, was already being reinterpreted to protect corporations and private property from state regulation.[110]

But laissez-faire alone didn't go far enough. Since prosperity now depended on the unimpeded reign of capital, liberals soon demanded a state with the capacity and will to use coercive power against its own citizens. Turning former slaves into a potential Southern proletariat precisely when Northern workers were becoming increasingly assertive, the Lincoln Republic had forced the issue of economic democracy. It was a short step from applauding the "redeemers" who restored racial order in the South to cheering on the coal operators who used Pinkertons to break the "Molly Maguires" strike in the Pennsylvania coalfields in 1875 to using federal troops against striking railway workers.

In March 1877 Rutherford B. Hayes became president despite having lost both the popular and electoral vote—to Democrat Samuel Tilden. (After months of wrangling, Hayes was allowed to take office in return for pledging to end the military occupation of the South.) That July, workers on the Baltimore and Ohio Railroad walked out after having their wages cut for the third time in a year; within a week the strike had spread to all of the major railroad lines. Thomas Alexander Scott, head of the Pennsylvania Railroad, suggested strikers should be given "a rifle diet for a few days." In Pittsburgh, the state militia fired on strikers, killing forty people.

In St. Louis, white railwaymen and black stevedores and boatmen walked out together in the nation's first general strike. Reading and Scranton, where the city's workers also called a general strike, were placed under martial law. In Illinois the governor called out the National Guard and the army.

Baltimore, which in 1861 had rioted against federal troops marching through to defend Washington, now frantically requested President Hayes deploy the army inside the city.[III] On July 21, with the Maryland National Guard trapped inside Camden Yards, Hayes sent in the marines to put down the strike. The same federal force that had only recently been withdrawn from the fight against racial terror in the South was now enlisted on the side of the robber barons.

From the Emancipation Proclamation to the Compromise of 1877, the life of the Lincoln Republic was barely fourteen years. Yet through the Gilded Age that followed, and the Progressive Era that followed that, the ghost of the lost republic would not lie still. The Big Money might be in the driving seat, Jim Crow the law of the land, but the dream of equality did not die. Broken by guns and bayonets, labor would rise again. So would the descendants of slaves. Like waves in the open ocean, from tiny disturbances and imperceptible ripples their gathering swell would grow and subside, retreat and recur, from Michigan to Mississippi, from that day to this, sustained not just by hope but by the memory of what the Lincoln Republic had been—and done. It happened once. It can happen again.

CHAPTER SIX

Waleed Shahid and Corbin Trent—A Tea Party of the Left?

June 10, 2014, was a hot, sunny day in Washington. Down in Richmond, the biggest city in Virginia's Seventh Congressional District, it was even hotter—and not just in degrees. That was the day the Tea Party, an upstart group born out of the ashes of Ron Paul's failed 2008 presidential campaign and previously known mainly for their costumed protests against President Obama's stimulus package, the Wall Street bailout, immigration reform, and the Affordable Care Act, managed to defeat Eric Cantor, the sitting Republican Majority Leader in the House of Representatives.

Cantor was no liberal. A favorite of corporate PACs and K Street lobbyists, he'd raised over $30 million for the National Republican Congressional Committee; his own campaign boasted a $5.5 million budget and twenty-three paid staffers, plus support from the National Rifle Association and the National Right to Life Committee—and hefty donations from the Blackstone Group and Goldman Sachs. His opponent was Dave Brat, an economics professor at Randolph-Macon College and Tea Party activist. Brat ran without any assistance from the party's national organization; he never got a single PAC donation either. Instead he raised just $200,000 from local donors—and didn't even spend all of it. Brat's campaign manager, Zachary Werrell, was a twenty-three-year-old Haverford graduate who slept on his boss's couch to save money. An internal poll on the Friday before the primary showed Cantor leading by thirty-four points; a Daily Caller poll put him ahead by thirteen points. Yet when the votes were counted it was the seven-term-incumbent Cantor who came up short—the first majority leader ever to be defeated by a primary challenger.

Brat's upset victory sent a current of fear through the Republican caucus in both houses of Congress, stiffening the party's leaders in their policy of noncooperation with the Obama administration, and killing off a bipartisan effort on immigration reform. Those at least were the headlines. But there was another response to Brat's unheralded triumph among activists and organizations on the left: envy. For years—in some cases decades—these groups had been stymied by a Democratic Party that seemed increasingly contemptuous of its base. Whether it was labor opposition to the North American Free Trade Agreement and the Trans-Pacific Partnership, African American and Hispanic objections to mass incarceration, or the growing influence of Wall Street bankers over what had once been seen as the party of working Americans, these activists had waged a long, sisyphean struggle against the party leadership. Now a ragtag bunch of Republicans had put the fear of the grass roots into their party.

Could the Left—both inside and outside the Democratic Party—emulate their achievement? Where might a "Tea Party" of the left come from? What would it look like? And what would be its signature issues?

▪ ▪ ▪

For a time, the Occupy Wall Street protest that began in September 2011 seemed like it might be the Tea Party's progressive counterpart. The two movements even shared a professed disdain for the crony capitalism epitomized by the 2008 Wall Street bailout. But while the Tea Party quickly attracted the support of right-wing celebrities like Sarah Palin and Glenn Beck, and institutional backing from Fox

News and the Koch brothers, OWS spurned celebrities—or leaders of any kind—and deliberately refrained from articulating clear demands or even engaging with electoral politics.

That doesn't mean it was a failure (though when I typed "Occupy Wall Street" into Google it added the word "failure" to my search). The group's invocation of the "99 percent" changed the national conversation, putting income inequality and political corruption on the political agenda for the first time in decades. OWS provided crucial momentum—and experience—to the effort to raise the national minimum wage. It reshaped—and dramatically broadened—the environmental movement, recruiting a new generation of activists to the fights against fracking and the Keystone and Dakota pipelines. Occupy's critique of the role of corporate money—especially finance capital—in electoral politics kick-started the movement to overturn the Supreme Court's ruling on *Citizens United*. And the millennials who thronged its encampments dragged the long-festering crisis over rising college costs and skyrocketing student debt into the media spotlight.

But if it is unfair, and inaccurate, to say that Occupy petered out with the wave of evictions from Zuccotti Park, the movement's influence on candidates, legislation, and elections isn't immediately obvious. Which doesn't mean it isn't there. Occupy's persistent focus not just on economic inequality but on "Wall Street" itself created the space for a counter-narrative to the anticipated coronation of Hillary Clinton during the Democratic primaries. As I traveled the country reporting on the Bernie Sanders campaign, I kept coming across articulate, passionate, dedicated activists for whom Occupy had served as a kind of political awakening.

At a "Bernie Fest" in St. Petersburg I met Amos Miers, a graphic designer who'd been involved in Occupy Tampa. Meirs went to his first Sanders meet-up "not prepared to jump in. We were in Occupy. We were against the two-party system. A lot of us were against electoral politics. But I still voted. I realized we *had* to be involved in politics." In Nevada, Tazo Schafer and other veterans of Occupy Las

Vegas fought the state's powerful Democratic machine to a draw in the caucuses. In Brooklyn, OWS tech activists Charles Lenchner and Winnie Wong founded People for Bernie, whose slogan "Feel the Bern" became a meme for the Vermont senator's insurgent candidacy. And in Philadelphia, I met Waleed Shahid, a talented young organizer who'd also been inspired by Occupy.

"When I think about who needs a political revolution in this country, I think of my dad." It was April 2016, a few weeks before the Pennsylvania primary, at the opening of the Sanders campaign's South Philadelphia field office. A mostly young, mostly white crowd was packed into a former clothing store listening to a thin young man with brown skin and a neat beard. "He came to this country as an immigrant from Pakistan. Worked as a parking attendant. Eventually promoted to manager."

Describing his father's pursuit of the American dream, Shahid said his parents had put all of their savings into a house—"because that's what everybody told them you should do." They lost it all in the crash of 2008. "Since then, he's had his hours and wages cut—by the same company he's worked for since 1974!"

At the time, Shahid was the political director of Pennsylvania's Working Families Party. Founded in New York in 1998 to take advantage of that state's "fusion" laws—allowing candidates to run on more than one ballot line—to push the Democratic Party to the left, the WFP has long campaigned on issues of economic justice and labor rights, reflecting the interests of the unions who provided the bulk of the party's financial support. But the relationship had never been stress-free. In 2014, the New York WFP recruited Zephyr Teachout, a Fordham law professor, to challenge Governor Andrew Cuomo in the Democratic primary, only to end up endorsing Cuomo under pressure from its union backers—and out of fear that Teachout wouldn't draw the fifty thousand votes required to keep the party's guaranteed line on the ballot. (Running without the WFP endorsement Teachout got 192,000 votes, a record showing against an incumbent governor.)

Perhaps in penance, the party polled its membership before endorsing Bernie Sanders for president in December 2015—a move that lost it the support of a number of major unions, who'd already committed to Clinton, but reflected the overwhelming preference of the group's members. Having spread beyond its New York roots to fourteen states and the District of Columbia, the WFP's early endorsement did more than just raise Sanders's profile. Everywhere I went in Pennsylvania that spring, I came across WFP activists staffing the local Sanders office—in Reading, Lancaster, even Bethlehem, where the shell of the former Bethlehem Steel plant—once the second-largest mill in the country—now houses a hotel and casino complex owned by Republican donor Sheldon Adelson. The same level of WFP engagement was true in Florida, Connecticut, and other states with a WFP presence.

Spending a day with Shahid's team canvassing the streets of West Philadelphia, I heard him remind the volunteers to "tell our story." Politics, he told me afterward, is partly a "war of narratives. We've had all these movements on the left: Occupy, Black Lives Matter, Fight for $15, Climate Justice. And now we have this candidate, Bernie Sanders. We need to tell people that these candidates are part of these movements. People don't understand that this is all part of the transformation of the Democratic Party. That's something folks on the right do understand about their people."

I asked Shahid about his own story. He talked again about his father, "who just wanted to be middle class. My father has been a citizen since the 1980s. Never voted—until 2008, when Barack Obama inspired him by telling a hopeful story. But he didn't see his life improving. Now he tells me 'I like Bernie because he's angry. I like the way he talks.' Bernie seemed willing to talk about the way things were messed up."

His mother worked in the public school system. "On September 11, 2001, I was in fifth grade. That day is still pretty vivid in my mind, because I lived in Arlington, which is where the Pentagon is, and my mom picked me, my brother, and my sister up from school early.

"The police had blocked off our street because it was an access road heading toward Washington, DC, and my mom and this police officer got into an argument. The officer got really angry at my mom. He said she wasn't listening to him and he wound up pulling his gun and pointing it at her head. I was in the front seat. I remember my little brother and sister screaming in the car. When we got home my mom told me to go put on a movie and take care of them. When I went back, my mom was in the kitchen and she was crying.

"What was crazy was that my mom felt really bad for the police officers, because they'd been out there all morning, so she went to McDonald's and brought them food. She organized a candlelight vigil on our front lawn, even though she was still upset. People had all these tiny American flags, and everyone was singing the national anthem. I didn't even know my mom knew the national anthem until that day. I think the reason she did the stuff with the police officers and organized this whole patriotic thing was that she wanted to show that she was scared too, and that she was an American, too."

▫ ▫ ▫

Corbin Trent never needed to show anyone he was an American. His grandfather, Col. B. Corbin Trent, was the head chaplain of the US Air Force Pacific Command. I first set eyes on the young Tennessee native on a steamy summer night in Nashville, during the lull between the end of the Democratic primary season and the nominating convention. But I'd been hearing about him for months, chasing his trail from Florida northward through all the late primary states as Sanders kept on racking up victories and his campaign refused to die.

Like a guerrilla operating in hostile countryside, Trent kept a low profile, sleeping on supporters' couches, eating and drinking with volunteers in each state, the long drives through strip-mall America and the hollowed-out towns that marked the death march of domestic manufacturing enlivened only by his own abundant store of anecdotes—and an endless capacity to listen to other people's stories. A product of the same southern soil that had produced Estes Kefauver and Albert Gore Sr.—two Tennessee populists who managed to make their mark on national politics despite being at odds with their state, and their times—Trent's easygoing frat-boy charm belied his fierce radical convictions.

Then there was Zack Exley. With the national Sanders campaign focused on the four "early states"—Iowa, New Hampshire, Nevada, and South Carolina—the rest of the country was left to the volunteers to organize. Wherever I found Sanders volunteers phone banking, canvassing, or holding house parties to recruit their neighbors, when I asked how they managed to do so much with so little direction from headquarters in Burlington, the answer was always the same: "This guy Zack Exley came down for a couple of days . . ."

I caught up with Exley in Nashville, too. A tall, lean man with spiky silver hair and geeky glasses that made him look more like a film director than a veteran political operator, he'd worked on Howard Dean's pioneering campaign and then for MoveOn.org. He'd been chief revenue officer for the Wikimedia Foundation before joining the Sanders campaign—Wiki's success in raising money from small donors proved that relying on corporate funding is a choice, not a necessity. Exley and Claire Sandberg, the campaign's director of digital organizing, were given a free hand to conjure up a campaign in forty-six states while the rest of the national staff focused on making Sanders credible with an early win (which they got in New Hampshire, and came very close to getting in Iowa and Nevada. If Sanders had won either of those as well, he might have picked up enough momentum to defeat Hillary Clinton). Soon they, too, were hearing about this guy, Corbin Trent, who'd organized Tennessee for Bernie seemingly single-handedly, and was getting a massive response from East Tennessee—a deep-red region in a deep-red state.

"I'd never really found electoral politics to be that inspiring," Trent told me. So what drew him to Sanders? Partly the memory of working in the family's furniture factory with his father. "My dad was a Vietnam War deserter. He went up to Canada and started an alternative newspaper—the *Toronto New Paper*." Mark Trent also founded an organization that found housing and work for American GIs in Canada. Eventually he came back to Bean Station, Tennessee, and took over the furniture business, where he soon discovered that thanks to cheap imports "if we wanted to survive, we basically had to become a distribution center for stuff we didn't make."

Instead Trent lit out for New York—and cooking school. "I graduated from the Culinary Institute of America, but when I came back home I soon realized there was no way to make money cooking in East Tennessee. So I made Crazy Good Burgers instead. Local beef. Fresh. Everything to order. I had a group of food trucks." He was doing well enough, but when Sanders declared his candidacy, Trent answered the call for volunteers.

"At first I just started driving around, talking to people doing Facebook groups. Seeing who was ready to work. There was a lot of activity. But also a resistance to being organized. People were afraid we were going to come in and take over"—a common experience of many volunteers in the Dean and Obama campaigns. Trent's response was to let people who were already doing effective work get on with it—but to integrate the groups into a coherent network, giving them the technological means to connect to each other, and share their discoveries about what worked and what didn't. He saw his own role as a kind of circuit rider, spreading encouragement and, where needed, giving advice and instruction. When Exley and Sandberg hired him, they asked him to do the same thing on a national scale.

The result was the Bernie Barnstorm—a two- or three-day-long concentrated training session that turned green volunteers into the disciplined organizers who went on to build the biggest grassroots electoral movement this country has ever seen. Combined with the software developed by programmer Saikat Chakrabarti that allowed volunteers across the country to connect with any of the sixty thousand events posted on map.berniesanders.com—from phone banking or sign holding to organizing and planning local groups—the campaign's "distributed organizing" model was a powerful tool for taking politics out of the hands of consultants. Especially after Becky Bond joined the team, applying the expertise she'd gained as political director at CREDO, the alternative mobile phone company, to scaling up the model across the country.*

▪ ▪ ▪

By the time we crossed paths in Nashville, Trent and Exley had left the Sanders campaign and were taking their barnstorming double act on the road, recruiting organizers and volunteers for a new group, Brand New Congress. Their pitch was simple: whoever won the nomination—at that point almost no one took seriously the possibility that Trump might actually become president—would still end up thwarted by a dysfunctional Congress in thrall to corporate interests. So why not harness the energy, enthusiasm, national organization, and fundraising muscle of the Sanders volunteers to elect a whole new Congress—all at once, in 2018 or 2020—committed to the same platform of greater economic equality, climate justice, civil rights, criminal-justice reform, and fair trade? Why not elect a Congress that not only looks like us—more women, more people of color—but will actually work for us instead of for lobbyists and special interests?

For decades, pundits have lamented the decline in voter participation, especially in midterm elections. Brand New Congress looked at those figures the way the Barrow Gang looked at backcountry banks—as opportunities. "Turnout in midterm primaries is typically between eight and thirteen percent," says Exley. In most districts, you only need thirty thousand votes to win the primary.

---

* In November 2016 Bond and Exley published *Rules for Revolutionaries: How Big Organizing Can Change Everything,* distilling the lessons they'd learned during the Sanders campaign, and offering a how-to guide to distributed organizing.

And if the idea of a small, ideologically cohesive force challenging the party establishment sounded familiar, that wasn't an accident. Like the Tea Party, BNC was the product of frustration with a status quo that paralyzes government's machinery while allowing insiders to prosper. Except while the Tea Party (aided, funded, and ultimately directed by donors like the Koch brothers) worked to pull the center of debate to the right, targeting only wayward Republicans, the BNC wanted not to take over the Democratic Party, but to do an end run around both parties, returning government to the people.

"It sounds like a crazy idea," Exley admitted. But when we met in Nashville, he was still hopeful the group would recruit "a couple of hundred seats"—and seriously contest at least forty to fifty seats. Trent was a little more grounded, playing the inside man to Exley's blue-sky visionary. Younger and more solidly built, with the stubbornness common to southern radicals who remain in the South, he'd be an asset in a bar fight. Sticking his neck out was in his blood—besides his father's example, "my granddaddy opened an integrated school" on Maxwell Air Force Base in Alabama; he'd also preached at Ebenezer Baptist Church at the invitation of Martin Luther King Jr.[112] And though Trent was willing to believe Exley's claim that the country had a secret supply of Republicans "who really believe that 'love thy neighbor' stuff in the Bible," he didn't think they'd be easy to find.

That turned out to be a considerable understatement. When I checked in with Trent a few months later, he admitted "we're having some trouble with recruitment." The plan was for people to nominate their neighbors and colleagues. "We want people with a deep history of service. People who had the chance to sell out—but didn't." It was the BNC's version of "leader identification"—a standard item in any organizer's toolkit. Only without the institutional structure of a workplace or a church group or a union, they kept getting self-nominated activists. "I finally had to say, 'Look, if you can't find one other person to nominate you, you probably shouldn't be running for office.' Also, while I still believe there are plenty of good-hearted Republicans out there, their focus is on direct service, not electoral politics."

The group's commitment to recruiting Republicans in red districts was based on two assumptions: that "among Republican, Democratic, and independent voters, there is an invisible majority waiting to be united around radical and practical solutions."[113] And that American politics was in a "post-partisan" phase that would allow this majority to be assembled, from scratch, by relative novices working outside the party structure. Bill Lipton, the WFP's New York state director, was always skeptical. "We've been working on this for almost twenty years," he told me. "You need a party—rooted in ideology, with an organic connection to a social base, and with a desire over the long term to systematically recruit people to run for office to contest state power." Even when the BNC found suitable Republicans, Act Blue, the online fund-raising platform, refused to accept contributions for them.

Instead of the post-partisan future Exley had predicted, Donald Trump's victory ushered in an era of hyper-partisanship, with Republicans turning a blind eye to the president's repeated disregard for the norms of civilized behavior—and contempt for the party's professed concern with the deficit—while Democrats seemed to view any criticism of their own party's leadership as tantamount to treason. By the end of 2017 Brand New Congress was little more than a website—listing just twenty-eight candidates, of whom only two were Republicans. Exley took time out for a fellowship at Harvard, and to work on policy ideas. Meanwhile Trent and most of the staff of BNC migrated to a new group, Justice Democrats, devoted to challenging and replacing corporate Democrats.

▫ ▫ ▫

The paradox of the Sanders campaign was that in revealing the unexpectedly large constituency for genuinely radical measures—universal health care, free tuition at public colleges and universities, a livable minimum wage, an end to the school-to-prison pipeline for minority youth, paid family leave—it also revealed the weakness of progressive organizations that in some cases had been advocating for such policies for years. "Bernie sparked this politics in a way that left organizing had never been able to do on its own," said Waleed Shahid. The question was how to harness that explosion of radical energy and enthusiasm outside the context of a presidential campaign.

"The political revolution needs to go local," George Goehl told me. As co-director of People's Action, a grassroots organization created out of the merger of community groups in twenty-nine states, Goehl's call for "ongoing issue and electoral activity" was echoed across the left. Our Revolution, the most direct inheritor of the Sanders mantle—and, crucially, the only group given access to the millions of donors to the senator's campaign—has endorsed candidates at every level, from school boards in California to the Somerville, Massachusetts, city council, to governors and senators.

Indivisible, a group founded by four former congressional staffers to resist the Trump administration by teaching people how to more effectively lobby their elected officials, has also grown rapidly, with more than 3,800 groups spread across the country.

But the risks of an electorally led strategy were summarized by Dan Cantor, co-founder of the Working Families Party, when he observed that "if you try to occupy the Democratic Party, the Democratic Party will end up occupying you." The party leadership might give way on specific issues—abandoning a trade pact, or opening the door to a public option on health care—but when it came to weaning itself from corporate influence, big donors, and the consultant culture they pay for, #TheResistance, as the lowest-common-denominator Democratic opposition to Trump called itself, seemed more slogan than strategy. Months before the election, when a Clinton victory still seemed inevitable, the scholar and activist Frances Fox Piven warned that "electoral politics can also smother movements."

The truth is that a lot of issue-oriented groups were geared up to push a Clinton administration in a progressive direction. Trump's surprise victory left them struggling to find their footing. The day before the election I'd spoken on the phone with Dan Cantor, who'd outlined an ambitious agenda—on trade, infrastructure spending, immigration, voting rights, health care—already gathering support among influential Democratic legislators. Two years later Democrats couldn't even force the administration into a deal to protect the DACA Dreamers. And while the Women's March on Washington did draw nearly half a million protestors onto the streets of the capital the day after Trump's inaugural—joined by an estimated four million more in other parts of the country—there was little coordinated follow-up. Even as a manifestation of feminist anger, the women's march was overshadowed by the #MeToo campaign against sexual harassment—which doubtless derived a considerable portion of its cultural force and political resonance from outrage over the harasser in chief in the White House.

Yet the focus on Trump himself could be a trap, too.[114] The president's longstanding bromance with Vladimir Putin, and the possibility that the Russian leader might have used so-called active measures to assist his American admirer served as an excuse for avoiding a more painful examination of the party's own failings, and the Clinton campaign's many disastrous errors in judgment. And the personal attacks on Trump let the system that created him off the hook.

As Becky Bond put it, "they only want to talk about Trump's racism. They don't want to talk about why so many people support him. Why so many people are hurting."[115] In the summer of 2016, with the excitement of the Sanders campaign still in the air—and Trump merely a toxic cloud on the horizon—the actor and activist Rosario Dawson declared, "Once you know something you can't un-know it. Now we know how powerful we are." A year later, the writer and activist Naomi Klein summed up some bitter lessons. Our movement, she said, was still "too white." For too long, issues of "race, gender, sexuality felt like add-ons" rather than central concerns. Yet Klein, too, was unable to unlearn the hope she'd felt watching America feel the Bern. Speaking at the People's Summit, she reminded the Sanders supporters, "Now that we know we can win, we have a moral obligation to win. Because our losses are measured in lives."

▫ ▫ ▫

Nobody I'd met knew that better—or felt that obligation more keenly—than Waleed Shahid. Aware from the first of Hillary Clinton's vulnerability—"when you have a candidate who is so clearly part of the establishment, it allows the Tea Party to claim to represent the people"—he had a young person's eagerness for the future to begin right now. "The Bernie movement has planted hundreds of seeds into the American soil. People will experiment and learn things," he told me several months before the election.

Arrested in September 2016 outside Paul Ryan's office after calling on the House speaker to denounce Trump's racism, Shahid led a group of young people who got arrested the week after the election—this time for protesting outside Chuck Schumer's office. "The party of Clinton and Schumer is also the party of Wall Street," he told reporters. "And now the party of Trump is the party of the KKK. So where is our party?"[116] He'd left the Working Families Party to start a new group, #AllOfUs. Founded by and for millennials, #AllOfUs was supposed to serve as a model for a new generation of left organization, more reliant on social media than a membership base, determined to bridge the political narrative between "Obama's compelling story about who 'we' are and Bernie's much better version of who 'they' are."

Like Brand New Congress, #AllOfUs offered a beguiling vision of political possibility. From #BlackLivesMatter to #MeToo, millennials had contributed a significant portion of every movement's ground troops. Shahid himself had been going on demonstrations since his days as a student at Washington-Lee High School, when

Wisconsin congressman James Sensenbrenner had proposed "a bill that would have made it a felony to aid and abet an undocumented immigrant." He'd long felt that no one was speaking directly to or for his generation. #AllOfUs wanted to fill that gap—and to furnish the many protest campaigns based on racial justice or economic justice or migrant rights with a unifying narrative. "#AllOfUs comes from a direct action background," Shahid said. "We're good at that. We know how to organize protests. But if you just keep protesting, eventually you burn out."

"We wanted to avoid foundation money," which had them chasing the same small-dollar donor base the other ex-Sanders people were after. Shahid discovered that while young people were always welcomed to help make up the numbers, "when we started out talking about ourselves as millennials and a new generation, progressive allies, donors, the press, didn't take us seriously." Starting from scratch without funding or an institutional sponsor turned out to be harder than he'd expected. And then his mother had a stroke.

Returning to political work in the fall of 2017 Shahid and his friends wound up #AllOfUs. "We thought we could push the anti-Trump energy into reforming the Democratic Party. We did help create a change in the political weather. But the Women's March and Indivisible—they out-organized us. Only they never gave their base a theory of political change.

"In an age of hard partisanship, with one the party of white resentment, the other the party of cosmopolitanism," Shahid scaled back his ambition. "For now I just want the progressive wing of the Democratic Party to have more power in Congress. It's not that I think elections are the only form of politics, but it is a terrain of struggle. A new generation, inspired by Bernie Sanders, is making ideas like tuition-free college, paid family leave, national health care . . . mainstream. That will only happen when we express our numbers and our power in the number of seats."

The 2018 midterms saw Shahid joining forces with Trent and Saikat

Chakrabarti at Justice Democrats.* Partly a tactical turn away from the BNC approach of searching for acceptable Republicans, the new group had a much simpler focus. Justice Democrats' platform included a twenty-two-item progressive wish list supporting single-payer health care, a green New Deal, and net neutrality, and opposing bad trade deals, warrantless surveillance, and discrimination on the grounds of race, gender, religion, sexual orientation, or immigration status. But the emphasis was on recruiting and funding primary challengers to corporate Democrats, including Democratic incumbents.

"We're working on building up the Left's fear-making capacity," said Trent. With over fifty candidates—including Alexandria Ocasio-Cortez, one of the group's leaders, a South Bronx native running against Rep. Joe Crowley, a ten-term incumbent who's never had a primary opponent—the group easily surpassed BNC's recruitment efforts. "We're trying to drag the party back to its New Deal roots, fighting for working people."

Raúl Grijalva, Arizona's maverick congressman, has joined Justice Democrats, as have California congressman Ro Khanna, who represents Silicon Valley, and Pramila Jayapal, the Seattle congresswoman who has been leading the opposition to the Trump administration's policy of separating undocumented immigrants from their children. And in late June 2018 the Left finally got its "Eric Cantor moment" when Ocasio-Cortez, running on a platform of economic justice, Medicare for All, and the abolition of US Immigrations and Customs Enforcement (ICE), easily defeated Crowley, who in addition to heading the powerful Queens Democratic machine had been widely touted as a possible successor to House minority leader Nancy

* In May 2018 Shahid, another young man in a hurry, became the director of policy for Cynthia Nixon's challenge to New York governor Andrew Cuomo's reelection campaign. With over $30 million of campaign funds in the bank, Cuomo remained a heavy favorite for a third term. Yet his eight years of cozying up to the state's Republican Party—likely in preparation for launching his own presidential bid in 2020—offered Shahid and the Working Families Party, who endorsed Nixon, an irresistible target for their critique of the Democratic Party's subservience to Wall Street.

Pelosi. Although press coverage of the resulting political earthquake made much of twenty-eight-year-old Ocasio-Cortez's youth, Puerto Rican heritage, and relative inexperience—including the fact that she'd recently been working as a bartender—and her endorsement by the Democratic Socialists of America (DSA), few accounts noticed that the young Puerto Rican activist had actually been one of Brand New Congress's first recruits. Or that her brilliant guerrilla campaign included a media coordinator with an East Tennessee exchange on his mobile phone: Corbin Trent.

"The DCCC [Democratic Congressional Campaign Committee, the campaign arm of the House Democratic Caucus] is scared stiff that after 2018 there will be a huge wave of progressive Democrats taking over the party that won't be accountable to their corporate interests," Chakrabarti, Justice Democrats' executive director, told a reporter for Mic digital news.[117] By demanding that its candidates agree to back the party's eventual nominee, regardless of their position on the issues, and by stipulating DCCC candidates spend most of their resources on paid advertising—providing income for paid consultants, but ignoring the potential for the kind of peer-to-peer networks Chakrabarti built for the Sanders campaign—the DCCC's criteria seem designed to exclude the insurgents recruited by Justice Democrats. And with its poster boy Crowley defeated by a candidate who refused a single corporate donation, it appears the DCCC has plenty to worry about.

▫ ▫ ▫

Still, as Waleed Shahid learned the hard way, building a Tea Party of the Left poses a different set of challenges than its namesake. "The actual Tea Party attracted big money donors committed to traditional conservative values. Even if there were left-wing versions of the Koch brothers, our values mean we have to avoid becoming part of the nonprofit industrial complex." Also, unlike the Republican Party, the Democratic Party is a multiracial coalition, which complicates any anti-incumbency movement by the Left, since many of the most senior Democratic incumbents are black or Hispanic.

If you look at the history, says Shahid, "the Tea Party operated most effectively in deep-red districts [where they could show the incumbent had abandoned the base—and where any Republican nominee would probably win]. Because of redistricting and racial gerrymandering, a lot of the deepest blue districts are represented by pillars of the Congressional Black Caucus and the Congressional Hispanic Caucus. These incumbents are very popular—and they do represent their communities, at least in terms of identity." Even when some of their members support policies that serve corporate interests and directly injure their constituents, Shahid says, these veteran legislators "are a lot less vulnerable to challenge from the left, and particularly by white leftists. We also have real urban political machines in a way the Republicans don't." Corrupt but effective, that kind of entrenched power has proven remarkably resistant to movement pressure.

Shahid and Trent still envy the Tea Party's influence—and the successes of Momentum, the left-wing caucus of Jeremy Corbyn supporters inside Britain's Labour Party. "Where were all the people on the left before us who should have built this stuff?" Shahid asks.

And they're both still devoted to the task of trying to articulate a progressive populism to counter the authoritarian vision offered by Trump—and the neoliberalism still endemic among the Democratic elite. Which for the moment means trying to win elections. "For people like my parents, voting is the only political activity they engage in," says Shahid.

The goal, he says, remains the same. "Racial justice. Economic justice. Bringing them together is the future of left-wing politics."

CHAPTER SEVEN

Chokwe Antar Lumumba—Black *Power* Matters

I just don't see anything to be substituted for having people understand their position and understand their potential power and how to use it.

—Ella Baker

In October 2016 a friend and I went to get some barbecue in Ferguson, Missouri. It was the day after the St. Louis presidential debate—one of the most bizarre encounters I'd ever witnessed. In the wake of the *Access Hollywood* tape, on which Trump is heard boasting of his success as a sexual predator thanks to his celebrity and his willingness to "grab 'em by the pussy," his campaign moved to neutralize the issue by inviting three women who'd made allegations against Bill Clinton, including Juanita Broaddrick, who claims the former president raped her back when he was running for governor of Arkansas, to the debate, where they were seated in the front row. As Trump stalked Clinton around the stage at Washington University, two dispiriting thoughts occurred to me almost simultaneously. The first was that Trump was incredibly fortunate to be running against the one candidate least able—precisely because of the way she'd defended her husband—to use Trump's sexual history against him. The second was that even though we were only a few miles from the spot where an unarmed African American teenager named Michael Brown had been shot and killed by the police, this debate, like all the previous debates I'd attended, was not going to confront the topic of race.

The killing of Michael Brown on August 9, 2014, and the subsequent decision by St. Louis county and federal authorities not to prosecute Darren Wilson, the Ferguson police officer who fired six bullets into Brown, a suspect in the robbery of a box of cheap cigars, set off violent protests in Ferguson, a formerly white suburb now with a black majority but where the police force and municipal government remained overwhelmingly white. Brown's death, along with that of Eric Garner, killed by New York City police after being arrested for selling "loosies" (single cigarettes) in Staten Island, and Sandra Bland, found hanged in a Waller County, Texas, jail after she was pulled over for failure to signal a lane change, had been taken up by Black Lives Matter, the group formed after the 2012 shooting of Florida teenager Trayvon Martin by a Neighborhood Watch volunteer.

In Ferguson and elsewhere Black Lives Matter had shown itself capable of mobilizing an effective, outspoken response. Yet the shootings continued—perhaps because America's conscience had become calloused, thickened by decades of indifference to the more intractable aspects of racial injustice that persisted long after the elimination of de jure segregation. A country more susceptible to appeals to conscience would have responded to the argument for reparations for slavery—a case that was in my view morally unassailable, regardless of the practical difficulties, and historically as strong as any appeal for restorative justice—with something other than an ill-tempered and impatient shrug of the shoulders. In North Carolina the Rev. William Barber's "Moral Mondays"—weekly demonstrations at the state capitol protesting the Tea Party–dominated legislature's assault on the poor and minorities—had impacted the 2016 governor's race, helping defeat the Republican incumbent. But Barber's effort to take up the banner of the Poor People's Campaign—Rev. Martin Luther

King Jr.'s final effort to build a populist movement uniting poor whites and blacks—was struggling to gain traction.

So I went to Ferguson, to see what had changed—and what hadn't. It wasn't a very original move—as I realized when, entering J & C BBQ and Blues, I recognized New Jersey senator Cory Booker leaving with his entourage. Still, finding myself in St. Louis it seemed like a kind of obligation. The co-owner, Jerome Jenkins, said the restaurant had twenty-six of its twenty-seven windows broken in the disturbances. But just a few doors farther down South Florissant Road, at Cathy's Kitchen (a more upscale spot named for his wife, who does the cooking), after a single window was broken protesters had linked arms to prevent further damage. A born entrepreneur, Jenkins had expansive plans. But as he described trying to grow his business in an area where blacks had been systematically denied political agency for decades, he didn't bother to disguise his bitterness. "Nothing here has really changed," he said, evincing little faith in protest—or elected officials.

But then he, like the rest of us, had seen the way America had seized upon the election of Barak Obama as the occasion for countless calls to "move on" from race. As if transcending our own history was ever going to be that easy.

"The problem of the twentieth century is the problem of the color-line," W. E. B. Du Bois had written. In the twenty-first century, race remains the central fissure in American life. For all his good intentions, Bernie Sanders's inability to reach across racial lines doomed his candidacy. Not, as some of his young white supporters insisted with impervious certainty, because the older black voters who resisted the Vermont senator's call for a political revolution were uninformed—or hadn't been sufficiently attentive to his rhetoric. But because his own tenacious focus on economic inequality, and his reluctance to engage with race—a reluctance that only diminished following a confrontation with protesters from Black Lives Matter—showed he still didn't fully appreciate the scale or the nature of the problem.

Older black voters had seen white liberals come and go, and while it was arguably perverse that Hillary Clinton, whose husband's presidency ushered in the era of mass incarceration for young black men, should be the beneficiary of that skepticism, that didn't excuse Sanders from the obligation to earn a trust he seemed to feel already entitled to claim.

African Americans—especially African American women—had long been the Democratic Party's most dependable voters. Yet ever since 1964, when the party convention refused to seat the Mississippi Freedom Democratic Party in place of that state's official all-white delegation (all of whom were opposed to President Lyndon Johnson's newly passed Civil Rights Act, and most of whom had already endorsed his opponent, Republican Barry Goldwater), such loyalty had seen scant repayment. Fannie Lou Hamer, who'd been beaten and jailed for trying to register voters, was pushed to the side in a sordid maneuver that saw the MFDP offered two seats as "guests" while the official delegation kept the votes. Despite pressure from white allies such as Walter Reuther, head of the United Auto Workers, and Hubert Humphrey—concerned that continued fighting might endanger his nomination as vice president—the MFDP rejected the deal.

Because it wasn't just about representation. It was about power. Frederick Douglass observed long ago that "power concedes nothing without a demand." As a white man, I'd found that note of demand uncomfortable to listen to. And it was always tempting to think that maybe there was another way—a cure for America's long history of racial oppression that didn't inconvenience anyone very much. That had been a part of Obama's appeal—at least to white voters—and was, I suspected, a considerable element in Booker's popularity among the same group.

Wary of my own bad faith as much as anything else, I resolved to try to avoid comforting solutions. Even so, when Stacy Abrams, an African American woman with impeccable progressive credentials, announced she was running for governor of Georgia in 2018, I was intrigued. Instead of campaigning as a moderate—as Doug Wilder had already done in Virginia—Abrams refused to water down her message to appeal to conservative voters, or Republicans offended by Donald Trump's manners. Yet the strikingly charismatic Abrams also seemed to base her candidacy on the assumption that, at least in Georgia, the Rising American Electorate of minorities, millennials, and unmarried women had arrived and would be sufficient to elect her.

Perhaps it would. Running a smart populist campaign Abrams won a stunning primary victory over a white, centrist opponent. And the symbolic importance of electing an African American woman in the heart of the old Confederacy was undeniable. Yet I knew that the very possibility of such a thing happening meant that Georgia was not the place I needed to go.

Instead I went to Mississippi—a state that, since slavery, has always been the hardest place. A state where, a century and a half after the Emancipation Proclamation, genuine equality between the races—equality of power—remains the radical idea it has always been. The challenge is not just to demand an end to the wholesale murder of black youth—though that of course is essential. Nor would it be enough to gain elective office—though that, too, is necessary. The challenge is to keep racial justice where it belongs—at the center of any movement for social change—and to move from protest to power. If the stirrings in Georgia and North Carolina are to be sustained, they'll eventually have to be sustained here. And if those efforts fall short, they'll fall short here.

▫ ▫ ▫

And so it is good to remind ourselves how things here once stood. On July 2, 1949, Malcolm Wright, a Mississippi tenant farmer, was driving his wife and children to town in their mule-drawn wagon when three white men in a Ford truck, enraged because they had to slow down to pass on the narrow road, pulled Wright from his seat and beat him to death with a bumper jack in front of his family. Well known in the area to both blacks and whites (Wright's father was white, as were his two half-brothers), Wright was exceptional only in that his killers, who'd turned themselves in to the local deputy sheriff, were arrested and charged with murder. They were speedily acquitted by an all-white jury.

On August 28, 1955, Emmett Till, a fourteen-year-old Chicago boy visiting relatives in Money, Mississippi, was kidnapped, mutilated, and murdered for the alleged crime of whistling at a white woman (though a half century later the woman, Carolyn Bryant, admitted she'd fabricated her account). Despite testimony from witnesses to the abduction—who'd been convinced to come forward by Medgar Evers, Mississippi field secretary for the NAACP—it took the all-white jury little more than an hour to acquit Roy Bryant and his friend J. W. Milam.

Evers himself, a World War II veteran who'd fought in both France and Germany, was shot in the back in the driveway of his own home in Jackson on June 12, 1963, by Byron De La Beckwith, a member of the White Citizens' Council. De La Beckwith, too, was set free after all-white juries deadlocked twice. Twenty years later, prompted in part by Myrlie Evers, who pressed authorities to reopen her husband's case when new evidence surfaced of jury tampering by the Mississippi Sovereignty Commission, a state agency, De La Beckwith was brought to trial again in 1994 and finally convicted of first-degree murder.

"This is where Medgar fell," said Frank Figgers, as we pulled up in front of a tan brick and pale green bungalow. I'd met Figgers in the local NAACP office. A fourth-generation Jacksonian who'd long been active in "the movement," he'd offered to give me a sense of the city's racial geography. "See the way the houses here don't have sidewalks? That's how you know this was a black area," he said. A minute later, and a block away, we pulled over again; the lawns were all bounded by a neat ribbon of concrete. "This is where the shooter was. In 1963, white folks lived in all these houses."

By now the white folks have mostly left. In 1960, before the Freedom Riders arrived, Jackson was 65 percent white. (In May 1961, a group of Freedom Riders who tried to integrate the restrooms at the bus terminal in Jackson were arrested, but—under the terms of a secret deal between Attorney General Robert Kennedy and Senator James Eastland—not beaten. Instead they spent the next two months locked up on death row in the Mississippi State Penitentiary at Parchman.) In 1970, when police fired on students protesting the Vietnam War at Jackson State, killing two of them, whites made up 60 percent of the city. Even in 1980 Jackson was still more than half-white. But once it tipped, whites fled in droves. In the last decade of the millennium Jackson lost thirty-five thousand whites—mostly to the suburbs of nearby Rankin or Madison Counties, which have both nearly doubled in population over the last thirty years. Middle-class and wealthy blacks were leaving, too. By 1997, when the city elected its first black mayor, Jackson was over two-thirds black. Twenty years later that figure is closer to 80 percent.

I'd come to Jackson to see the new mayor, Chokwe Antar Lumumba. We'd spoken briefly at the People's Summit in Chicago—a June gathering of the Bernie Sanders tribes, who'd shouted and stamped their feet when Lumumba said he wanted to make Jackson "the most radical city on the planet." I wanted to find out what he meant. And to see what he was up against.

Barack Obama's presidency allowed his white supporters to imagine the country had transcended race—an illusion whose cruelty was only revealed on November 9, 2016. Yet conventional wisdom said there was no other way. For decades white liberals—usually men—have argued that any form of "identity politics," whether based on race or gender or ethnicity, is always divisive, always an impediment to progressive action on the economic issues fundamental to any fight for social justice. Lumumba, whose parents were both black nationalists, came out of a very different tradition. I also wanted to find out what impact the mayor's background had on his politics.

▫ ▫ ▫

The first thing I see when I walk into the mayor's office here is an easel with an artist's rendering of a movie theater. At one time this city had nearly a dozen, including the Alamo, a Streamline gem on Farish Street, the center of segregated Jackson's black business district, where a diet of Westerns and second-run features once shared the stage with B. B. King, Louis Jordan, and Nat King Cole. But Farish Street today is deserted, and Jackson—the capital of Mississippi, with a population roughly the size of Fort Lauderdale or Providence—has not a single cinema inside the city limits.

"Most people don't see the value in what you're trying to build until you build it. Once you build it, then people see the value in it." Tall and slender, with a neatly trimmed beard, the mayor explains that while previous administrations have tried, and failed, to entice the national cinema chains back to downtown Jackson, he plans to tackle the problem from a different angle.

"My vision is that the city can use its bully pulpit in order to encourage the development of cooperative businesses. So it would be more than just a movie theater. The city wouldn't own it—it wouldn't be socialism in that sense. But we can write a check that will go into a nonprofit organization . . . If we just got thirty thousand people—that's fewer than voted in the primary—to put twenty dollars each, which is less than the cost of taking a date to the movies, you'd have a six-hundred-thousand-dollar initial investment.

"People tend to like to eat before they go the movies, right? So it now becomes a place for someone to invest in a restaurant. Especially franchise restaurants that some people in South Jackson would like to see. And when you have people eating, preparing to watch the movie, sometimes they like to do a little shopping . . ."

When I tease the mayor about trying to build socialism in one city, he laughs, then comes back with: "I recently had the opportunity to go to Barcelona and talk with the mayor there about the cooperative businesses that they've developed over time." FC Barcelona, as every soccer fan knows, is owned and operated by its supporters. It also happens to be one of the most valuable and successful sports franchises in the world.

"I actually played soccer," he continues. "I was a fat kid. My father put me in soccer to run and to work out. They were like, 'He takes up a lot of space. We're going to put him in goal.' I was good at it, but I never liked it."

Lumumba tells me he's more of an American football fan. His political inspiration, too, lies a lot closer to home. "Cooperatives are not a new idea. Fannie Lou Hamer [a Student Nonviolent Coordinating Committee (SNCC) activist who went on to help found the Mississippi Freedom Democratic Party] used to talk about cooperative businesses, cooperative farms, as one of the ways poor people could pool their resources to further their goals. And when you look at the United States, Ace Hardware is a cooperative. Land O'Lakes Butter is a cooperative. And what's the greatest community-owned cooperative business? The Green Bay Packers!"

Green Bay, Wisconsin, Lumumba points out, is only two-thirds the size of Jackson. "So my view is that if the city of Green Bay can figure out how to own their own professional football team, we can figure out how to own a movie theater!"

Assuming he gets his movie theater, what would "the most radical city on the planet" look like in ten years? "In ten years, what we should see is a city that was not only able to correct its ills, but one that could serve as a model for other cities—by abandoning the traditional model of how you develop a city."

Jackson has many of the same resources that have allowed northern cities like Pittsburgh and Cleveland to reinvent themselves. Besides the State of Mississippi—the city's largest employer—Jackson is home to several major hospitals, and a half-dozen colleges, including Jackson State and Tougaloo. Of course, the "eds and meds" magic may not work when the colleges are historically black. Even where it has worked, the price has been displacement—already an issue in Jackson along the "medical corridor" connecting the hospitals to the downtown area.

Nsombi Lambright, a Jackson native who used to be the executive director of the Mississippi ACLU, and currently runs One Voice, a public-policy shop focusing on economic and community development, points to Atlanta as an example of a city where "you have a lot of development. And a lot of displacement."

"Traditional models speak to creating great edifices and nice new housing and pricing people out," says Lumumba. "Moving people from one state of misery to the next. Instead of moving people away, we're going to lift them up. As we look at initiatives, we're asking, 'How are we going to create jobs in this process? How are we going to match an underskilled work force with the work that we need to do? How do we turn our crumbling infrastructure into an economic frontier? How do we create incubator funds to support small, homegrown businesses?'

Cooperation Jackson has spent the past four years trying to answer exactly those questions. Kali Akuno, the group's co-founder, told me that his members have been slowly taking over abandoned buildings and vacant lots, planting fruit and vegetables and creating a community land trust, and opening a catering kitchen to train workers for the restaurant and hospitality sector.

"Black politicians in major cities had to go with the neoliberal program to get resources—which left a lot of folks disillusioned," says Akuno. He, too, thinks Jackson can become a showcase for a whole new economy, a Mondragon* in Mississippi leading the way out of capitalism and exploitation.

Alongside economic self-sufficiency, the other big idea the mayor keeps coming back to is co-governance. Rukia Lumumba, who co-chaired her brother's election campaign, explains: "The idea is that the people retain power, which the government responds to. So that the residents control the city. Not my brother sitting on the hill."

According to both Rukia and her brother, the main vehicle for achieving this is the People's Assembly. Held every quarter, these assemblies are meant to be opportunities for the community to both critique and inform their elected officials. "Three minutes on a microphone does not make community participation," the mayor acknowledges. "Instead it should be an information exchange, where we go to the community and say, 'This is what's going on. This is what's going to impact your community.' And the community can say, 'This is what is happening on the street. This is what you need to be concerned about.' It's literally the process of connecting pothole to pothole to pothole—and community to community."

"Antar has very radical ambitions," says Lambright, who like all the mayor's friends and colleagues refers to him by his middle name. "But he's not going to get there without the support of the community."

▫ ▫ ▫

If the new mayor's ambitions offer a surprising perspective on politics in the Magnolia State, the obstacles in his path are depressingly familiar: rotting infrastructure, failing schools, and a white power structure that has been hollowing out Jackson for decades.

You don't have to go very far here to see the scale of the problem:

---

* Founded in 1956 in the Basque region of Spain, the Mondragon Corporation today is the country's tenth-largest enterprise, a federation of worker cooperatives manufacturing everything from bicycles to elevators, as well as owning a supermarket chain, an insurance business, and its own bank.

driving south on Mill Street toward my hotel a few blocks from the Governor's Mansion I counted a dozen potholes in as many minutes, many of them deep enough to swallow an entire wheel—or, in some cases, a small car. In Belhaven, the leafy historically white neighborhood that served as a location for the film *The Help*, the potholes even have their own Facebook page.[118]

The same Yazoo clay whose shifts undermine Jackson's streets also wreaks havoc on the city's aging water pipes and culverts. Throughout the fall, Jackson residents regularly received "boil notices" from the state health department warning them not to drink the tap water. Back in 2012, Jackson entered into a consent decree with the US Environmental Protection Agency requiring $400 million in repairs to bring the city's water and sewer systems into compliance with federal standards. According to the EPA, during the previous five years Jackson's sewers overflowed more than 2,300 times, sending untreated waste into the Pearl River.

Five years—and a 100 percent rise in sewer rates—later, the city is desperately trying to renegotiate both the time allowed for the work to be completed and the method used to finance it.[119] At the same time, Rankin County, which has been paying Jackson upward of $4 million a year for access to the city's water and sewers, recently won permission from the state to build its own treatment plant on the Pearl River.

Though couched in the antiseptic language of suburban growth and urban decay, the dispute is really about race. Phil Bryant, Mississippi's current governor, is a Tea Party Republican who used to represent Rankin County in the state legislature—whose upper and lower houses both have Republican majorities. In Jackson, as in other cities where a history of racial strife preceded the election of black or Hispanic office holders, the state's response to the city's challenges can be summed up in the phrase "We broke it; now you fix it." It's a forced choice familiar from Detroit, or Cleveland: raise taxes on already hard-pressed businesses, or preside over continuing decline. What sets Lumumba apart is his refusal to play by the old rules.

Despite Jackson's status as state capital it has been left to the city's shrinking tax base to remedy decades of neglect and disinvestment. At the same time the state has not been reluctant to interfere, for example by expanding the number of exemptions to the 1 percent sales tax Jackson voters approved in 2014 to fund infrastructure repairs, cutting the city's expected proceeds in half. Of the ten members on the commission overseeing how sales tax proceeds are spent, the city gets just three nominees, while the governor, lieutenant governor, and the speaker of the state House of Representatives—all white Republicans—are given one each. The remaining four places are filled by the Jackson Chamber of Commerce.

The state also recently moved to seize control of Jackson-Medgar Wiley Evers International Airport. Built on land the city bought and annexed in 1963, the airport contributed $3.76 million to the city's bottom line in 2015. The bill—drafted by a Rankin County state senator who is also a commercial real estate broker, and signed by Bryant in 2016—would give the governor, rather than the city, control over the airport board, while also reserving seats for appointees from Rankin and Madison Counties.

The most bitter, most blatant instance of the way Mississippi's long history of racial oppression continues to shape events is the battle over Jackson's public schools. Before the Supreme Court's *Brown v. Board of Education* decision, Mississippi maintained two separate and decidedly unequal school systems. Not only were black students shunted into ramshackle facilities with inadequate equipment, the Mississippi school calendar was built around the cotton season, with black schools only in session five months of the year.[120]

Brown was handed down on May 17, 1954—labeled "Black Monday" on the floor of Congress by Rep. John Bell Williams, who fourteen years later was elected governor of Mississippi; the *Jackson Daily News* called the ruling "the worst thing that has happened in the South since carpetbaggers and scalawags took charge."[121] In December 1954 the Mississippi legislature voted to close the state's public schools—all of them. That year also saw the founding of the White Citizens' Council. In addition to pursuing, as the historian Charles M. Payne put it, "the agenda of the Klan with the demeanor of the Rotary Club," the group opened Council McCluer High in Jackson. Governor Bryant is a Council McCluer graduate.[122]

Though such schools were privately run, the state provided tuition grants for white students. After the 1965 Civil Rights Act made it clear that de jure segregation was a hopeless cause, Mississippi adopted "freedom of choice"—giving all students the right to choose which school to attend. Black parents who tried to send their children to all-white schools were no longer arrested. They merely faced the loss of their jobs, cancellation of mortgages or evictions, cross burnings, and other "unofficial" violence—often at the hands of city and state police.

After the Supreme Court ruled—in *Alexander v. Holmes County Board of Education* (1969)—that the South had to desegregate its schools without further delay, whites in Mississippi simply abandoned them. In 1963 there were only seventeen private schools in the whole state; by 1970 there were 263. They also did everything they could to avoid paying for public education. The Mississippi Adequate Education Program—a 1997 state law supposedly mandating an "adequate education" for every child in the state—has been fully funded just twice in the past twenty years. In 2015, Proposition 42, a citizen-driven ballot initiative that would have given the courts the right to enforce full funding, was defeated—thanks in part to Americans for Prosperity, the Koch brothers group that donated $239,000 to the campaign against it.[123] Which means that while wealthy areas can make up their funding shortfall out of property taxes, pupils in Jackson schools must continue to do without.

That hasn't stopped the state from declaring Jackson—the second-largest school system in the state—a failing district. Nor did the fact that a previously agreed Corrective Action Plan still had months to run prevent the state from threatening to take over the Jackson schools. To Nsombi Lambright, the whole process is a sinister farce.

"For years the state has been taking over majority-black districts, which have been given failing ratings while, at the same time, those districts have never received full funding," she said. "What they want is something like the Recovery School District in Louisiana," where all the schools in New Orleans were removed from local control and turned into charter schools.

In Mississippi, says Lambright, talk of charter schools, vouchers, and "school choice" all add up to "the same thing"—a covert campaign to rig the system "so white families won't have to pay private-school fees anymore."

▫ ▫ ▫

Edwin Taliaferro's parents both came to Michigan as part of the Great Migration of blacks leaving the South. Studying at Kalamazoo College in the late 1960s, he'd been involved in protests over the paucity of black faculty members and the absence of African American studies programs. The young activist changed his name to honor the Chokwe people of Central Africa and the murdered president of the Belgian Congo, Patrice Lumumba. He also joined the Republic of New Afrika (RNA).

Chokwe Lumumba senior often told the story of the day—March 28, 1971, more than ten years before his son Antar was born—he was in the lead car of a caravan from Detroit to Bolton, Mississippi, a small town about twenty miles west of Jackson, where the RNA had agreed to buy twenty acres of land. There the group planned to establish a base from which to spread the RNA message that African Americans should resettle in the five Black Belt states of the Deep South—Mississippi, Louisiana, Alabama, Georgia, and South Carolina—demand reparations for slavery, and, eventually, petition the United Nations for recognition as an independent country. Lumumba was the RNA's vice president.

When the procession arrived in Bolton that afternoon they found local, state and federal law enforcement blocking the road. All were armed—as were the RNA. Yet in a turn of events Chokwe Lumumba always recounted with amazement, "that roadblock opened up. Just like the Red Sea," allowing the planned Land Celebration Day festivities to go ahead.[124] Five months later, however, Jackson police, accompanied by the FBI—and with a tank parked outside for emphasis—raided the RNA's Jackson headquarters, setting off a gun battle that left one officer dead and two more wounded. Chokwe Lumumba, who was away that day, returned to law school in Detroit, where he worked in the public defender's office, and eventually set up his own practice. His clients were a who's who of black nationalism, including Geronimo Pratt—a Black Panther who spent twenty-seven years in prison before receiving a $4.5 million settlement for wrongful imprisonment—Assata Shakur, and Tupac Shakur.

The Lumumba children were born in Detroit. "When I was around two years old," the mayor told me, "my father moved us to Brooklyn. He represented Mutulu Shakur, Tupac Shakur's stepfather, in the Brink's truck robbery." The family lived on DeKalb Avenue, in an apartment so small, recalled Rukia Lumumba, five years older than her brother, "that our dresser had to be in the living room."

After the Brink's trial ended, Lumumba told his children, "We have unfinished business in Mississippi," and the family moved to Jackson. For ten-year-old Rukia the culture shock was immediate. "Jackson then was very segregated. There was an underlying fear that I recognized early on. You couldn't talk about race, because it was offensive.

"I was used to being in a city where you could see yourself in successful positions. If I went with my father to court in Detroit, the judge looked like me. In New York, I saw people that looked like me in positions of power. Down here they weren't even going to let my father take the bar exam."

It took three years for Chokwe Lumumba to be admitted to the Mississippi Bar. Yet the family never felt alone. "My mother really believed in this concept of community as family and family as community. When I was in high school, two of my friends lived with us. So Antar grew up in a house full of teenagers," she said.

Their mother, Nubia, was a flight attendant for Northwest Airlines. "My mother wore high heels every day. She was very stylish," says Rukia, adding that "Antar inherited our mother's fashion sense." Which she regards as fortunate, since "my father was still wearing an Afro in the 1980s."

Their mother was also the stricter parent. "If she gave you a dollar, she'd say, 'I want my dollar back tomorrow.' My father was more 'I trust you until you give me a reason not to.' If he saw someone hitchhiking on the highway he'd stop and pick them up. With me or my brothers in the car. Which would drive my mother crazy!"

Though both siblings grew up steeped in the politics of black nationalism, Rukia insists, "My parents didn't force anything on us. You could go to the meeting—or not."

Her brother tells it a bit differently, remembering "Kwame Ture [formerly Stokely Carmichael] coming to the house. When I was in junior high, we had Rosa Parks eat dinner at the house. I used to talk to Tupac about Sega Genesis. Did I make a conscious decision that I'm going to be an activist? I don't think that I ever felt I had a choice."

I asked the mayor how his parents described the movement that took up so much of their lives. "I think they saw it as a movement for self-determination. How to have more control over our lives. The goal wasn't: 'One day, we're going to run for political office.' In fact, you could say that we were kind of antagonistic to the electoral piece."

Over time, Chokwe Lumumba attracted a critical mass of activists to Jackson, where, working with like-minded locals, he helped found the Malcolm X Grassroots movement. It was the government's response to Hurricane Katrina—when evacuees in the Mississippi Coast Coliseum were bussed out of state to make room for a Disney On Ice production of *Finding Nemo*—that prompted Jackson's activists to reassess their dismissal of electoral politics. After Katrina the group issued something called the Jackson-Kush Plan, named for the ancient African kingdom. In many ways reminiscent of the Republic of New Afrika, it called for "regional self-determination" starting in the eighteen contiguous counties of western Mississippi with majority-black populations. The aim was to develop "a network of people's assemblies" and eventually move the region to "a broad-based solidarity economy."[125] But there was no mention of secession. And this time the group decided to run candidates for electoral office. In 2009 Chokwe Lumumba was elected to Jackson City Council. Four years later, he became the city's mayor. Nine months after the election he was dead.

▫ ▫ ▫

Chokwe Antar Lumumba inherited his father's name—and his unfinished political agenda. But he did not inherit his office. In the special election to complete Chokwe Lumumba's term his son, barely five years out of law school, ran—and lost. After three years of an administration dogged by allegations of corruption, with little evidence of improvement either in the city's infrastructure or in the lives of its citizens, he ran again. Endorsed by both Our Revolution and the Working Families Party—which sent two organizers to Jackson—Lumumba defeated nine challengers in the 2017 Democratic primary, cruising to victory in the general election with 92 percent of the vote.

Given the challenges he faces, Antar Lumumba's attempt to foster what used to be called "sewer socialism"—the kind of municipal experiments that once flourished from Reading, Pennsylvania, to Milwaukee, Wisconsin—can seem heartbreakingly modest. "People want to know he's really gonna fix those potholes," says Safiya Omari, the mayor's chief of staff—a job she also held under Chokwe Lumumba. But his ultimate goal is the same as his father's: building power. "We want to make Jackson an example of what government *for* the people can be."

Kali Akuno, who served as Chokwe Lumumba's director of special projects, worries that with so many fires to fight on the horizon—schools, water, infrastructure, the airport—Antar Lumumba's administration might be too pinned down to ever begin anything radical. Still worse, he says, would be what he calls "the Syriza trap, which is having a left-wing government come in to administer the worst forms of austerity."

Lumumba clearly recognizes the scale of the challenge. "When people ask me, 'How do you feel about Donald Trump being president?,' I tell them, 'On the Wednesday after the election, I woke up in Mississippi.' No matter whether Donald Trump is the president or Barack Obama was the president, we've always been at the bottom."

And the implacability of the opposition: "The United States is infected with a disease called racism. The anti-racism movement has had some seminal victories. But you have a racist movement that is fighting at the same time. When we win something, they don't go home and say, 'Oh, we lost' and go to sleep. So we can't rest."

Michelle Colon, a clinic escort at Jackson Women's Health—the last abortion provider left in the state—told me, "We fight like hell in Mississippi. We don't have the luxury of some other states." We met in Fondren, Jackson's tiny hipster district, where she described the state legislature's continuing efforts to pass a "personhood amendment," giving legal force to the view that human life begins at conception.

In 2011, Colon said, "we had no money. I traveled the state from one end to the other." The amendment lost, with 58 percent voting against it—only to have the same bill reappear in 2015. "They haven't given up," she says.

Yet she, too, felt a flickering of possibility from the new administration. "Everyone thinks of Mississippi as being so backwards. It would be great if Jackson could be a model."

Were such hopes more than just wishful thinking? Safiya Omari moved from California to Jackson to join the fight for racial justice, then left a tenured position teaching psychology at Jackson

State to work in the city hall that slaves had built—and where their descendants were now in charge. "We want a shot" at fixing Jackson's schools, she told me. Rukia Lumumba spoke passionately about alternatives to incarceration for young offenders and her own eagerness to "transform the way we deal with justice." Frank Figgers took me on a tour of abandoned factories to demonstrate the industrial base the city once had—and could have again.

That seemed unlikely. I also wondered whether restoring an industrial economy built on cheap labor was really the high road to economic independence. Yet as I left Jackson I kept thinking about Figgers, a soft-spoken man who'd graduated from Lanier High School in Jackson—as we drove by the school he counted off the many classmates who'd also joined the movement, taking special pride in those who "stayed with the work." Not at all coincidentally, during the 1980s Lanier had been the proving ground for the Algebra Project, former SNCC field secretary Robert Moses's pioneering effort to give low-income students and students of color the mathematical literacy they need to exercise full citizenship in a technologically based society. Selling paint and office supplies to support his family, Figgers taught at the Georgetown Liberation School, tutored in the Algebra Project, and served two terms as county election commissioner.

"When black power hit, in 1966, that caught hold of me," Figgers told me. Like most white liberals, I'd grown up thinking of black power as at best a historical curiosity, at worst a dead end on the road to a post-racial society. Charles Payne writes persuasively about the need to reexamine "the idea that Civil Rights and Black Power represented two fundamentally different movements, the one to be lionized—at least in retrospect—the other vilified."[126] One of the things I learned in Jackson was that in Mississippi it had never been like that.

The civil rights struggle in Mississippi had little to do with the textbook story of Martin Luther King Jr. and other charismatic clergymen enduring beatings and arrests to end segregation. To begin with, it was obvious that segregation in Mississippi had never ended. Nor had local activists completely embraced nonviolence. *This Nonviolent Stuff'll Get You Killed* was the title of one Mississippi veteran's memoir—and an attitude shared widely by those who worked in the state.[127]

And while there were some Mississippi ministers who welcomed the movement, most were too afraid. Which didn't surprise Ella Baker, the veteran activist who'd founded SNCC—in part out of frustration with what she saw as an excess of caution by traditional black leaders. "Strong people," Baker used to say, "don't need strong leaders." In Jackson, as elsewhere in Mississippi, the movement instead relied on a partnership between older activists—often either farmers who owned their land, and were harder to intimidate, or skilled workers—and young people who hadn't yet learned to be afraid. Like Hollis Watkins. As a seventeen-year-old high school student Watkins had been recruited by Medgar Evers to join the NAACP Youth Chapter. Two years later, Watkins came to a meeting above a supermarket in Macomb where he thought Martin Luther King would be speaking. Instead he met Robert Moses, and became one of the first Mississippians to join SNCC.

His memoir, *Brother Hollis*, is a bracing corrective to anyone who believes that persuading white college students to come south for a "Freedom Summer" was the secret of SNCC's success. "The term 'black power' was as much a question as a declaration," writes Watkins. "Most people don't realize that . . . 'black power' was aimed as much at the old guard Negro leadership as it was aimed at white America."

Fifty years later, Watkins is still in Jackson, still raising awkward questions. In his book he describes "packing, cracking, and stacking"—the three methods used to dilute the black vote: "Packing" crams black voters into a single district to minimize black representation. "Cracking" draws lines to fragment or displace black voters. "Stacking" links black voters with white communities who do not share their concerns. Watkins was lead plaintiff in the 1991 lawsuit challenging the state's redistricting plan.[128]

A friend to Chokwe Lumumba and a mentor to his son, Watkins

told me that for him the struggle—the movement—has always been a fight for self-determination. "The threat is 'You can't do it without us.' If you buy into that—'It can't be done'—you're locked into the self-exploiting process. Because you believe it can't be done, it won't be done."

Jackson, Mississippi, may seem like an unlikely place to look for the seeds of the next republic. But as I talked with Watkins and other activists there, I noticed two things. One was negative: almost everywhere else in America—especially among communities of color—the issue of police violence was at the top of the agenda. In Jackson it simply never came up. When I asked Nsombi Lambright why that was, she replied that Lee Vance, a twenty-seven-year veteran of the force named chief of police by the previous administration, "has been doing a pretty good job." Coming from a former head of the ACLU, that was practically an endorsement.

The topic of race, on the other hand, was part of every conversation I had here. That may have been because I was a white man asking questions. Mostly, though, I think it was because the people I spoke to in Jackson knew exactly who they were, what they—and their community—had been through, and what they had accomplished.

They were under no illusions that further progress would come easily. Discussing the state's threat to take over Jackson's schools, Kali Okuno said, "We may need to use their own racism against them" by threatening to send Jackson's students to suburban schools. Perhaps coincidentally, a few days later the mayor and governor announced an agreement—brokered by the W. K. Kellogg Foundation, a Michigan-based educational charity—that lets Jackson maintain local control of its schools.

It was a small victory, on a battlefield where most of the successes have been modest, and the odds have never been favorable. Yet the same could be said of many of the civil rights struggles of the 1960s. Who would have thought then that the right to eat at a lunch counter, or keep your seat on a city bus, were levers that would change the world? Because while racism is "baked in" to our history, from the three-fifths clause in the Constitution to racial gerrymandering and the prison-industrial complex, so too is the legacy of resistance, from the slaves who revolted and the abolitionists—black and white—who defied the Fugitive Slave Act, to the Mississippi Freedom Democratic Party and Black Lives Matter.

"It's a war on many fronts," said Hollis Watkins. "But it's not a war that can't be won."

CHAPTER EIGHT

Whatever Happened to the Roosevelt Republic?

The New Deal was a genuine revolution, whose deepest purpose was not simply reform within existing traditions, but a basic change in the social, and, above all, the power relationships within the nation. It was not a revolution by violence. It was a revolution by bookkeeping and lawmaking.

—Whittaker Chambers, *Witness*

By the third day of the Republican convention everybody agreed that Donald Trump's campaign was a car crash. Between Melania Trump's plagiarized rendition of a Michelle Obama speech and Senator Ted Cruz's pointed failure to endorse the party's nominee during his prime-time speech, pundit Nate Silver spoke—as he so often does—for the collective wisdom of the press corps when he said the Republicans were "flirting with disaster."[129] Sitting in the bleachers in Cleveland it was hard to disagree, yet something besides the heartburn I'd picked up at the Quicken Loans food court was keeping me awake nights.

Perhaps it was my choice of bedside reading. At 682 pages, *Who Voted for Hitler?* hardly made for light entertainment. Author Richard F. Hamilton took on the received view of the Nazi Party's rise to power—that Hitler's electoral success stemmed from a "panic in the middle class" brought on by the depression and the threat of "economic marginality"—and reduced it to smithereens. "Sometimes the facts that everyone knows prove to be the least known," he wrote. Hamilton showed that all of Germany's traditional parties were "unattractive to important segments of the electorate." But by carefully analyzing vote counts and mapping the results against German census data, Hamilton also proved that the Nazis' actual base of support lay among the better off, with their share of the vote rising with income.

Of course I knew that Trump was no Adolf Hitler.* But after watching scores of delegates who'd arrived at the convention passionately #NeverTrump depart chanting "Lock her up!," I found myself haunted by Hamilton's answer to the question: "What does a Conservative voter do when his first-choice candidate is removed from the race?" The Nazis, after all, never won a majority. Indeed, in the last two free elections held in Germany, the party's share of the vote actually declined, from 37.3 percent in July 1932 to 33.1 percent that November. (The Socialist share also went down, from 21.6 to 20.4 percent, while the Communists increased their vote from 14.3 to 16.9 percent.) It was the failure of the Left to unify—and the moral collapse of German conservatives who thought they could "control" Hitler—that opened the door to the Nazis. "Almost all of [the] Conservative support," wrote Hamilton, "went to an extremist candidate, to Adolf Hitler."

So in September I went back to Ohio. Hillary Clinton had been ahead in the polls all summer, until, on September 9, at a fundraiser in New York City, she'd consigned half of Trump's supporters to a "basket of deplorables"—a phrase that was already turning

* I first interviewed Donald Trump in the early '80s, when I was writing a profile of Sandy Lindenbaum, the lawyer who'd steered Trump's first Manhattan real-estate project, the former Commodore Hotel, through New York's labyrinthine zoning process. (Lindenbaum's father, Abraham "Bunny" Lindenbaum, had been chair of the City Planning Commission—and Fred Trump's political "fixer.") Whatever his other abundant faults, Trump himself is not a Jew hater.

up on T-shirts by the time I caught up with Trump's campaign in Canton.

Occupying the high ground was clearly a new—and disconcerting—experience for the Republican nominee. "Hillary Clinton calls people who aren't supporting her 'deplorable' and 'irredeemable.' I call people who aren't supporting me American citizens—who are entitled to the same respect as anyone else," he told the crowd, quickly shifting to a more familiar theme. "It used to be cars were made in Flint, and you couldn't drink the water in Mexico. Now the cars are made in Mexico, and you can't drink the water in Flint."[130]

A few weeks earlier, in Akron, Trump had also spoken about the decline of manufacturing jobs since Bill Clinton pushed through the North American Free Trade Agreement, shouting, "Hillary Clinton's donors own her," promising to "stop the Trans-Pacific Partnership" before it could do similar damage, and vowing to "put the miners and steelworkers back to work." Addressing "the forgotten men and women of America," Trump told them, "I am your voice."

In Wooster I met John O'Brien, a Long Island transplant who used to be a union rep with Local 66 of the Laborers' Union. "Worked thirty-one years in heavy construction. I did my time in hell," he said. A volunteer at the local GOP headquarters, O'Brien was doing a brisk business in Trump lawn signs.

In Columbus, community organizer Molly Shack described her city as "the poster child for corporate Democrats." Alongside its flourishing arts scene and thriving university are whole blocks of vacant houses. "Four out of five kids in the public schools qualify for free lunches," said Shack. The same dynamic was on display in Cincinnati's Over-the-Rhine, a hipster enclave that until recently was 80 percent African American. Tourists can enjoy seventeen-dollar burgers on the very blocks that, fifteen years ago, saw some of the twentieth century's worst urban riots.

In Cleveland, at a meeting of the Amalgamated Transit Union, bus driver Anshel Epstein told me, "Forty percent of the guys in my garage are considering voting Trump." The next day Fred Ward, who runs an Afrocentric bookstore on the East Side, took me on a ride through pitted streets piled high with rotting garbage and abandoned furniture. The original John D. Rockefeller once lived here, and GE Lighting still has its headquarters in the neighborhood—but with factory jobs long gone, East Cleveland has been ravaged by predatory lending, white flight, and waves of deindustrialization. Four months later, when Trump invoked "American carnage" during his inaugural, I remembered East Cleveland.

But as I traveled across Ohio that fall, I kept noticing something else: the ruins of a prosperous past. Some, like the columns from Daniel Burnham's Union Station in Columbus, were mere fragments. Others, like the Rubber Bowl football stadium in Akron, were awaiting demolition. Most, like the once-elegant Forest Hill Park Footbridge I drove past with Fred Ward, were just badly in need of repair. On the corner of Third and Cleveland in Canton, the imposing sandstone columns of the mostly vacant Frank T. Bow Federal Building beckoned to me from the entrance; inside, a series of thirteen decaying murals depict the rise of the local steel industry. Even more striking was the triptych inside the Cleveland Public Library titled *Dominance of the City*, whose central panel shows a steel bridge thrusting out over the Cuyahoga River. A granite cornerstone in the east wing of Columbus City Hall bore an inscription that finally pointed to the lost civilization whose relics these were: "PWA Project 1454."

One of the fruits of President Franklin D. Roosevelt's first hundred days, the Public Works Administration built roads, bridges, dams, airports, and public buildings. Intended to "prime the pump" and restart the nation's faltering economy during the Great Depression, the PWA and its sister agency, the Works Progress Administration—which, unlike the PWA, was charged with directly putting the millions of unemployed to work—built much of the nation's infrastructure. From the Lincoln Tunnel and LaGuardia Airport, where

I'd begun my travels, to Cleveland Hopkins Airport and the parks in Cincinnati where I ended, the PWA's handiwork was everywhere. Daniel Burnham died two decades before Franklin Roosevelt's election, but Teddy Roosevelt had been an ardent admirer of Burnham's Chicago Plan. As was Harold Ickes, the Bull Moose Republican from Chicago who as FDR's secretary of the interior was in charge of the PWA. It was Burnham's famous admonition to "Make no little plans; they have no magic to stir men's blood" that best sums up that agency's ambitious ethos.

What had become of that confidence? Though Trump's campaign promise to "rebuild our roads, bridges, tunnels, highways, airports, schools, and hospitals" would turn out to be empty rhetoric, and his pledge that "American ships will patrol the seas. American steel will send new skyscrapers into the clouds. American hands will rebuild this nation—and American energy, harvested from American sources, will power this nation. American workers will be hired to do the job" was merely a cynical parody, his repeated invocations of the New Deal never failed to rouse his audiences.[131]

Something was missing. Something, people felt, had been taken from them. White privilege, male privilege—these surely accounted for some, perhaps much, of Trump's appeal. But to stop there was to dismiss the anguish of millions—at least some of whom voted twice for Barack Obama, and for Marcy Kaptur (a woman) and Marcia Fudge (an African American woman) in 2016. From Akron to Youngstown, I kept hearing about broken promises. "When I'm elected president I won't forget you," Bill Clinton told the autoworkers of Youngstown in 1992. After the election Clinton's pledge to bring seven thousand jobs to the area was promptly abandoned—"unless they're all disguised as trees," said Jim Graham, the former president of UAW Local 1112, who recalled standing next to Clinton on the dais that day.

"This used to be a place where you could quit your job in the morning and get another after lunch," Graham told me. Youngstown's decline goes back long before Clinton. Before Ronald Reagan, too. As Bruce Springsteen sang, "these mills they built the tanks and bombs / That won this country's wars."[132] When Youngstown Sheet and Tube shut down in September 1977, a coalition of church and union groups put together a proposal to buy the plant and run it as a worker-owned co-op. The Carter administration backed the plan—then refused the federal loan guarantees that would have made it work. From a peak population of some 170,000 in the 1930s, Youngstown now has barely 65,000 inhabitants. *Forbes* called it one of "the fastest-dying cities" in America—but there's a lot of competition.

What had become of the Roosevelt Republic?

▫ ▫ ▫

> *I was become a stockholder in a corporation where nine hundred and ninety-four of the members furnished all the money and did all the work, and the other six elected themselves a permanent board of direction and took all the dividends. It seemed to me that what the nine hundred and ninety-four dupes needed was a new deal.*
>
> —Mark Twain, *A Connecticut Yankee in King Arthur's Court*

Accepting the Democratic nomination in 1932, Franklin Roosevelt told the delegates in Chicago, "I pledge myself to a new deal for the American people." What he meant, however, remained unclear until after his inauguration, when in a burst of activity he sent Congress the Emergency Banking Act stabilizing the country's banks and providing federal insurance on savings deposits, along with fourteen other pieces of major legislation. Some, such as the Federal Emergency Relief Administration, which spent $500 million on soup kitchens, blankets, and aid to the destitute, or the Civilian Conservation Corps, which put the unemployed to work planting trees, preventing soil erosion, and fighting forest fires, were temporary measures. Others, such as the Tennessee Valley Authority, which combined flood control and rural electrification, the Securities Act, which subjected the stock market to federal regulation, and the Glass-Steagall Act separating commercial and investment banking—and banning banks from gambling with depositors' money—were intended to remain permanent.[133]

But if the roots of the New Deal can be traced to the extraordinary crisis that followed the Wall Street crash of October 1929, when stocks lost nearly 25 percent of their value over two days, and so damaged the real economy that by the time of FDR's inaugural fifteen million Americans—a quarter of the country's workforce—were still unemployed, the roots of the Roosevelt Republic go much deeper.

The Gilded Age that followed the end of Reconstruction was an era of corruption, speculation, and brutal industrial concentration. Farmers, squeezed between the banks who mortgaged their land and the elevator companies and railroad barons who demanded extortionate rates to bring their harvests to market, first organized into the Grange movement. Though effective on some issues, such as the campaign for rural free delivery of the mail, the Grange was hampered by its reluctance to engage in electoral politics—and by keeping its network of cooperative stores on a cash-and-carry basis, which put them out of the reach of most farmers.

Founded to fight the crop-lien system, whereby farmers, especially in the South, obtained seed and supplies from merchants (who were often also their landlords) on loans, which gave them first call on the crop, the Farmers' Alliance attacked the problems of credit and political impotence head-on. By 1882 the Alliance had branches across Texas, the Dakotas, the Midwest, and the cotton South. Eight years later, in coalition with the Colored Farmers' Alliance, which claimed over a million members across the "Black Belt" of the former Confederacy,[134] the first genuinely multiracial mass movement since the abolition of slavery convened in Ocala, Florida, to demand a graduated income tax, direct election of senators, government ownership of the means of mass communication and transportation, and a series of measures designed to increase the supply of money and improve access to credit. Two years further on, in Omaha, the same coalition—augmented by the remnants of the Knights of Labor, the first major American labor organization, and elements of the anti-monopoly Greenback Party, who opposed the hard money policies pursued by both Republicans and Democrats—gave birth to the People's or Populist Party.

Declaring "the interests of rural and civil labor are the same; their enemies are identical," the Omaha Platform added calls for women's suffrage, an eight-hour workday, and the secret ballot in state elections to the group's aims. But the stakes were far higher than mere reform: "We ask all men to first help us to determine whether we are to have a republic to administer before we differ as to the conditions upon which it is to be administered." Convinced that the growing power of organized wealth menaced the very survival of the republic, the Populists "believe[d] that the power of government—in other words, of the people—should be expanded . . . to the end that oppression, injustice, and poverty shall eventually cease in the land."[135]

Intending to "march to the ballot box, take possession of the government . . . and run it in the interest of the people," the Populists were not an electoral success.[136] (Though their record in 1892 of over a million votes—8.5 percent of the total—winning four states and twenty-two electoral votes was far better than the rounding error fate of most new third parties.) Southerners, in particular, seemed unwilling to abandon the "party of the fathers," whose bosses deployed white supremacy and electoral fraud in equal measure to keep voters in line. Having failed to beat them, in 1896 the Populists joined the Democrats in nominating William Jennings Bryan, a former Nebraska congressman and editor of the *Omaha World-Herald*. The fusion campaign reduced the Populist platform to an attack on the gold standard; the party's vote evaporated. In the wake of Bryan's defeat, his Populist running mate, Georgia newspaper editor Tom Watson, one of the most powerful advocates for organizing across the color line, turned to racism, anti-Semitism, and anti-Catholic bigotry to revive his political career, giving Populism's opponents ammunition for decades to come.

Yet much of the Omaha Platform would reappear, little altered, in the Socialist Party manifesto of 1912. Populism's critique of capitalist corruption would also provide the more mainstream Progressive reformers with both an agenda and a source of inspiring rhetoric in their efforts to make government more responsive (if not exactly more democratic). It was the Republican Progressive Theodore Roosevelt, not his Democratic cousin, who in a speech in Portland, Maine, in 1918 called for laws to "secure to the tenant not merely a right to his improvements, but a certain right to the land which he cultivates." The state, said TR, should encourage farm cooperatives. Urban workers, he insisted, should also be helped to become "in some sense a real partner" in their factories, with partial government ownership of large businesses to make "ours an industrial as well as a political democracy."

To ensure that "labor, the working man . . . have their full share in prosperity," Roosevelt recommended "a heavily increasing" excess profits tax and "a proper and heavily progressive inheritance tax on large fortunes." (The original typescript of the speech shows the word "heavily" added in pencil both times.) He also called for old-age pensions, workmen's compensation, and unemployment insurance—all measures eventually enacted by his Democratic namesake.[137]

Whatever its electoral shortcomings, as a vehicle for mass democratic protest, Populism represented "a cultural achievement of the first magnitude." By giving ordinary people the analytical tools, and the confidence, to throw off "inherited forms of deference" Populism produced "a new way of looking at society." Which in turn, by providing the means to spread this new thinking, called forth not just a movement, but a "movement culture" capable of seriously shaking, if not toppling, the established order.[138]

▫ ▫ ▫

Populism's movement culture never went away. Though some of the Alliance suspicion of finance capital got diverted into various currency panaceas, or anti-Semitic paranoia, Midwestern radicalism remained strong enough to push the circulation for *Appeal to Reason*, the Kansas-based socialist weekly, above half a million in 1910. The Industrial Workers of the World (IWW)—better known as "Wobblies"—fought for industrial democracy and the eight-hour day with massive strikes in Lawrence, Massachusetts, Patterson, New Jersey, and on Minnesota's Iron Range. Socialists organized the needle trades in New York, aided by middle-class women reformers. Wall Street climbed to new heights in a banquet whose fruits went overwhelmingly to the already rich, but as speculators celebrated, falling consumer demand set off a wave of factory closures across the country. In Philadelphia nine thousand families were evicted in 1928; in April 1929 more than 10 percent of that city's workers were already unemployed. Prosperity was not around the corner.

Yet while Republicans promised "a chicken in every pot and a car in every garage" in 1928, Democrats offered no opposition to Wall Street rule. Instead nominee Al Smith, focusing on the repeal of Prohibition, turned his campaign over to John J. Raskob, an official with DuPont and chief executive of General Motors whose political philosophy was summed up in an article he'd written for the *Ladies' Home Journal* entitled "Everybody Ought to Be Rich." Smith's failure to challenge Republicans on the economy was labeled "a grave mistake" by Franklin Roosevelt, whose election as governor of New York was a rare item of good news for Democrats that year.[139]

As governor, FDR instituted old-age pensions, established the New York Power Authority, set up the first unemployment relief program in the country, funded public works projects through borrowing, and argued for Social Security. Four years later, with the country still deep in the Depression, Roosevelt kicked off his own presidential bid by blasting "trickle-down" economics, invoking "the forgotten man at the bottom of the economic pyramid," followed a few weeks later by the promise of "bold, persistent experimentation."

Few believed him. The writer Matthew Josephson, hard at work on *The Robber Barons*, his 1934 muckraking exposé of America's great fortunes, dismissed the Democratic candidate as "the logical alternative of the Republican . . . just as Tweedledum is the logical alternative of Tweedledee—for the same job."[140] Norman Thomas, the Socialist Party candidate (and Princeton graduate) patronized Roosevelt as "a nice person who once graduated from Harvard, has a good radio voice, and is as sincere as old party politics would permit."[141] The philosopher John Dewey shared Thomas's skepticism, as did theologian Reinhold Niebuhr and journalist I. F. Stone, who all backed the Socialist ticket. But many intellectuals—including novelist John Dos Passos, poet Langston Hughes, philosopher Sidney Hook, and critic Edmund Wilson—agreed with Josephson that the only way to bring about real change was to "join in the revolutionary struggle . . . under the leadership of the Communist Party."

Yet radicals needed to eat, too, and the plethora of "alphabet agencies"—the Agricultural Adjustment Administration (AAA), Civilian Conservation Corps (CCC), Civil Works Administration (CWA), Federal Aviation Administration (FAA), Farm Credit Administration (FCA), Federal Deposit Insurance Corporation (FDIC), Federal Emergency Relief Administration (FERA), Home Owners' Loan Corporation (HOLC), National Recovery Administration (NRA), Public Works Administration (PWA), and the Tennessee Valley Authority (TVA) in 1933 alone—offered the generation of young left-leaning professionals who swarmed down to Washington a chance "to advance their convictions, as well as their careers."[142]

Like FDR's candidacy, the first New Deal, which ran from 1933 to 1934, benefitted from a division in the ranks of capital caused by the financial crisis. Though heavy industry, with its high labor costs and large domestic market, remained loyal to the high tariff policies and hostility to organized labor traditionally associated with the Republican Party, an emerging bloc of capital-intensive industries and commercial banks began to look elsewhere. With America transformed by World War I from a debtor to a creditor nation, these bankers understood that in order for European countries to pay off their loans, they needed access to the American market. Meanwhile US oil companies and other firms who sold their own products abroad chafed under Hoover's protectionist regime. [143]

Sidney Weinberg, the Goldman Sachs managing partner dubbed "Mr. Wall Street" by the *New York Times*, was Roosevelt's biggest fund-raiser. But the Bank of America's A. P. Giannini, Gerard Swope of General Electric, and sugar refiner Ellsworth Bunker all chipped in. R. J. Reynolds, Liggett and Myers, American, and Lorillard tobacco all backed FDR, as did Walter C. Teagle, president of Standard Oil of New Jersey. Chase National, the Rockefeller-controlled bank associated with the oil industry, loaned the Democratic National Committee $100,000.[144]

This first, administrative New Deal, with its emphasis on "adjustments" to production and financial regulation, also drew on *Quadragesimo Anno*, Pope Pius XI's 1931 encyclical rejecting laissez-faire capitalism in favor of corporativist collaboration among business, workers, and the state.[145] Between Catholic social thought and the purported triumph of Stalin's first five-year plan, the managed economy was very much in vogue. Under the NRA's ubiquitous blue eagle, competitors in a given industry were allowed to negotiate "voluntary agreements" fixing wages, hours, and prices.

The only problem is that they didn't work. The first New Deal did address the banking crisis. Taking the US off the gold standard allowed the treasury to increase the supply of money and credit. The FDIC ended the threat of bank runs, and by taking millions of acres out of production, the AAA put a floor under farm prices. (Directing payments to landowners rather than their tenant farmers, the AAA also further immiserated southern sharecroppers, especially in the cotton belt, where many were simply forced off the land. Indifference—at best—to the plight of African-Americans, who in order to satisfy the president's white southern supporters in congress were systematically excluded from the benefits of Social Security, federal housing, and other New Deal programs would be the Roosevelt Republic's Achilles heel.)

Unemployment remained above 20 percent of the labor force at the end of 1934. "Millions of Americans want reforms more basic, measures more liberal than those which the New Deal has so far developed," proclaimed a November 1934 editorial in the *New York Post*, then one of the most liberal—and pro-FDR—newspapers in the country.[146] They would soon get them.

▫ ▫ ▫

By the time the Supreme Court declared the NRA unconstitutional in May 1935, the blue eagle had become a political embarrassment. There was, however, one portion of the law that had proven its worth: Section 7(a), which guaranteed workers "the right to organize and bargain collectively through representatives of their own choosing." Drafted by Leon Keyserling, an aide to Senator Robert Wagner, the section survived as part of the 1935 National Labor Relations Act (better known as the Wagner Act). It was John L. Lewis, however, the pugnacious head of the United Mine Workers, who best summarized Section 7(a) in the slogan he used to organize Pennsylvania's coalfields: "The President wants you to join a union!"

Like the Emancipation Proclamation, which was both the result of slaves' actions and the trigger for a mass exodus toward Union lines, Section 7(a) turned the steady flow of union activity into a rising tide of organization and agitation. From 7.6 percent of the workforce in 1930, union membership more than doubled, to 16.6 percent in 1935.[147] Lewis brought 90 percent of the nation's soft coal production under UMW auspices. In November 1935, he joined with Sidney

Hillman of the Amalgamated Clothing Workers and David Dubinsky of the International Ladies' Garment Workers' Union to form the Committee for Industrial Organization, which soon cast aside the American Federation of Labor's (AFL) long-standing practice of organizing by craft—putting carpenters, plasterers, and painters each in separate unions—in favor of an industry-wide approach.

The move was prompted by the AFL's tepid response to a wave of strikes in 1934. Beginning in Huntsville, Alabama, a textile strike spread across Georgia and the Carolinas and then north through New York and New England, eventually bringing four hundred thousand workers out. In May 1934 employees at Electric Auto-Lite in Toledo struck after management refused to recognize the union. Though the governor called out the National Guard, the Lucas County Unemployed League, led by the pacifist preacher A. J. Muste, defied the injunction, which led to a citywide general strike. That same month, the Minneapolis local of the International Brotherhood of Teamsters shut down that city despite opposition from their national union leadership and brutal police violence. Later that summer, striking longshoremen shut down every port on the West Coast; when San Francisco police killed two men, and California's governor mobilized the National Guard, International Longshoremen's Association leader Harry Bridges persuaded the city's Labor Council to call a general strike.

That Bridges was close to* the Communist Party, while the Minneapolis Teamsters were led by the Trotskyist Dunne brothers, and the Toledo strikers marched under the banner of the socialist American Labor Party, suggests that when the Communist International officially endorsed the "Popular Front" strategy of cooperation among left forces in August 1935, it was merely ratifying a practice

---

* When Bridges first emigrated from Australia in 1920 he'd briefly joined the IWW. The charge that he was a secret member of the Communist Party began during the 1934 general strike and followed him for the rest of his career. But Bridges always denied it, and though the government repeatedly tried to deport him—once on the grounds of membership in the CP, and once for allegedly committing perjury by lying about it—the Supreme Court twice found the evidence insufficient.

that was already well established at the grass roots.[148] "Consider the feelings of socialists in Arkansas and Tennessee, who were trying, at the risk of their lives, to organize sharecroppers," wrote Irving Howe, never a warm admirer of the CP. "Didn't it make sense to work with anyone sharing their immediate objectives, no matter which idiotic theories Stalin advanced and his New York followers repeated?"[149]

Not all of the strikes were successful—at least in terms of immediate objectives. But in standing up and fighting back, the strikers were developing their own movement culture, which, like the Populists before them, had the force of revelation. Before Minneapolis, the writer Meridel Le Sueur had "never been in a strike." A member of the Communist Party, in a strike led by Trotskyists, "I felt my feet join in that strange shuffle of thousands of bodies moving with direction, of thousands of feet, and my own breath . . . As if an electric charge had passed through me . . . I was marching."[150]

Spurred both by conditions at home and by the spread of fascism in Europe, the movement did not yet have a name. But it did have what might be called an ethic of solidarity. And an evolving culture, breaking out everywhere from college campuses to concert halls—at the end of one Young People's Concert, Leopold Stokowski, the conductor of the Philadelphia Orchestra, led the audience in singing the "Internationale"—to shop floors in Detroit and farmworkers' camps in California. Contrary to later portrayals depicting the whole enterprise as a cover for Soviet foreign policy, or the class-based agitation of the American CP, much of this movement activity focused on combatting racism, with a boycott of German goods in the Northeast, anti-lynching campaigns and the founding of the Southern Tenant Farmers' Union* in the South, and battles against anti-Mex-

* Formed in 1934 partly in response to landowners' implementation of the AAA policy, the STFU represented another attempt to build a coalition across racial lines. Spreading from Arkansas across the South, the union grew to twenty-five thousand members, only to fall victim to a combination of planter terrorism and ideological warfare between socialists and communists inside the organization.

ican and anti-Asian discrimination on the West Coast.[151] Throughout the 1930s, the fight to free the Scottsboro Boys—nine black men falsely accused of raping two white women—brought together activists across racial and sectarian lines. Similarly, Billie Holiday's rendition of "Strange Fruit" reached audiences far beyond the patrons of the New York cabaret where the song closed her set every night for nine months.[152]

Whether inspired by Section 7(a), John L. Lewis, or by the newfound unity on the left, the next wave of strikes was different. Beginning at Firestone Rubber in January 1936, American workers wielded a new tactic in their confrontations with capital: the sit-down. Pioneered by the IWW, developed in Akron and perfected in Detroit, the sit-down soon became labor's winning weapon. In December 1936, the United Automobile Workers—founded less than two years earlier, the UAW joined the Steel Workers Organizing Committee (SWOC) in the new Congress of Industrial Organizations (CIO)—sat down at the General Motors Fisher Body Plant Number 2 in Flint, Michigan, bringing production from 15,000 cars a week down to 150.[153] By February, the strike had spread to Chevrolet. Michigan governor Frank Murphy refused to call out the National Guard, and under pressure from President Roosevelt, GM agreed to negotiate with the union, whose membership went from 88,000 to 400,000 over the next eight months.[154] A month later the mere threat of a strike was sufficient to unionize US Steel. But elsewhere the sit-down continued to spread; by year's end 400,000 workers had participated in 477 sit-down strikes covering everything from hospital workers, gravediggers, and garbage collectors to engineers, architects, and baseball players.[155]

▪ ▪ ▪

In his first inaugural, in 1932, Roosevelt assured Americans "the only thing we have to fear is fear itself." Accepting renomination in Philadelphia four years later, the president warned that although "we have conquered fear," the country now faced a peril as old as the republic, an updated version of the same "tyranny of political autocracy" against which the revolution had been fought. Instead of Hanoverians like King George III, the current danger came from "a new industrial dictatorship" composed of "economic royalists." Thanks to the rise of corporations and banks, "the political equality we once had won was meaningless in the face of economic inequality."

The second New Deal addressed that inequality—and the entrenched power that protected it. It also reflected the changing basis of the New Deal coalition. As the "progressive" wing of capital deserted the Democrats, their numbers (and funds) were more than made up by the four million workers brought into the party via the CIO and Labor's Non-Partisan League, founded by Sidney Hillman and John L. Lewis at the height of the 1936 strike wave. From the Works Progress Administration, which, starting in May 1935, gave jobs to 8.5 million Americans, to the National Youth Administration, which employed another 4.5 million, to the various federal artists' and writers' projects, government took up the role of employer of last resort. The result was an electoral landslide, as FDR won every state apart from Maine and Vermont.

With the Housing Act of 1937, drafted by fair-housing advocate Catherine Bauer Wurster, Washington also provided states with both the funds and the legal tools to build housing for the poor. The Social Security Act, with its old-age pension, unemployment insurance, aid to dependent children, and support for the blind, laid the foundations of the American welfare state. The Fair Labor Standards Act of 1938 instituted the eight-hour day and the forty-hour week—labor aims for half a century—as well as a minimum wage and time-and-a-half pay for overtime.

The Second New Deal also represented a shift from the "planners" and cartels encouraged by the National Recovery Administration (NRA) to the critique of concentrated corporate power represented by the revival, under Thurman Arnold, of the Justice Department's moribund Antitrust Division. Initially targeting the "bottlenecks" he said caused higher prices for consumers, Arnold brought cases against milk distributors in Chicago, tire and newsprint manufacturers, and the Alcoa aluminum company. He forced Hollywood studios to divest their ownership of movie theaters, won price-fixing cases against the major oil producers, and secured a criminal conviction against the American Medical Association for illegally boycotting a Washington, DC, neighborhood clinic that let patients subscribe to a prepaid health plan (analogous to a modern-day health maintenance organization).[156]

Finally, in its attempts to boost "mass purchasing power," the Second New Deal struck directly at economic inequality. The Revenue Act of 1935 introduced a Wealth Tax that raised the rate on the highest incomes to 75 percent and imposed a 70 percent estate tax. Two years later, in response to joint congressional hearings on tax evasion, the administration revised the act to close various loopholes. The undistributed profits tax, which targeted retained corporate earnings, aimed both to raise revenue and to force companies to pay more to workers and suppliers. Over five years the effective income tax rate on the top 1 percent more than doubled, from 6.8 percent in 1932 to 15.7 percent in 1937.[157]

By then the movement had a philosophy: anti-fascism. And a name: the Popular Front, inspired in part by French Socialist Léon Blum's *Front populaire* coalition government, and by the Comintern's newfound policy of cooperation with other anti-fascist parties—itself a response to the disastrous ultra-left Third Period, which saw Communists and Social Democrats battling one another in the streets of Germany as the Nazis seized power. And it had a cause: Spain, where the elected government of the Spanish Republic was fighting for its life against Franco's legions.

In Detroit, this meant recruiting experienced Communist organizers like Wyndham Mortimer, who represented the UAW at negotiations in Flint; in Pittsburgh the SWOC sent Ben Careathers and Ernest McKinney, two African American Communists, to organize the workers at Jones and Laughlin.[158] In New York, it meant cooperation with Mayor Fiorello LaGuardia and support for Congressman Vito Marcantonio—and the declaration, by Party General Secretary Earl Browder, that "Communism is Twentieth Century Americanism."[159] Indeed, there is some justice to Mike Davis's description of the CPUSA passing directly from sectarianism to sycophancy.[160]

In Washington, the close working relationships sanctioned by the Popular Front drew a handful of liberals into associations they later had cause to regret—even when they didn't cost them their careers. At the same time, the Second New Deal's tenacious attack on economic inequality convinced a generation of American radicals that it might actually be possible to realize the social democratic vision of a mixed economy in which a vital public sector balanced the private sector.[161]

While it lasted, the Popular Front was as much a cultural as a political phenomenon, regularly filling Madison Square Garden for pageants and rallies for Spain or the Scottsboro defendants. The web connecting politics and culture was indeed one of the Popular Front's hallmarks—in productions like *The Cradle Will Rock*, composer Mark Blitzstein's dramatization of a union drive, or *Pins and Needles*, a musical staged by the ILGWU that became the longest-running show on Broadway, or Duke Ellington's *Jump for Joy*, a revue whose numbers included "I've Got a Passport from Georgia"—containing the line "Good-bye, Jim, and I do mean crow."[162] The same sensibility is reflected in the diaries of Mary Dublin Keyserling,* an economist, consumer advocate, and advisor to Eleanor Roosevelt, who recorded attending a *Nation* magazine benefit for southern sharecroppers, another benefit for the Spanish Loyalists, two recitals by the singer Paul Robeson, cocktails for H. G. Wells, Orson Welles, the labor

* Leon Keyserling was her husband.

journalist Mary Heaton Vorse, the British Labour politician Harold Laski—and a performance of *Pins and Needles*.[163]

▫ ▫ ▫

It was the Nazi-Soviet pact of August 1939 that killed the Popular Front. Though most of the American Communist Party eventually swallowed Soviet foreign minister Vyacheslav Molotov's claim that opposition to fascism was merely "a matter of taste," fellow travelers were another story.[164] American Jews who'd seen German synagogues burn on Kristallnacht, or African Americans who'd watched as Mussolini gassed and bombed civilians in Ethiopia, had little patience for such rationalizations. Billie Holiday may have added "The Yanks Aren't Coming" to her set list, with the anti-war "Ballad of October 16"* replacing "Viva La Quince Brigada" in Almanac Singers' concerts as the party line switched overnight from "collective security" to "no imperialist war." But to most of the party's anti-fascist former allies it was obvious the Yanks were coming—the sooner the better. When they did, the Roosevelt Republic really hit its stride.

War and the mobilization for war not only rescued FDR from the wreckage of the court-packing plan that nearly stalled his second term; it called into being a state muscular enough to manufacture the means to wage war—and provided the rationale for progressive taxation on a scale large enough, over time, to draw down and redistribute much of the accumulated fortunes of the robber barons and their heirs. By 1944 the top tax bracket, which had been a largely

---

* Written to satirize the announcement, on October 16, 1940, that 16,500,000 men had registered for the draft, Millard Lampell's chorus became even more of an embarrassment when, after Hitler invaded the Soviet Union in June 1941, the party returned sheepishly to the ranks of the all-outers:

> *Oh, Franklin Roosevelt told the people how he felt*
> *We damned near believed what he said*
> *He said, "I hate war, and so does Eleanor*
> *But we won't be safe till everybody's dead."*

symbolic 79 percent of incomes above $5 million, had become a far more significant 94 percent of incomes above $200,000.[165] The top 0.1 percent, who'd owned a quarter of the nation's wealth in 1928, saw their share fall to 10 percent by 1945.[166] FDR's War Labor Board incorporated many of the trade union movement's prewar objectives into its mandates, making paid vacations, seniority and grievance systems, sick leave, mealtime pay, and a supplement for night work standard for an ever-growing portion of the working class.[167]

Labor didn't get everything its way. But even its setbacks reveal a scale of ambition unprecedented in American history. In May 1940 FDR asked Congress for fifty thousand planes a year—at a time when Curtiss-Wright, the largest US manufacturer, struggled to produce ten a day. With aircraft manufacturers happy to accumulate a backlog of orders rather than expand production, and automakers determined to keep turning out cars, Walter Reuther, a UAW organizer who'd been beaten up by Henry Ford's thugs, came up with a plan to build five hundred planes a day. Reuther's detailed proposal to turn the whole auto industry's spare capacity into an aircraft production line got him a meeting with FDR, who praised the plan. It also terrified the Big Three automakers, who rightly saw it not only as a challenge to management's power—made in the name of efficiency and the public interest—but as a precedent applicable to any strategic industry. (George Romney, Mitt Romney's father, called Reuther "the most dangerous man in Detroit, because no one is more skilled at bringing about the revolution without seeming to disturb the existing forms of society.")[168]

"There is only one problem," Treasury Secretary Henry Morgenthau told Reuther. "It comes from the 'wrong' source."* Endorsed by ardent New Dealers from Sidney Hillman (newly appointed co-di-

* Though credited to Reuther, who was indeed its intellectual architect, the plan might have had an even rougher reception if its actual draftsman had been known. Four decades later the radical journalist I. F. Stone told Reuther's biographer, Nelson Lichtenstein, the plan "went through my typewriter."

rector of the Office of Production Management) to Under Secretary of War Robert Patterson, Reuther's plan was sent to William Knudsen, chairman of the War Production Board, with a note from FDR asking him to give it "a good deal of attention." Knudsen, who'd been president of General Motors when Reuther led several successful strikes against the company, had no intention of allowing workers an equal say in production—or in promoting industrial democracy. "We had to stall," he later admitted, by pretending Reuther's proposal was impractical. Yet within months of Pearl Harbor, the industry was integrating to a far greater degree than anything Reuther had imagined. Detroit stopped making cars entirely; two-thirds of machine tools were converted to aircraft production. The difference was that labor had no role in managing those factories.[169]

If labor never became a full partner in production, the war was still swingtime for the Roosevelt Republic. In 1944, the CIO's Political Action Committee mobilized war workers in Texas and Alabama shipyards to defeat such notorious reactionaries as Martin Dies (co-founder and first chairman of the House Committee on Un-American Activities) and Joe Starnes (who'd insisted on segregation in federal housing projects). In Winston-Salem, unionization of the largely African American workforce at R. J. Reynolds Tobacco transformed the city's NAACP chapter into the largest along the southern coast, opening up black participation in local electoral politics for the first time since the Populist era.[170] The threat of a march on Washington by A. Philip Randolph, head of the Brotherhood of Sleeping Car Porters, prompted FDR to issue Executive Order 8802, which established the Fair Employment Practices Committee (FEPC) prohibiting racial discrimination in federal training programs and in defense industries, followed by Executive Order 9346, which gave the FEPC authority over all federal contracts.

Thanks to groups like the Southern Conference for Human Welfare and the Highlander Folk School—whose work carried on through the demise of the Popular Front without interruption—and unions like the Food and Tobacco Workers and the Mine, Mill and Smelter Workers, which both had significant black membership, the struggles of organized labor and the movement for black freedom became increasingly intertwined. In a series for *The Crisis*, the NAACP journal, Harold Preece reported, "The South has not known such a force since . . . the great days of the Reconstruction era."[171] Operation Dixie, conceived by the CIO in September 1945, aimed to use the tactics of the Steel Workers Organizing Committee—and a cadre of some two hundred experienced organizers—to unionize the South, particularly the textile industry.

Operation Dixie is usually regarded as a failure—and in terms purely of trade union membership in the South the evidence is clear.[172] Though the CIO invested a million dollars and opened offices throughout the South, the organizing drive was undercut by the AFL, which launched a rival campaign promoting "American" unionism, and by political infighting between rival CIO unions, some of whom used blatantly racist appeals to recruit Ku Klux Klan members and to launch destructive raids on more militant unions (which tended to have a higher black membership and a leadership more closely aligned with the Communist Party).[173]

But Jack O'Dell, an organizer in the National Maritime Union at the time who went on to become a key advisor to both Martin Luther King Jr. and Jesse Jackson, paints a more complicated picture. Describing Operation Dixie's early successes—the Longshoremen and the Marine Cooks and Stewards were both established in New Orleans, while Eastern Airlines skycaps in Miami joined the Transport Workers Union—O'Dell calls the effort "an early casualty of the Cold War." Yet as his own career demonstrates, the massive investment in black activism and civil rights represented by Operation Dixie would continue paying dividends for decades to come.[174]

The war years saw blacks and women entering the workforce—including the white-collar workforce—in unprecedented numbers. From Rosie the Riveter with her polka-dot bandana to Frances Perkins in the cabinet, the public image of women was changing. By 1944, women were filling 30 percent of factory jobs; in defense industries, employment of women rose by 462 percent.[175] One result was the growth of a labor feminism in which economic justice was as important as the struggle for political and legal rights.[176]

Though often overlooked by historians, this movement, which grew out of collaboration between working-class activists and middle-class reformers in response to garment strikes or tragedies like the Triangle Shirtwaist fire,* also reached new levels of influence in the Roosevelt Republic.[177] "For a brief historical moment," writes historian Landon R. Y. Storrs, reviewing the careers of Mary Keyserling, Catherine Wurster, Elizabeth Wickenden (who ran the relief program for transients and later, at the WPA, supervised the young Lyndon Baines Johnson), the pioneering consumer advocate Caroline Ware, and civil rights lawyer Pauli Murray (a friend of Eleanor Roosevelt, Murray would be listed as co-author by Ruth Bader Ginsburg on her brief for *Reed v. Reed*, the Supreme Court case that first held that discrimination on the basis of sex was unconstitutional), "left feminists were positioned to shape American policymaking."[178]

▪ ▪ ▪

Like the Lincoln Republic, the Roosevelt Republic didn't reach its apogee until after the death of its founder. When Harry Truman took office in April 1945, the military Keynesianism that powered America's economic recovery was still in high gear. Union membership among nonagricultural workers hit 35.4 percent—an all-time high. Perhaps equally significant, in a Gallup poll that August nearly 80 percent of Americans thought the "law guaranteeing collective bargaining" was a good thing.[179] The end of the wartime no-strike pledge

---

* Labor Secretary Frances Perkins, who as a young social worker had witnessed women jumping to their deaths from the burning factory, said the Triangle fire marked "the day the New Deal began."

saw labor flexing its muscles as over five million workers walked off the job during the year following V-J Day. In the fight to shape the postwar order, the tide appeared to still be running strongly to the left.

The National Resources Planning Board's 1942 report *Security, Work and Relief Policies,* often described as the "American Beveridge Report" after economist William Beveridge's blueprint for Britain's postwar welfare state, actually went beyond Beveridge to propose not only social insurance and a national health plan but "the right to work, usefully and creatively through the productive years."[180] The CIO's *People's Program for 1944* called for big-power cooperation, full employment, and economic planning—the thinking behind the "Full Employment Bill of 1945," which by the time it reached President Truman had dropped the word "Full" from the title, along with any commitment stronger than the goal of promoting employment.*

Such hopes did not die quietly. *Saving American Capitalism,* a 1948 collection of essays by Leon Keyserling, Chester Bowles, and other New Dealers, advocated a peacetime Keynesian management of the economy to keep consumer spending high in order to ensure that "capitalism is not but a passing phase in the historical process from feudalism to socialism."[181]

Starting in 1943, and again in 1945, Senator Wagner had introduced bills to add national health insurance to the Social Security program. In November 1945—two months after Japan surrendered—President Truman sent a revised version to Congress—where it would be reintroduced every year for the next five years. But the same coalition of Republicans and Southern Democrats who vetoed efforts to provide economic security to American workers fought even harder—and with even greater success—against the specter of universal health care. So perhaps the old question, "Why is there no socialism in the United States?" should be reduced to Bernie Sand-

* But only "in a manner calculated to foster and promote free and competitive enterprise."

ers's more modest: Why is the US "the only major country on Earth that doesn't guarantee health care to all people as a right?"

Republican senator Robert Taft, who'd labeled Eveline Burns, the author of *Security, Work and Relief Policies*, "a socialist disciple of Harold Laski," introduced his own bill calling for grants to the states to subsidize private health insurance. The American Medical Association accused Truman of following "the Moscow party line" in a campaign backed by the American Legion and the American Bar Association. Before Joseph McCarthy ever set foot in the Senate, "Medical McCarthyism" was being deployed by a "medical establishment that had a vested interest in . . . linking advocates of compulsory health insurance with disloyalty."[182] Opponents also benefitted from division in the ranks of labor, as John L. Lewis withdrew his support after the UMW successfully struck for an employer-funded health plan. In years to come, distrust and resentment would fester between the largely young, often minority or female non-union workforce denied such protections, and older, unionized, blue-collar workers who effectively paid a double tax, supporting both their own, negotiated benefits and a state welfare system funded by increasingly regressive payroll taxes.[183]

If the failure to enact national health insurance marks the limits of the Roosevelt Republic, the Taft-Hartley Act sounded its death knell. Passed in 1947, the bill was partly a response to the postwar strike wave, partly a product of Cold War panic, and partly an opportunistic move once Republicans gained control of the Senate. Its ban on secondary boycotts, provision allowing states to enact their own "right to work" laws, and requirement that union leaders file sworn affidavits declaring they were not supporters of the Communist Party had been on the conservative wish list since the 1930s. And while President Truman opposed the bill, his decision to follow Republican senator Arthur Vandenberg's advice to "scare hell out of the American people" to drum up support for the Truman Doctrine of confronting Communism overseas made the kind of domestic red-baiting that FDR had always laughed off much harder to dismiss. It also afforded rhetorical cover to Southern Democrats who viewed Operation Dixie as a threat to white supremacy. A total of ninety-three Democrats voted in favor of Taft-Hartley.

Truman's surprise victory in 1948 gave labor one last chance. Repeal of Taft-Hartley was in the 1948 Democratic platform, but when the bill reached the House floor sixty-nine Southern Democrats voted against labor—a lesson in futility that doubtless contributed to the decline in working class voting.[184] Taft-Hartley did more than cripple the labor movement. Along with Executive Order 9835, which established the Federal Loyalty Security Program, it delivered the Roosevelt Republic into the hands of its enemies. How often this was literally the case is impossible to say; most records of the more than five million federal employees subject to security screening—including the 25,000 subject to "full field investigation" by the FBI, the 12,000 who subsequently resigned, and the estimated 2,700 who were dismissed—were destroyed.

But the historian Landon Storrs, working only on the largest files—more than an inch thick—preserved in a single record group, concluded that in case after case "direct repression of progressive policymakers . . . stifled and stigmatized social democracy in the United States."[185] Unlike HUAC or the McCarthy hearings, loyalty boards generally remained secret. For example, neither Leon Keyserling nor his wife, Mary Dublin Keyserling, ever spoke publicly about their ordeal; nor did they preserve documents related to it in their papers. Yet as Storrs demonstrates, after being cleared by the board in 1948 Leon Keyserling changed his emphasis from redistribution and mass purchasing power to economic growth; by 1949 he explicitly supported increases in military spending, providing the fiscal rationale for National Security Council Paper Number 68 calling for a massive military buildup to "check and roll back the Kremlin's drive for world domination."[186]

Mary Keyserling left government service for a decade, and when

Lyndon Johnson nominated her to head the US Women's Bureau, the red-baiters started up again. Johnson stuck with her—and perhaps in return both Keyserlings were supportive of the president's war in Vietnam. Pauli Murray, whose scholarship is responsible for the inclusion of the word "sex" in the 1964 Civil Rights Act, had her appointment as counsel to the Equal Employment Opportunities Commission blocked out of fears that her brief membership in the Communist Party thirty years earlier would make the commission vulnerable to attack.[187] Public housing advocate Caroline Bauer Wurster; child welfare expert Elizabeth Wickenden and her husband Arthur Goldschmidt, a public power advocate who helped create the WPA; economist Thomas Blaisdell, one of the architects of the Marshall Plan—none of them had ever been Communists, yet the loyalty program caught them all in its net, and when they emerged very few remained in government service. Or publicly on the left.

▪ ▪ ▪

These were not just personal tragedies. As Storrs shows, the anti-Communist crusade pushed a generation of left feminists into adopting the language of the ideological center. The CIO had begun tearing itself apart in its own purges even before Taft-Hartley. But the decapitation of the labor movement's most militant leadership—and many of its most experienced organizers—had a devastating effect, while labor's inability to repeal Taft-Hartley starkly exposed the limits of its "inside-only" relationship with the Democratic Party. When push came to shove, labor had nowhere else to go.

The effect of the Cold War on the struggle for racial justice is more complicated. Competition with the Soviet Union increased the pressure on America to live up to the promises made in fighting fascism, when, as Wendell Willkie observed, "the mocking paradoxes in our own society become so clear they can no longer be ignored." From Gunnar Myrdal's 1944 identification of racism as the "American dilemma" to Frank Sinatra singing "All races and religions / That's America to me" in "The House I Live In,"* to Jackie Robinson's debut with the Dodgers, racial equality was on the national agenda.[188]

At the same time, the Cold War frame narrowed the range of civil rights activism, sidelining any linkage of race and class, or of domestic racism with America's conduct in Africa, Asia, or Latin America. It also destroyed lives, and deprived the civil rights activists of the 1950s and 1960s of experienced mentors.[189]

"To say that the Cold War was 'good' for the civil rights movement strikes me as like saying that Hurricane Katrina was good for the building trades in the Gulf Coast," writes one historian.[190] As if by design, the postwar red scare "guaranteed the defeat of more democratic policy alternatives," writes Storrs, "by removing or crippling their government advocates . . . [F]orcing these civil servants to alter or hide their convictions, the loyalty program also severed transmission between the generations. . . . Scarred survivors . . . kept their distance from the radicals of the late 1960s, who in turn saw their forbears as part of the problem rather than part of the solution."[191]

And yet it moved. In 1955 the economist Simon Kuznets noted that between 1929 and 1950 the share of income going to the bottom two-fifths of the population rose from 13.5 percent to 18 percent, while the share taken by the top fifth fell from 55 to 44 percent over the same period; the share of the richest 1 percent dropped even more sharply, from 19.1 to 7.4 percent.[192] By the 1950s, America's income distri-

* In the film version, a ten-minute short that won an Oscar in 1946, this verse is left out. The film was written by Albert Maltz, later blacklisted as one of the Hollywood Ten; the music was written by Earl Robinson, a veteran of the Federal Theatre Project, who was also blacklisted. The lyrics were by Abel Meeropol, who also wrote "Strange Fruit," and who with his wife, Anne, adopted the two sons of Julius and Ethel Rosenberg, executed after being convicted of spying for the Soviet Union. Outraged by HUAC's attacks on the film, Sinatra, who thought he was still living in the Roosevelt Republic, protested: "How long will it be before the committee gets to work on freedom of the air?" Five years later, deserted by his record label, his movie studio, and his agent, a penitent Sinatra announced: "I don't like Communists and I have nothing to do with any organization except the Knights of Columbus."

bution, wrote C. Wright Mills, had become "less a pyramid with a flat base than a fat diamond with a bulging middle."[193] The "Great Compression" in American wages identified by Claudia Goldin and Robert Margo shows a steep decline in the gap between the top and bottom of the wage scale from 1939 to 1950, with inequality not rising significantly until the 1970s.[194] The super-rich—the top 0.1 percent—didn't significantly increase their share until the early 1980s.[195]

Along with Social Security and Medicare—consistently the two most popular government programs—the long tail of the Roosevelt Republic would also include public aid to higher education.[196] Thanks to the GI Bill and the Pell Grants program, the share of young adults who completed four years of college tripled, from 8 percent in 1950 to 24 percent in 1980.[197] Not only did grants then cover the full cost of tuition. Students in New York City, New York State, and California also had access to systems that were virtually free.

So, what happened? In *The Unwinding*, writer George Packer argues, "When the norms that made the old institutions useful began to unwind, and the leaders abandoned their posts, the Roosevelt Republic that had reigned for almost half a century came undone. The void was filled by the default force in American life, organized money."[198] But as we have seen, the process was far more deliberate than that. From the 1950s onward, the concentration of power that President Eisenhower would label the military-industrial complex successively disarmed countervailing forces, starting with organized labor and progressives in the 1950s and ending with the very regulatory structures of the New Deal in the 1990s. Yet until the Bernie Sanders campaign, merely pointing this out was enough to disqualify a politician from high office.

Whether Sanders runs again or not, his persistent popularity, the lingering legacy of the Occupy Wall Street protests, and the growth in groups like the Democratic Socialists of America have put the issue of inequality back on the agenda for the first time since Franklin Roosevelt. Something had indeed been taken from us—all of us. The destruction of the Roosevelt Republic's ethic of solidary not only allowed for a resurgent oligarchy to seize a greater share of the national wealth than at any time since the Gilded Age. It also condemned us to our separate and very much unequal struggles: for Black Lives, women's liberation, immigrant rights, gender equality; against police violence, poverty, environmental degradation, sexual exploitation. The question is whether, this time around, the many streams of the next republic can come together in a mighty force that will both restore the things that have been taken from us—economic security, mutual respect, solidarity—and carry us, together, into a future of peace, justice, and sustainable prosperity.

CHAPTER NINE

Zephyr Teachout—Corruption and Its Discontents

Here's something you probably don't know about Zephyr Teachout: she used to go to Tea Party rallies. Teachout, a professor at Fordham University School of Law, is one of the Left's rising stars. In 2014 she challenged Governor Andrew Cuomo in the New York Democratic primary. Despite having no name recognition, no money, and no organization to speak of—the Working Families Party, which recruited Teachout to run, was so afraid she might not get the fifty thousand votes needed to maintain the party's line on the ballot they ended up endorsing Cuomo—Teachout got 182,000 votes, over 34 percent of the total, carrying half the counties in the state. Not enough to win, but more than enough to give the previously indestructible Cuomo a bloody nose. Lately she's been in the news as lead plaintiff in the lawsuit accusing Donald Trump of violating the Constitution's emoluments clause, meant to prevent federal officials from accepting gifts from foreign governments.* In between, she ran for Congress and waged a one-woman crusade against overweening corporate power.

But in 2009, after watching the Obama campaign transform its grassroots online platform Obama for America (OFA) into a tooth-

* In May 2018 Teachout announced her candidacy to succeed Eric Schneiderman as New York State attorney general.

less propaganda megaphone for the president's Wall Street bailout plan, Teachout found herself drawn to Tea Party rallies. "At the time, the Tea Party had lots of different angles," she says. "Rallies on the border with Joe Arpaio [the Arizona sheriff whose persistent racial profiling got him convicted of contempt of court—and then pardoned by President Trump] that were obviously all about race.

"At the same time, there were others where a deep story was being told about the Wall Street crash. 'Things are falling apart'—this is the Tea Party speaking—'I can tell you who did this to you. Who did this to you was government. Government destroyed you. Government made you insecure.' Remember, I used to be a death penalty lawyer. If you have any kind of criminal trial, and your client is accused, you can always say your client didn't do it. But it's a hell of a lot better to say somebody else did it."

Building on the model Teachout and Zack Exley developed for the Howard Dean presidential campaign, OFA had amassed a list of thirteen million names and e-mails, and raised $778 million—double the total raised by John McCain. After the election David Plouffe,* Obama's campaign manager, sent an e-mail to all thirteen million names—inviting them to hold house parties to watch the debut video of Organizing for America, OFA's successor, in which the case for the bailout would be made by the newly anointed chair of the Democratic National Committee, one Tim Kaine.

"I predict," wrote Teachout, "that there will be perhaps a thousand such parties, then hundreds, then dozens. I think OFA will fail in its mission . . . And I think this is a very good thing . . . This is a good thing because it is not intended to be a representative organization, where people have real power."[199]

---

* After he left the White House Plouffe was fined $90,000 by the Chicago Board of Ethics for failing to register as a lobbyist before contacting Mayor Rahm Emanuel on behalf of Uber, the ride-sharing company, who'd hired him as a strategic advisor. In January 2017 Plouffe became head of policy and advocacy at the Chan Zuckerberg Initiative, the charity set up by Facebook founder Mark Zuckerberg and his wife.

Being right didn't make Teachout happy. "So much of the Democratic Party's response for so long was, 'It's not our guy! And by the way, it's nobody else, either.' They had no basic story for 'Who did this to me? Who did this to America?' There is a true answer to that question: Monsanto and Bank of America and Wells Fargo and Pfizer. They have, one, totally monopolized industries, so that people are just little serfs coming to beg to work for them, and so you can't bargain for benefits; two, been big drivers pushing for what they call free trade, which is basically a global regime run by big corporations. They did this on purpose, and they did it through taking over big parts of the Democratic Party, and they did it through taking over huge parts of the Republican Party." And in 2009 you'd have a better chance of hearing such an analysis—or getting a hearing for such an analysis—at a Tea Party rally than at a Democratic Party meeting. So Teachout went to Tea Party rallies. To talk. But mostly to listen.

Two years later she was doing the same thing at Occupy Wall Street, where she spent several months attending the nightly general assemblies at Zuccotti Park, participating in the Spokes Council, and becoming an active member of the Occupy Wall Street Activist Legal Working Group. What she found there was more inspiring—a movement that "created an imaginative opening in the political and economic possibilities for the country." But also deeply frustrating, as over time Occupy's consensus rules "not only stopped decisions, but also led to a kind of fetishizing of 'the process,' [leading] away from action."[200]

When Bernie Sanders declared his candidacy in 2015, Teachout, who grew up in Vermont, was one of his earliest backers. Explaining that she'd first met Sanders "at a brown bag lunch" in Montpelier in 1993, where he'd spoken to voters about how the newly enacted North American Free Trade Agreement (NAFTA) would jeopardize their rights, Teachout said she was endorsing Sanders "because of my deep patriotism, my belief that democracy is possible and a thriving economy is possible, and we don't need to beg at the feet of the wealthiest donors to have a collective life worth living."[201]

One of the harder lessons history teaches us is that the good guys don't always win. I spent election night 2016 in the Rhinecliff Inn, watching Teachout watch as Hillary Clinton's anticipated victory collapsed. Her own race, in a historically Republican rural district, had been lost hours before, but with a much larger disaster unfolding, Teachout told her supporters, "Once in a generation, we are called upon to restore American democracy. You've seen what's happened across the country tonight. It's urgent, and it's going to take all of us. We may have lost this race, but we are not going away."

▪ ▪ ▪

Persistence is a trait Teachout has been cultivating all her life. At thirteen she ran in the New England cross-country championships. "You're not supposed to run out front. But nobody told me that," she says. Racing against high school students several years her senior, nobody bothered to tell her she wasn't supposed to win, either. So she did, and went on to win the state title several times. Jim Eakin, her high school coach, recalled Teachout racing through the long winters without long sleeves or tights. "She had a lot of natural talent," said Eakin, "but her greatest strength was her toughness."

When Teachout talks about her childhood she describes an almost nineteenth-century tableau of town meetings and church on Sundays, growing up on a farm near Norwich, Vermont, with sheep and chickens and chores for her and her four siblings: Woden, Chelsea, Cabot, and Dillon. Given the unusual names, I'd always assumed her parents were part of the back-to-the-land movement that, beginning in the 1960s, transformed Vermont from one of the most conservative states in the country to the most progressive—attracting and then molding incomers like ex–New Yorkers Howard Dean and Bernie Sanders. But Teachout corrects me.

"That wasn't my parents' world." The Teachouts—the name is

Dutch—have been in Vermont for generations. As a law student, her father, Peter Teachout, had spent a summer registering voters in rural Louisiana. An early opponent of the Vietnam War, he was drafted and offered the option of enlisting as an officer because of his law degree. He served three years in Army intelligence, once, says his daughter, giving "a speech in Japan to a bunch of officers and enlisted men about why we were violating the Geneva Conventions in Vietnam, and all the officers stood up and walked out because they were so offended." For the last forty years, he's taught constitutional law at the Vermont Law School.

Her mother, Mary Miles Teachout, is a superior court judge. Her parents "will never answer the name question," she says, "but I often think of it as more a sense of humor than a seventies ethic. They aren't particularly political. Because my dad cared a lot about it, we did end up talking about race a fair amount, even in this very small, very white community. The deep ethos, I would say, of my family was very much that nobody's the boss of anybody else." Apart from the face-to-face democracy of the New England town meeting, Teachout says her own politics were shaped by the experience of "growing up in a Congregational church. One of the distinct features . . . is that the members have power over the minister."

Born in 1971, Teachout attended her first demonstration "on my own. I took the bus from White River Junction to DC to the Women's March on Washington" in April 1989. Yet when she graduated from Yale four years later, neither politics nor the law beckoned. "I wanted to become a journalist, or a teacher." In the meantime, she was working as a waitress. But on the way to hear Sanders speak in Burlington she ended up sharing an elevator with Howard Dean's chief of staff, who suggested she come to work on his gubernatorial campaign.

"There were only three of us there, so I was able to learn every part of it. I wrote the polls. I created the literature. I think he spent $250,000 on the whole thing." After Dean won, Teachout traveled to Morocco, where, still interested in education, she put together a database of English-language textbooks. Returning to the US, she worked as a personal assistant and applied to Duke, which had a joint program in law and political science.

"I didn't become deeply political until after going to law school. I was very troubled by the high levels of incarceration [in North Carolina]. I thought, 'Well, maybe part of the reason is because you have life sentences which seem trivial compared to a death sentence, and there's all these problems with the death penalty, so why don't [I] work on the death penalty?' So many things you just wander into, and then it has a profound effect. It had a very profound effect on me."

"There was a guy, Clifton White, about to be executed. This was in my first few months of really working as a lawyer. We'd submitted a request for a pardon to the governor and the governor summarily denied it. But the governor had also been Clifton White's prosecutor in a prior life, who had pushed for him getting death. That seemed like a pretty basic equal protection clause violation. If you're going to allow for somebody to be pardoned, they should not [need to] be pardoned by their own prosecutor. You either provide the process or you don't, but if you do provide it, it can't be somebody who's already got his thumb on [the scale].

"A lower court stayed the execution at nine thirty at night. The Supreme Court of North Carolina got together on the phone that same night and dissolved the stay. Clifton White was executed six hours later. It was awful—this incredible carelessness of the North Carolina Supreme Court that they wouldn't even have a hearing. They just got together on the phone. I had come in a bit neutral . . . on capital punishment, but not neutral on whether the procedure should be fair. I'm no longer neutral on capital punishment. You realize the degree to which law is profoundly political."

▫ ▫ ▫

Watch Teachout pressing the flesh at a fund-raiser for Upper Hudson Planned Parenthood, or giving an impromptu stump speech to supporters in New Paltz, and she seems like a natural politician. She's composed, articulate, and feisty, pulling off the difficult trick of projecting warmth without coming across as fake. Yet she only arrived at politics late and with a certain reluctance. "I love poetry, I like painting, I like art. I hadn't really thought of myself as a political person—I think in part because I thought everything was okay.

"Like a lot of people in my generation—the [Berlin] Wall came down in '89—there was a sense that the fundamental problems of democracy had been solved. I came to college and divestment [from South Africa] was happening. These were success stories." Her death penalty work showed her that things were not okay—and would not improve by themselves. "The worst kind of progressive, I think, is the one who believes that history will solve itself."

So when, in 2003, Dean announced he was running for president on a platform of universal health care and opposition to the Iraq War, "I thought, 'Oh, if he gets to become president, I can really have a voice here.' I auctioned off all the stuff in my apartment in North Carolina" and headed back to Vermont. Despite her rudimentary programming skills, Teachout became Dean's director of online organizing. "I hired the first programmers for a presidential campaign. At the time, people were still just putting up pamphlets on the Internet. It was unbelievably exciting. At first, there were five hundred meetings around the country. Then there's a thousand. Then there's tens of thousands . . . This at a time when Bill Clinton said Dean couldn't be a serious candidate [because of his opposition to the war in Iraq]."

Though Dean's campaign eventually ran aground in Iowa, campaign manager Joe Trippi's experiment in "online populism" lasted long enough for proof of concept. Dean for America—the website Teachout's team created—became a ten-thousand-dollar-an-hour fund-raising machine, while at the same time providing "Deaniacs" with chat rooms, blogging platforms, and a continuous stream of user-generated content celebrating their candidate. On DeanLink, supporters who typed in their zip codes were given the names of every registered Deaniac in their community, with options to send messages or add them to their list of friends. Clicking on "Go Local" took you from virtual to actual, with invitations to fund-raisers, envelope-stuffing sessions, and door-knocking forays—in your own neighborhood, or, for the more adventurous or dedicated, in Iowa and New Hampshire.

Zack Exley, who took a leave from his job as organizing director at MoveOn.org to advise the campaign, described the Dean staffers as "the antithesis" of typical careerist political operatives. "They just *really* wanted to take back their country."[202] For Teachout, the campaign was a continuing education in how conventional politics had broken down—and how much could be accomplished outside the conventional model.

"We raised more money than Bill Clinton had—but from low-dollar donations. At the same time, you could see how—in non-explicit ways, without the candidate even necessarily being involved—policy is responsive to big donors. I wrote up an open-source policy* and somebody said, 'Just run it by the head of public policy for Microsoft. He doesn't have to approve, just see what he thinks.' All these soft conversations, not explicitly quid pro quo, just a sense that these are important people because they are in our big fund-raising world. Honestly, I thought we were changing everything . . .

"We'd shown how a distributed method of fund-raising could compete. And a model for distributed organizing. I also had a moment of coming up short, thinking, 'These are really important tools.' They could either be tools of centralization or decentralization." In 2008, Barack Obama's campaign used distributed fund-raising to amass the biggest war chest ever seen in American politics. But the campaign itself was famously top-down.

---

* Readers interested in a geek's-eye-view from the outside might want to find *Linux Journal* editor Doc Searles's dispatches from the campaign trail, all archived at www.linuxjournal.com.

"If you don't allow people to connect and create their own power sources," says Teachout, "two things follow. One, you actually learn less. But also you build less power.

People disengage.

"They'll make the phone calls you ask them to for the six months before an election, or show up and do the canvasing that you want them to, because they care so much. But they haven't then built a political community with real clout that can effect things on the local or state, or even national level." Which is what happened to the Democratic Party during the eight years Obama was in the White House. "There really was no political organizing, and that hurt our country in a lot of ways," says Teachout.

After Obama's reelection in 2012, Teachout tracked several local groups of Obama supporters. "The groups that lasted the longest were often the groups that the Obama campaign never got around to sending staff to, which makes a lot of sense. Nobody told them to start, so nobody could tell them to stop. In Durham, there was an active group that ended up working on local incarceration issues because they had figured out how to be effective . . ."

It wasn't until the Bernie barnstorms of 2016, and Becky Bond and Zack Exley's "Big Organizing" model,[203] that distributed organizing got another chance to show what it could do. In the meantime, Teachout became preoccupied with a related problem: Since devolving power away from the center is not only good politics, but also effective politics, why is it so rarely practiced?

▫ ▫ ▫

In her 2015 TED Talk, "What is Corrupt?," Teachout begins with a confession: "I grew up killing chickens." Not exactly what the audience expected from the immaculately coiffed law professor in a blue suit. But a clever way to introduce one of the most important concepts in her political lexicon: "chickenization," which is Teachout's shorthand for the forces corrupting our politics and strangling our economy.

"I think you can look at the chicken industry as both a truth [for agriculture], and also a metaphor for what's happening everywhere. The chicken industry looks like, on paper, a profoundly competitive, thriving industry. There are tens of thousands of contract farmers. They are their own business owners. They run chicken farms. They compete against each other. They produce a lot of cheap chickens."

"In fact, what has happened is the big three—Tyson, Pilgrims Pride, and Sanderson—have effectively divided up the country into little fiefdoms. If you're a chicken farmer in Tyson's territory, you can't sell to anybody but Tyson. Or if you do, the terms are no better.

"Tyson says, 'We are not going to buy your chickens unless you use our feed, [from] an affiliated company, unless you use our eggs, unless you use our watering system, unless you use our light and dark system.' Basically, unless you use their entire scheme. Our image of the chicken farmer as this entrepreneur who's figuring out how to build a better chicken—someone we might be able to go to and say, 'Hey. I think this is inhumane,' and who might have the moral agency to say, 'I hear you. I'll change this.'— That is not true.

"But then it gets worse, because Tyson then also requires the chicken farmer to sign a contract that says he can't talk to his neighbors, who are also chicken farmers, about their practices. One of the things about a functioning market is that there's a lot of competition, but there's also a lot of communication. Not here.

"Tyson can then use these chicken farmers, because they can't communicate with each other, to experiment, to say, 'Okay, let's send this person some different feed.' But all the learning happens at Tyson. The learning doesn't happen at the local level because they've just been using them as guinea pigs."

Farmers also take on hundreds of thousands of dollars in debt to build chicken houses to the company's specifications. Meanwhile, processors like Tyson pay their contract farmers through the "tournament system," which "pits farmers against one another by pegging their pay to their ranking, with no accountability or transparency. Farmers know that if they protest or challenge the company, it can cut them off—and sink their livelihood.[204] There's great reporting by Chris Leonard on this in his book *Meat Racket*.* I've talked to people in the dairy industry who've experienced the same thing.

"This procedure, which works very well for Tyson, is called chickenization. It's called chickenization because the beef and pork industry are taking it up. But I would say this is also Amazon, this is Google. A lot of our big companies are chickenizing all of the people they work with. You want to sell a book? You'd better follow Amazon's rules and Amazon's contract, and Amazon can use its contract to learn, to spy on publishers. These distributors have [an] incredible amount of power. It looks like a market, but it's not a market—and it leads to political fear. Just try to find publishers that are willing to speak up against Amazon."

Political fear is something Teachout has seen at first hand. As a senior fellow at the New America think tank's Open Markets program, she wrote policy papers blasting Tom Wheeler, the Obama-appointed chair of the Federal Communications Commission, for wobbling on net neutrality, and criticizing conservative chief justice John Roberts. No problem. Then Barry Lynn, the program's head, wrote a blog post in June 2017 praising the European Union after it fined Google €2.42 billion for abusing its dominance as a search engine to promote its own products.

Teachout explains: "The classic example is Yelp in this country. It's really hard to prove, but there've been some white papers on this. Organically, TripAdvisor should show up. Then Google decided it wanted to get in the game, so now Yelp is the top search result. This is something that all the anti-monopolists from the Granger period

* Christopher Leonard, *Meat Racket: The Secret Takeover of America's Food Business* (New York: Simon and Schuster, 2014).

understood. It's like, 'Oh, we own the railroad? We are going to make it cheaper for our companies to ship things on this railroad.' Google flexed its muscles, and within three days Lynn was asked to leave New America, with eight staffers and a few of us fellows." As Teachout notes, New America's main conference room is named the Eric Schmidt Ideas Lab, after Google's chairman, who between his family foundation and the corporation donated some $21 million to New America.[205]

"I can't tell you the number of people who have said to me, 'I can't help you if you're working on your Google project because my sibling has a project that depends on Google money.' These are the normal choices people make. They care more about their sister than they care about taking on the monopoly. That makes perfect sense, but the problem is the system that allows for this incredible fear of these companies, who have the capacity to retaliate."

Once you start noticing it, the chickenization of the American economy is hard to miss. In Millerton, New York, Teachout introduces me to Lou Saperstein, whose family store has dominated the town's Main Street for half a century. "I've been doing business with OshKosh for twenty, twenty-five years," Saperstein told me. "I used to go to their offices in the Empire State Building to make my orders. Then they started sending me sheets in the mail. Then they sent a disk in the mail. After they got bought by Carter's in 2012, I got a letter saying they were canceling my order."

To retain the privilege of selling OshKosh jeans, Saperstein's would "need to order a minimum of five thousand dollars" in the spring of 2013, said Lou, "rising to twenty thousand dollars in the fall and fifty thousand dollars a year thereafter." This in a town with a population of 958.

"There's a lie that Main Streets all over America are dying because local businesses can't compete," says Teachout. "If there was an open market, Saperstein's could compete. But there isn't."

▫ ▫ ▫

"We are at a revolutionary moment right now," says Teachout, "about what kind of society we want to live in. An enormous number of people—left and right—are saying, 'Definitely not this.' Monopoly and antitrust aren't just technical sideline issues. These are fundamental swords that you can use to restrict excessive power.

"We just kind of lost the language. It's like we actually lost the words. After 2008 I was involved in efforts to use Dodd-Frank [the Dodd-Frank Wall Street Reform and Consumer Protection Act] to try to break up eight banks. Even people I really agreed with, they'd say, 'That's not antitrust.' Well, what is it? If you have really important political tools that have no name, then they don't get used."

With her professorial suits and Pepsodent smile, Teachout doesn't exactly fit the image of a radical firebrand. This is a woman who uses "Gee willikers!" to express anger, who on the campaign trail sometimes described herself as a "Teddy Roosevelt Republican"—though to me she referenced a different Roosevelt: "I'm a second-term FDR person." That would be the term that saw the Democratic Party transformed into the party of immigrants, city dwellers, and African Americans—and the rise of the Roosevelt Republic.

What makes Teachout radical—and indispensible for understanding both what has happened to our country and how to redeem it—isn't her manner, it's her message. Which isn't just that the system is rigged, but how it's rigged, who rigged it, and why. Not some paranoid fantasy about black helicopters and federal bureaucrats. Or a capitalist conspiracy with Wall Street puppet masters pulling strings (though Wall Street, particularly the banking industry, is a frequent target). But a clear, persuasive, historically informed whodunit laying out exactly how the unchecked exercise of corporate power is destroying our country—and why, back when Donald Trump was still just a reality TV star with improbable hair—things had already gotten so much worse.

"People don't necessarily know the meaning of 'antitrust' or 'monopoly,' but they know something is wrong," she says. The Founding Fathers, Teachout says, were obsessed with the fragility of republican government. They'd all read Gibbon's *History of the Decline and Fall of the Roman Empire*. In drafting the Constitution, the founders were acutely aware of what had happened not just to the Roman republic, or the Venetian republic, but to Britain, which they perceived as a failed republic in which the forms of representative government had been hollowed out by *corruption*, embodied, in the language of the time, by the king and his "placemen"—the term used to describe subservient political appointees.

"By corruption," Teachout writes, the Founders "meant excessive private interests influencing the exercise of public power. An *act* was corrupt when private power was used to influence public power for private ends.[206] A *system* was corrupt when the public power was excessively used to serve private ends instead of the public good. A *person* was corrupt when they used public power for private ends."

Teachout's 2014 book *Corruption in America* is a postmortem for the Roosevelt Republic. Beginning with the story of Benjamin Franklin's snuffbox—intended as a parting gift from Louis XVI to Franklin after his service as ambassador to France, the diamond-encrusted gold box with an enamel portrait of the king prompted a crisis in the young republic, resolved only after Franklin submitted it to Congress, which after some debate granted him permission to keep it—Teachout traces the decay of our democracy from a country in which lobbying was literally illegal* to today's post–*Citizens United* dystopia.

Of course the threat of corruption has always been with us. As early as *Fletcher v. Peck*, an 1810 Supreme Court decision holding that even though the Georgia legislature made certain land grants

* The Georgia constitution made lobbying a crime; the 1879 California Constitution made it a felony.

in return for bribes, the sale of those lands was a binding contract, which a later, reforming legislature could not revoke. The Supreme Court, as this case shows, has long been prepared to protect business interests at the expense of equity (or, in this case, the Native American tribes whose land had been sold out from under them). The Founders may have taken bribery seriously enough to make it one of the only crimes—along with treason and piracy—mentioned by name in the Constitution. Yet Boise Penrose, the early twentieth-century Republican who bought his seat in the US Senate by spreading half a million dollars among the 254 members of the Pennsylvania legislature—his opponent, John Wanamaker, was under the mistaken impression that $400,000 would be sufficient—was hardly an isolated case.[207] Thwarting such common practice was why the Populists demanded, and the Progressives delivered, direct election of senators in the Seventeenth Amendment to the US Constitution, ratified in April 1913.

Though they've been on the books throughout our history, bribery laws, the muckraking journalist Robert Sherrill pointed out, have mostly ensnared "the small-time operator, the unpopular politician, the fringe power broker. They are not generally used to bring the big-time operator to a shameful end." Indeed, by Richard Nixon's day, the sale of ambassadorships for campaign contributions—a bribe in all but name—was sufficiently well established that Nixon "even set up a kind of 'complaints' window. Givers who expected an ambassadorship and didn't get one"—like Cornelius V. Whitney, who donated $250,000 in hopes of becoming ambassador to Spain, but was opposed by the State Department—"could receive a refund."[208]

That's because, like the War on Drugs, a "War on Corruption" is nearly impossible to win through the criminal justice system—especially when the lines between a bribe and a gift and a campaign contribution are so easily blurred. Instead, the Founders relied on what Teachout calls "incentive structures" like Article 1, Section 9, Clause 8—the "emoluments clause"—of the Constitution, which bars all federal office holders from receiving "any present . . . of any kind whatever" from a foreign government without the consent of Congress.[209]

Yet beginning with *Buckley v. Valeo*, a 1976 ruling that struck down limits on campaign spending, the Supreme Court has successively dismantled every effort to contain the influence of money—and hence of corporate power—over our politics. "The hallmark of corruption is the financial quid pro quo: dollars for political favors," wrote Chief Justice William Rehnquist in 1985.[210] Where the Founders regarded mere gifts as dangerous and in need of close supervision—in an era when the giving of gifts was an accepted part of the political culture—the court's 2010 *Citizens United* decision restricted corruption to actual bribery, since, as Justice Anthony Kennedy wrote, "favoritism and influence are not . . . avoidable in representative politics."[211]

The view that government had no interest in preventing influence peddling so long as there was no explicit quid pro quo was reinforced by the Roberts Court in 2014 with *McCutcheon*, which dismantled the last remaining limits on individual donations.[212] The decline reached its denouement two years later, when the court overturned the conviction of Bob McDonnell, a former governor of Virginia, who with his wife had taken $177,000 in loans and gifts from a Richmond businessman. Though Jonnie Williams had given the governor a Rolex watch, the use of his Ferrari, and $20,000 toward his daughter's wedding reception, paid for the McDonnell family vacation, and loaned the governor $120,000, the court found that Williams was merely paying for "access"—which is apparently no longer a crime.[213]

▪ ▪ ▪

Corruption matters. A candidate who refuses to recognize corruption—who insists, as Hillary Clinton did repeatedly in 2016, that "America is already great"—will never be trusted by voters who can smell the stench all around them. Donald Trump's inaugural promise that "we are transferring power from Washington, DC, and giving it back to you, the people" may have been a lie. But at least it didn't pretend the system worked. Offered a forced choice between two paths to their own extinction—the gently managed, technocratically assisted suicide offered by the Democrats, or the savage Darwinian winner-take-all sweepstakes of the Republicans—is it really so surprising that millions of Americans decided not to play along, whether by voting for the candidate who promised an end to business as usual, or simply by staying home?

That Trump's victory ushered in what may be the most corrupt administration in American history—where oil companies eviscerate environmental regulations, corporate foes of public schools dismantle federal aid to education, billionaires and their congressional placemen rewrite the tax code, and influence peddlers domestic and foreign line up to patronize Trump's businesses—will remain merely a bitter irony so long as the larger corruption at the heart of our democracy remains unacknowledged. Putting a kleptocrat in the White House only underlines how far we have fallen from a government of the people, by the people and for the people.

Corruption, not conspiracy, is the thread that connects the Flint water scandal (where General Motors was given access to clean water from Lake Huron while city children were poisoned) to congressional paralysis in the wake of mass shootings (thanks to NRA lobbying), to the high cost of prescription drugs, to the lack of accountability for police shootings, to the criminalization of marijuana, to the suppression of climate science. A movement that opposes racism and sexism and militarism and economic oppression while ignoring corruption is fighting with its hands tied. Which is why, Teachout says, she's trying "to bring corruption back. Not as a societal ill—but as an idea.

"Everything I do is about, in some ways, fighting against concentrated power. People might disagree on this. But for me at least, the problem is not the corporate form. The problem is the big corporation."

She traces her distrust of bigness to her hero, Louis Brandeis. "For many years, the Brandeis-influenced, decentralized power part of the left has been suppressed." For socialists in love with central planning, bigness seemed like a virtue. Teachout says she always asks such people, "In your ideal society, who will make the shoes?" Any answer that involves concentrated power, she says, "terrifies the hell out of me, and not just because of the Soviet history. This is perhaps where I'm a little more conservative than some people. Because I believe things can get even worse."

In her own campaign for Congress, Teachout felt the power of Big Money at the sharp end. Though she raised nearly $1 million more than her Republican opponent, former lobbyist John Faso—mostly from small donors giving an average of twenty-one dollars each—the difference was more than made up for by just two billionaires, Robert Mercer and Wall Street financier Paul Singer. The $6.7 million in super-PAC money against her financed an onslaught of hostile television, radio, and Internet ads Teachout was unable to answer. "If you lived in the district and went on Pandora, you had to watch an attack ad on me." Despite losing her race, she jokes, "I have the same job I was applying for—except without the staff or the authority."

Yet Teachout remains hopeful. "One of my fears after the election is that people running from Trump would run into the arms of the oligarchs. 'Save us, Facebook. Save us, Google. Save us, Jeff Bezos.' This fear is not coming to pass."

Instead, she's noticed "some strange bed follows, like labor and small business, which had been seen as antagonistic. Because if your approach to labor is essentially bureaucratic, it's much easier to organize GM than to organize ten different companies making something. Then there's net neutrality, which is kind of shocking in how it became a grassroots movement. Thousands of people marching and sitting in and pressuring the FCC? That's kind of interesting. I feel like it's post-crash politics.

"There's no shortcut to a better society," Teachout says. "It requires rebuilding a structure of local power of Democrats and progressives. It requires taking on these big companies. It will require some really difficult coalitions—the old populist platform coalitions. That can seem a little hard because there's Trump over here."

While some commentators have abandoned populism to Trump and his supporters, Teachout is not among them. The sense of revelation she felt reading Lawrence Goodwyn's *The Populist Moment* after Dean's defeat has never left her. "What's the opposite of populism?" she asks. "Technocratic elites making decisions? It's not like there's this wonderful history of enlightened elites making the best decisions for the rest of us. Actually, technocratic elites also have a long tradition of incredible corruption and racism. If you disrespect people, some form of reaction will arise."

A week after her defeat, and Trump's victory, the *Washington Post* asked Teachout to reflect on what had happened. She was blunt. "In the 1990s, Democrats pretended they could fund their campaigns with cash from Wall Street titans and still remain the party of the American worker and American farmer and American independent business owner. Well, that didn't work, did it? The rising tides of Wall Street didn't lift all boats. What it did do was flood the country, washing away our homes and our jobs and our dignity and our sovereignty . . ."

"What should the Democratic Party stand for? In a word, democracy, with equal dignity for each person. That means becoming the party that resists every effort by small groups of well-organized wealthy men to take over our families and our communities and our nation."

A year later, she gave me a longer to-do list: "Pass an absolute ban on staffers or members of Congress taking jobs in the influence industry. Any [state] legislature can pass laws banning legislators and staffers from holding stock in companies affected by legislation. Congress can clearly define coordination so that independent corporate spending is actually independent. The public can oppose any Supreme Court nominee that supports the logic of *Buckley*, *Citizens United*, and *McCutcheon*. To my mind, the two most important solutions that require no Supreme Court blessing are ideas advocated by Teddy Roosevelt: publicly funded elections and trust-busting."

Losing an election isn't always a defeat, much less a reason to quit fighting. "There are no saviors here," she told me. "That desire to be saved by anybody is itself anti-political and anti-democratic. We actually have to rebuild power." The good guys don't always win. Zephyr Teachout learned that the hard way. What matters is what happens next.

ACKNOWLEDGMENTS

Although I don't remember it, my mother always said she'd wheeled me around Springfield, Massachusetts, in my stroller while knocking on doors for Senator John F. Kennedy's 1960 presidential campaign. Whether it was then or later, at some point I got the bug, and have been fascinated by presidential elections since long before I was old enough to vote. In fact I still have vivid memories of the first campaign I volunteered on myself—working the phones (I was still too young to drive) and canvassing for George McGovern in Memphis, Tennessee, in 1972. (When I phoned the Shelby County Democratic Party that spring they asked if I wouldn't rather volunteer for Hubert Humphrey or Ed Muskie. After I insisted they agreed to put me in touch with the McGovern people. At the first meeting there were just five of us—and one was the friend who had driven me.)

So when Katrina vanden Heuvel, my boss at the *Nation*, asked me what I wanted to write about after we'd finished our very pleasant collaboration on the magazine's 150th anniversary issue in 2015, I decided to push my luck. To my great delight she not only agreed to let me cover the election, sending me to all the early primary states and most of the debates, but then kept me on what she called the "insurgency beat" after November 2016, reporting on the people and movements who were working not just to resist Trump, but to move the country forward. That reporting, beginning in August 2015 and still ongoing nearly two years after Election Day, is the basis for the book you have just read. I thank her not just for her encouragement and enthusiasm, and her friendship, but for her deep engagement with the topic, and the countless e-mails, phone calls, and Skype conversations that guided my coverage.

Dan Simon, my editor at Seven Stories, understood what this book should be about even before I did. It was Dan who, gently but implacably, turned me away from the campaign book I thought I wanted to write toward something that looked forward instead of backward. Throughout he has been a first-rate intellectual *provocateur*, a patient and meticulous reader, and a hard taskmaster when it came to meeting a very tight deadline. I'm deeply grateful to him for all of those things, and for his energy and enthusiasm. I've also benefitted enormously from the eagle eye and deft pencil of Lauren Hooker and the contagious enthusiasm of Ruth Weiner and Silvia Stramenga, also at Seven Stories.

My agent, Andrew Wylie, has stuck with me through four books and over twenty-five years. This book demanded unusual persistence, so I'm particularly thankful to Andrew, Jin Auh, and Jessica Friedman for their support.

The people profiled in this book live very busy lives, and I am indebted to each of them for taking the time to meet with me, to talk at length, and for patiently answering my many follow-up questions by phone or e-mail. Some have become good friends, and I look forward to continuing the conversation with all of them in the years to come.

At the *Nation* my editor, Richard Kim, was intellectually exigent, stylistically meticulous, and remarkably tolerant of my neuroses. Every piece I published in the magazine was improved by his editing, and much of the thinking behind this book was shaped by our conversations. My colleagues Joan Walsh and John Nichols were always generous with opinions and advice and contacts; George Zornick and Julianne Hing made even the Republican Convention fun. Emily Douglas and Annie Shields took copy at absurdly late hours. Sandy McCroskey repeatedly saved me from solecism.

My comrade Steve Cobble conducted a one-man seminar throughout the 2016 campaign that immeasurably deepened my understanding of election strategy and political movements—and the relationship between the two. Winnie Wong, one of the founders of People for Bernie, patiently explained the significance of Donald

Trump's Facebook metrics to a net-non-native; she also invited me back to the People's Summit in Chicago, where I first met some of the people profiled in this book. Claire Sandberg, Becky Bond, and Zack Exley have been remarkably tolerant of my ignorance about the mechanics of distributed organizing, and generous with their insights. My Philadelphia *landsman*, Larry Cohen, the former head of Labor for Bernie and current chair of Our Revolution, has always been candid, and (crucially for a reporter) available. I've learned a lot talking to him and to his colleague Rand Wilson.

I've admired Dan Cantor of the Working Families Party for as long as I've known him—since we were both undergraduates. He and Bob Master understood—and explained—the complex, at times abusive, relationship between the Democratic Party and progressive movements better than anyone else I've met. Bill Lipton and Joe Dinkin, also of the WFP, have always been generous with their time and their insights, for which I am grateful.

My debts to Staughton Lynd and Eric Foner go far beyond the endnotes—though I hope those suggest the extent to which I relied on their work. Staughton and Jane Lynd gave me a lovely lunch and a lively briefing on the Ohio economy, but his book on the intellectual origins of American radicalism, which I only read after we met, came as a revelation. Lynd's exclusion from the academy since the 1960s—tantamount to blacklisting—is not only a huge loss to the historical profession, but also an enduring stain on American intellectual life. Eric Foner, happily, remains one of the ornaments of American intellectual life, as well as a friend and mentor. I cherish his friendship, but am even more grateful for his work, which illuminates the politics of the Civil War and Reconstruction with wit, clarity, and passion.

My travels around the country were made not only pleasant but possible thanks to Don Share and Jacqueline Pope, who put me up in Chicago; Larry Friedman and Randi Mozenter, who did the same in St. Louis; Sid and Jill Holt, likewise in Old Salem, New York, and Peter Cariani, Becky Heaton, Brent Cochran, Angela Raffel, and Karen Cariani, who always made my passages through Boston a delight. Albert Scardino put me up in Beaufort, South Carolina, fed me oysters, and enlightened me about the politics not only of that state but of his native Georgia as well. Makani Themba provided wise counsel and generous introductions in Jackson; Sofia Jawed-Wessel and Megan Hunt were splendid guides to Omaha. Dave Leshtz and Jeffrey Cox not only initiated me into the mysteries of the Iowa Caucuses; they also planted ideas that continue to bear fruit long after we met. Jeff Klein provided a crucial assist in Buffalo. Arguing politics with Rick MacArthur—something we've been doing since our days on the *Columbia Spectator*—sharpened my thinking.

My dear friends Rosemary Moore and Josh Shneider and Tom Mellins and Judy Weinstein made me feel at home, and taken care of, on frequent stays in Brooklyn and Manhattan. Since all work etc. . . . I also thank Nanci Levine and Joel Sanders for always finding time to play on my visits to New York.

If my reporting skews a bit east, that may be because I have a daughter in New York and a home in Vermont. Besides keeping the *Nation*'s travel expenses down, this also meant I was able to try out some of the ideas in this book last fall at a benefit for Kopkind, the summer residency program for journalists, filmmakers, and community organizers down the road in Guilford. Begun as a memorial to our beloved neighbor Andy Kopkind, the great radical journalist, Kopkind continues to exemplify Andy's pessimism of the intellect and his optimism of the will—as well as his fondness for good food and brilliant company. I'm grateful to JoAnn Wypijewski for inviting me, and John Scagliotti for years of gentle provocations across the kitchen table. Also to Verandah Porche, David Hall, Harry Saxman, Sue Lederer, Eric and Dale Morse, Richard Wizansky, Todd Mandel, Susan Bonthron, and Gilbert Ruff for always welcoming me home.

In London my friends Sally Angel, Erin Cotter, Sarah Dunant, Jonathan Freedland, Ben Freedman, Maurice Glasman, Jonny Levy,

Sue Prevezer, and Gillian Slovo have repeatedly forgiven my absences, for which I thank them all.

My travels over the last few years have meant that my wife, Maria Margaronis, had to hold the fort at the *Nation*'s London bureau, which she has done with her usual grace, while also making a series of brilliant radio documentaries for the BBC. I thank her for being so understanding about my work, and for the inspiration provided by her own. I look forward to being home a bit more in the coming months.

Finally I am more grateful than I can say to our children, Alexander, Zoe, and Theo, for filling the years with such deep pleasure, and for growing up into such delightful adults who no longer need to be driven to school every day. As Greek-Jewish-British-Americans, they belong to many cultures and can pick and choose as they like. But insofar as they are interested in America, I hope they find these pages useful in understanding their father's country, which is also, in part, their country too.

NOTES

INTRODUCTION: IN SEARCH OF THE LOST REPUBLIC

1. Eric Foner, *Tom Paine and Revolutionary America* (Oxford: Oxford University Press, 1976, 74–75.
2. D. D. Guttenplan, "Texas Showdown," *Nation*, June 4–11, 2018, 12–18.

CHAPTER ONE: JANE MCALEVEY—WINNING UNDER CONDITIONS OF EXTREME ADVERSITY

3. https://janemcalevey.com/wp-content/uploads/2013/08/scan_ramapo.jpg. Accessed September 26, 2017.
4. Thomas Knipe, *Golden v Ramapo: Lessons in Growth Management*, May 14, 2010, accessed September 28, 2017, https://tomknipe.files.wordpress.com/2010/07/ramapo-v-golden-lessons-in-growth-management.pdf.
5. "Hazel Hansen McAlevey," *Journal News* (White Plains, NY), December 18, 1969, 2.
6. James O'Sullivan, "SASU Pres. Released from Jail Friday Morning," *Albany Student Press*, September 20, 1985, accessed September 29, 2017, http://library.albany.edu/speccoll/findaids/issues/1985_09_20.pdf; Bill Jacob, "SUNY Votes to Divest as S. African Stocks Drop," *Albany Student Press*, October 1, 1985, accessed September 29, 2017, http://library.albany.edu/speccoll/findaids/issues/1985_10_01.pdf.
7. Hillary D. Rodham, "'There Is Only the Fight . . .': An Analysis of the Alinsky Model," (BA thesis, Wellesley College, 1969), accessed September 29, 2017, http://www.hillaryclintonquarterly.com/documents/HillaryClintonThesis.pdf.
8. Jane McAlevey, *No Shortcuts: Organizing for Power* (Oxford: Oxford University Press, 2016), 40–47. McAlevey cites Frank Bardacke, *Trampling Out the Vintage: Cesar Chavez and the Two Souls of the United Farm Workers* (London: Verso, 2011); she also credits both Gary Delgado, founder of the Center for Third World Organizing, and his successor Rinku Sen for shaping her critique of Alinsky.
9. Saul Alinsky, "Playboy Interview," *Playboy* (March 1972). Widely available online.
10. McAlevey, *No Shortcuts*, 46.
11. Danny HoSang, "All the Issues in Workers' Lives," *Shelterforce*, May 1, 2000, accessed September 29, 2017, https://shelterforce.org/2000/05/01/all-the-issues-in-workers-lives/.
12. Jane McAlevey, "What Angelina Jolie Didn't Tell You About Breast Cancer and That Gene," *Alternet*, May 30, 2013, accessed September 29, 2017, http://www.alternet.org/personal-health/angelina-jolie-and-breast-cancer.

CHAPTER TWO: THE WHISKEY REPUBLIC

13. "Full Transcript: Donald Trump's Jobs Plan Speech," *Politico*, June 28, 2016, accessed September 4, 2017, http://www.politico.com/story/2016/06/full-transcript-trump-job-plan-speech-224891.
14. Charles McCollester, "The Next Page: The Nixon-Kennedy Debate . . . in McKeesport, 1947," *Pittsburgh Post-Gazette*, accessed September 4, 2017, http://www.post-gazette.

com/local/east/2011/11/27/The-Next-Page-The-Nixon-Kennedy-debate-in-McKeesport-1947/stories/201111270212.

15. John F. Kennedy, "Remarks at City Hall, McKeesport, Pennsylvania, October 13, 1962," Papers of John F. Kennedy, JFKPOF-041-001, John F. Kennedy Presidential Library and Museum, Boston, accessed September 5, 2017, https://www.jfklibrary.org/Asset-Viewer/Archives/JFKPOF-041-001.aspx.
16. Justin Champion, *Republican Learning: John Toland and the Crisis of Christian Culture, 1696–1722* (Manchester: Manchester University Press, 2003), 112.
17. Bernard Bailyn, *The Ideological Origins of the American Revolution* (Cambridge: Belknap Press, 1967), 36.
18. Bailyn, *Ideological Origins*, 304.
19. Henry N. Brailsford, *Levellers and the English Revolution* (London: Spokesman Books, 1976).
20. Stanley N. Katz, "Republicanism and the Law of Inheritance in the American Revolutionary Era," *Michigan Law Review* LXXVI (1977), 1–29.
21. William Hogeland, *The Whiskey Rebellion: George Washington, Alexander Hamilton, and the Frontier Rebels Who Challenged America's Newfound Sovereignty* (New York: Simon and Schuster, 2006), 82.
22. Staughton Lynd, *The Intellectual Origins of American Radicalism* (Cambridge: Cambridge University Press, 1968, 2009), 170, citing Thomas Paine, "Rights of Man, Part Second," *Complete Writings*, ed. Philip S. Foner (New York: 1945), vol. 1, 358.
23. Gordon S. Wood, *The Creation of the American Republic* (Chapel Hill: University of North Carolina Press, 1969), 84–85.
24. Donald Ratcliffe, "The Right to Vote and the Rise of Democracy, 1787–1828," *Journal of the Early Republic* 33 (Summer 2013), 219–254.
25. Gordon S. Wood, *The Creation of the American Republic* (Chapel Hill: University of North Carolina Press, 1969), p. 84-85.
26. Wood, *Radicalism*, 341.
27. Mary K. Bonsteel Tachau, "The Whiskey Rebellion in Kentucky: A Forgotten Episode of Civil Disobedience," *Journal of the Early Republic* 2, no. 3 (Autumn 1982), 239–259.
28. Thomas P. Slaughter, *The Whiskey Rebellion: Frontier Epilogue to the American Revolution* (Oxford: Oxford University Press, 1986), 14–17.
29. Slaughter, *Whiskey Rebellion*, 98.
30. Hogeland, *Whiskey Rebellion*, 66–67.
31. Wood, *Radicalism*, 306.
32. Hogeland, *Whiskey Rebellion*, 69–70.
33. Hogeland, *Whiskey Rebellion*, 8, 37–39, 97.
34. "Military History of James McFarlane (c. 1751—7/17/1794)," The State Society of the Cincinnati of Pennsylvania, accessed September 10, 2017, https://ooohjrt.wcomhost.com/Names/JamesMcFarlane.html.
35. Hogeland, *Whiskey Rebellion*, 150–154.
36. Hogeland, *Whiskey Rebellion*, 240; see also Edward Redmond, "Washington as Land Speculator," George Washington Papers, Library of Congress, accessed September 10, 2017, https://www.loc.gov/collections/george-washington-papers/articles-and-essays/george-washington-survey-and-mapmaker/washington-as-land-speculator/. Hogeland (138) says Washington's holdings across the Appalachians totaled sixty thousand acres.
37. Murray N. Rothbard, "The Whiskey Rebellion," *Free Market*, September 1994, accessed September 11, 2017, https://www.lewrockwell.com/1970/01/murray-n-rothbard/when-the-feds-first-attacked-the-americans/.
38. Alfred F. Young, *Liberty Tree: Ordinary People and the American Revolution* (New York: NYU Press, 2006), 70.
39. Lynd, *Intellectual Origins*, 84, 101.

CHAPTER THREE: JANE KLEEB—THE ACCIDENTAL ENVIRONMENTALIST

40. Karlo Barios Marcelo et al., "Young Voter Registration and Turnout Trends," The Center for Innovation and Research on Civic Learning and Engagement (Washington, DC: February 2008), 14.
41. Saul Elbein, "This Land is Our Land," *New York Times Magazine*, May 18, 2014, MM 34–38.
42. Robynn Tysver, "Newcomer is Thorn for State GOP," *Omaha World-Herald*, February 20, 2011, accessed January 25, 2018, http://boldnebraska.org/owh-profiles-kleeb-and-bold/.
43. Don Walton, "Kleeb Works to Transform Nebraska," *Lincoln Journal-Star*, December 19, 2009, accessed January 25, 2018, http://journalstar.com/news/local/govt-and-politics/kleeb-works-to-transform-nebraska/article_96f06a00-ec28-11de-8881-001cc4c002e0.html.
44. Richard Kirsch, *Fighting for Our Health: The Epic Battle To Make Health Care a Right in the United States* (Albany: Rockefeller Institute Press, 2012), 296.
45. ChangeThatWorksNE, "24/7 Project," YouTube, last updated July 24, 2011, accessed January 25, 2018, https://www.youtube.com/playlist?list=PL19BA00A5595B699B.
46. "Record of Decision and National Interest Determination: TransCanada Keystone Pipeline, L.P. Application for Presidential Permit," US State Department, November 3, 2015, accessed January 25, 2018, https://2012-keystonepipeline-xl.state.gov/documents/organization/249450.pdf.
47. Jeffrey A. Schneider, "Environmental Investigations: The Great Underground Sponge: Ogallala," accessed January 25, 2018, http://www.oswego.edu/~schneidr/CHE300/envinv/EnvInv12.html.
48. Steven Mufson, "Keystone XL pipeline may threaten aquifer that irrigates much of the central U.S.," *Washington Post*, August 6, 2012.
49. John Stansbury, "Analysis of Worst-Case Spills from the Proposed Keystone XL Pipeline," accessed January 25, 2018, https://www.motherjones.com/files/stansbury-worst-case-keystone-spills-report-summary-key-findings.pdf.
50. Charles P. Pierce, "This Is the Way Movements Are Supposed to Work," *Esquire*, June 22, 2016, accessed January 25, 2018, http://www.esquire.com/news-politics/politics/news/a46090/jane-kleeb-elected/.
51. Winona LaDuke, "The Black Snake Hears a Song: Declaring War on the Keystone Pipeline," *Indian Country Today*, November 21, 2014, accessed January 25, 2018, https://indiancountrymedianetwork.com/news/opinions/the-black-snake-hears-a-song-declaring-war-on-the-keystone-pipeline/.

CHAPTER FOUR: CARLOS RAMIREZ-ROSA—CHICAGO RULES

52. David Weigel, "The Socialist Movement Is Getting Younger and Turning Into a Left-Wing Force," *Chicago Tribune*, August 6, 2017, accessed November 30, 2017, http://www.chicagotribune.com/news/nationworld/politics/ct-socialist-movement-bernie-sanders-20170806-story.html.
53. Stuart Hall, "New Ethnicities," in *Stuart Hall: Critical Dialogues in Cultural Studies* (London: Routledge, 1996), 445.
54. Ryan Smith, "Beyond the 'Bernie Bro': Socialism's Diverse New Youth Brigade," *Chicago Reader*, August 23, 2017, accessed November 30, 2017, https://www.chicagoreader.com/chicago/socialism-democratic-socialists-of-america-convention-millennials-carlos-ramirez-rosa/Content?oid=29358708.

CHAPTER FIVE: WHEN THE REPUBLICANS WERE "WOKE"

55. Carl Sandburg, *Abraham Lincoln: The Prairie Years* (New York: Harcourt, Brace, 1926), 264. See also C. A. Tripp, *The Intimate World of Abraham Lincoln* (New York: Basic Books, 2006).
56. Sean Wilentz, "Constitutionally, Slavery Is No National Institution," *New York Times*, September 16, 2015, accessed January 3, 2018, https://www.nytimes.com/2015/09/16/opinion/constitutionally-slavery-is-no-national-institution.html; David Waldstreicher, "How the Constitution Was Indeed Pro-Slavery," *Atlantic*, September 19, 2015, accessed January 3, 2018, https://www.theatlantic.com/politics/archive/2015/09/how-the-constitution-was-indeed-pro-slavery/406288/.
57. Joan Brodsky Schur, "Eli Whitney's Patent for the Cotton Gin," National Archives, accessed January 3, 2018, https://www.archives.gov/education/lessons/cotton-gin-patent.
58. Roger L. Ransom, "The Economics of the Civil War," EH.net Encyclopedia, ed. Robert Whaples, August 24, 2001, http://eh.net/encyclopedia/the-economics-of-the-civil-war/. See also Ta-Nehisi Coates, "Slavery Made America: The Case for Reparations: A Narrative Biography," *Atlantic*, June 24, 2014, accessed January 4, 2018, https://www.theatlantic.com/business/archive/2014/06/slavery-made-america/373288/.
59. "'Cotton Is King': Speech by Sen. James Henry Hammond of South Carolina to the United States Senate, March 4, 1858," Causes of the Civil War, accessed January 4, 2018, http://civilwarcauses.org/King%20Cotton%20speech.htm.
60. Eric Foner, *The Fiery Trial: Abraham Lincoln and American Slavery* (New York: W. W. Norton & Company, 2010), 14.
61. John Quincy Adams, *The Memoirs of John Quincy Adams, Comprising Portions of His Diary from 1795–1848* (New York: Scribner, 1951), accessed January 4, 2018, http://college.cengage.com/history/ayers_primary_sources/adams_calhoun_discuss_compromise.htm.
62. Staughton Lynd, *Intellectual Origins*, 131. See also Paul Finkelman, "Garrison's Constitution: The Covenant with Death and How It Was Made," *Prologue Magazine* 32, no. 4 (Winter 2000), National Archives, accessed January 4, 2018, https://www.archives.gov/publications/prologue/2000/winter/garrisons-constitution-1.html.
63. Lynd, *Intellectual Origins*, 137, citing *Liberator*, June 21, 1839.
64. Horace Seldon, "The 'Woman Question' and Garrison," The Liberator Files, accessed January 4, 2018, http://theliberatorfiles.com/the-woman-question-and-garrison/.
65. Eric Foner, *Politics and Ideology in the Age of the Civil War* (New York, Oxford University Press, 1980), 68–69.
66. Foner, *Politics and Ideology*, 67.
67. Eric Foner, *Free Soil, Free Labor, Free Men: The Ideology of the Republican Party Before the Civil War* (New York: Oxford University Press, 1970), 73.
68. Karl Marx, *Capital: Volume One* (New York: Vintage, 1977), 142, n. 18. For a more thorough discussion of what Marx owed Franklin see John R. Aiken, "Benjamin Franklin, Karl Marx and the Labor Theory of Value," *Pennsylvania Magazine of History and Biography* 90, no. 3 (July 1966), 378–384.
69. "Historical Highlights: The House 'Gag Rule,'" History, Art & Archives, United States House of Representatives, accessed January 10, 2018, http://history.house.gov/Historical-Highlights/1800-1850/The-House-of-Representatives-instituted-the-%E2%80%9Cgag-rule%E2%80%9D/.
70. Wilentz, *The Rise of American Democracy*, 7; William Gienapp, *The Origins of the Republican Party, 1852–1856* (New York: Oxford University Press, 1987), 413.
71. "Cooper Union Address," Abraham Lincoln Online, accessed January 10, 2018, http://www.abrahamlincolnonline.org/lincoln/speeches/cooper.htm; "Speech at Springfield, Illinois," Collected Works of Abraham Lincoln, accessed January 10, 2018, https://

quod.lib.umich.edu/l/lincoln/lincoln2/1:438?rgn=div1;singlegenre=All;sort=occur;subview=detail;type=boolean;view=fulltext;q1=Equality+between+the+races.

72. "The Wide Awakes," *Hartford Courant*, accessed January 10, 2018, http://www.courant.com/opinion/op-ed/hc-wide-awake-hs-1950-530-odt1-jpg-20141114-photo.html.
73. Jon Grinspan, "Young Men for War: The Wide Awakes and Lincoln's 1860 Presidential Campaign," *Journal of American History* 96, no. 2 (September 2009), 357–378.
74. Wilentz, *The Rise of American Democracy*, 704.
75. Foner, *Politics and Ideology*, 10, 19.
76. Ulysses S. Grant, *Memoirs and Selected Letters* (New York: Library of America, 1990), 766.
77. W. E. Burghardt Du Bois, *Black Reconstruction* (New York: Harcourt Brace, 1935), 700.
78. James M. McPherson, *What They Fought For: 1861–1865* (New York: Anchor Books, 1995), 32, 41.
79. James M. McPherson, *For Cause and Comrades: Why Men Fought in the Civil War* (New York: Oxford University Press, 1997).
80. Foner, *Free Soil*, 2.
81. David Olusoga, "The History of British Slave Ownership Has Been Buried," *Guardian*, July 11, 2015, accessed January 10, 2018, https://www.theguardian.com/world/2015/jul/12/british-history-slavery-buried-scale-revealed.
82. "Legacy of the Civil War," National Park Service, accessed July 1, 2018, https://www.nps.gov/features/waso/cw150th/reflections/legacy/page2.html.
83. Nancy Cohen, *The Reconstruction of American Liberalism: 1865–1914* (Chapel Hill: University of North Carolina Press, 2002), 27.
84. "Address of the International Working Men's Association to Abraham Lincoln, President of the United States of America," Marx & Engels Internet Archive, accessed January 10, 2018, https://www.marxists.org/archive/marx/iwma/documents/1864/lincoln-letter.htm. Robin Blackburn, "Lincoln and Marx," *Jacobin*, August 28, 2012, is a fascinating survey of the relationship between the two men.
85. Matthew Josephson, *The Robber Barons* (New York: Harcourt Brace: 1934), 52.
86. Sam Pizzigati, *The Rich Don't Always Win* (New York: Seven Stories Press, 2012), 19.
87. McPherson, *For Cause and Comrades*, 126.
88. Karl Marx, "Revelations Concerning the Communist Trial in Cologne," afterword to the 1875 edition. See also Al Benson Jr. and Walter Donald Kennedy, *Lincoln's Marxists* (Gretna, LA: Pelican Publishing Company, 2011), for a hostile view.
89. David Montgomery, *Beyond Equality* (New York: Knopf Doubleday Publishing Group, 1981), 1,930–1,935, Kindle.
90. McPherson, *For Cause and Comrades*, 128.
91. "The Great Festival," *Nation*, July 6, 1865, 4.
92. Montgomery, *Beyond Equality*, 1,118–1,121, Kindle.
93. Montgomery, *Beyond Equality*, 1,378–1,379, Kindle, citing Thomas F. Woodley, *Great Leveler: The Life of Thaddeus Stevens* (New York, 1937), 375.
94. Montgomery, *Beyond Equality*, 1,455–1,458, Kindle.
95. Cohen, *The Reconstruction of American Liberalism*, 29.
96. Foner, *Politics and Ideology*, 134.
97. Foner, *Politics and Ideology*, 144, citing *New York Times*, July 9, 1867.
98. Foner, *Politics and Ideology*, 108–109, 111.
99. Robin Blackburn, *An Unfinished Revolution: Karl Marx and Abraham Lincoln* (London: Verso, 2011), 77; Timothy Messer-Kruse, *The Yankee International: Marxism and the American Reform Tradition, 1848–1876* (Chapel Hill: University of North Carolina Press, 1998), 194–195.
100. Marx, *Capital*, 414.

101. Montgomery, *Beyond Equality*, 1,855–1,858, Kindle.
102. Montgomery, *Beyond Equality*, 4,667, Kindle.
103. Cohen, *The Reconstruction of American Liberalism*, 39.
104. E. L. Godkin, "How Protection Affects Labor," *Nation*, May 25, 1871, 352–353.
105. Wendell Phillips, "The Foundation of the Labor Movement," September 4, 1871, accessed January 12, 2018, http://www.deleonism.org/text/hd000008.htm.
106. Godkin, "The Problem at the South," *Nation*, March 23, 1871, 192–193.
107. Cohen, *The Reconstruction of American Liberalism*, 133, citing Godkin, "The Tilden Commission," *Nation*, May 22, 1877, 171–172.
108. "The South and the Election," *Nation*, November 14, 1872, 308.
109. "The Third Term," *Nation*, October 8, 1874, 230–231.
110. Montgomery, *Beyond Equality*, 7,286–7,291, Kindle.
111. Foner, *Politics and Ideology*, 126.

CHAPTER SIX: WALEED SHAHID AND CORBIN TRENT—A TEA PARTY OF THE LEFT?

112. Clayborne Carson, ed., et al., *The Papers of Martin Luther King, Jr. Volume V: Threshold of a New Decade, January 1959–December 1960* (Berkeley: University of California Press, 2005), accessed February 1, 2018, https://kinginstitute.stanford.edu/king-papers/documents/cynthia-and-julius-alexander.
113. "FAQs," Brand New Congress, accessed February 1, 2018, http://brandnewcongress.org/faqs/.
114. D. D. Guttenplan, "Weapons of Mass Distraction," *Nation*, February 27, 2017, accessed February 1, 2018, https://www.thenation.com/article/weapons-of-mass-distraction/.
115. Becky Bond, interview by D. D. Guttenplan, Chicago, June 18, 2016.
116. Nick Pinto, "17 Arrested Protesting Senator Chuck Schumer and 'the Party of Wall Street,'" *Village Voice*, November 15, 2016, accessed February 1, 2018, https://www.villagevoice.com/2016/11/15/17-arrested-protesting-senator-chuck-schumer-and-the-party-of-wall-street/.
117. A. P. Joyce, "Is the Democratic Congressional Campaign Committee Stifling Dissent Within the Party?," *Mic*, December 7, 2017, accessed February 1, 2018, https://mic.com/articles/186648/is-the-democratic-congressional-campaign-committee-stifling-dissent-within-the-party.

CHAPTER SEVEN: CHOKWE ANTAR LUMUMBA—BLACK POWER MATTERS

118. Bellhaven Pot Hole Gardener (@belhavenpotholegardener), Facebook, https://www.facebook.com/belhavenpotholegardener?fref=ts.
119. "City of Jackson—Mississippi Clean Water Act Settlement," United States Environmental Protection Agency, November 21, 2012, https://www.epa.gov/enforcement/city-jackson-mississippi-clean-water-act-settlement#violations; Anthony Warren, "New Deal?," *Northside Sun*, https://www.northsidesun.com/front-page-slideshow-breaking-news/new-deal#sthash.ctYIMmmM.dpbs.
120. Charles M. Payne, *I've Got the Light of Freedom: The Organizing Tradition and the Mississippi Freedom Struggle* (Berkeley: University of California Press, 2007), 17.
121. Carole Cannon, "Black Monday: Mississippi's Ugly Response to 'Brown v. Board' Decision," *Jackson Free Press*, May 12, 2004, http://www.jacksonfreepress.com/news/2004/may/12/black-monday/.

122. Robert Luckett, "From Council Schools to Today's Fight for Public Ed," *Jackson Free Press*, February 15, 2017, http://www.jacksonfreepress.com/news/2017/feb/15/council-schools-todays-fight-public-ed/.
123. Arielle Dreher, "D.C.-Based PAC, Outside Money Funded Initiative 42's Demise," *Jackson Free Press*, December 9, 2015, http://www.jacksonfreepress.com/news/2015/dec/09/dc-based-pac-outside-money-funded-initiative-42s-d/.
124. Katie Gilbert, "The Socialist Experiment," *Oxford American*, September 5, 2017, http://www.oxfordamerican.org/item/1296-the-socialist-experiment.
125. "The Jackson Plan: A Struggle for Self-Determination, Participatory Democracy, and Economic Justice," Malcolm X Grassroots Movement, accessed November 5, 2017, https://mxgm.org/2012/07/07/the-jackson-plan-a-struggle-for-self-determination-participatory-democracy-and-economic-justice/.
126. Payne, *I've Got the Light of Freedom*, xvi.
127. Charles E. Cobb, *This Nonviolent Stuff'll Get You Killed: How Guns Made the Civil Rights Movement Possible* (Durham, NC: Duke University Press, 2015). See also Akinyele Omowale Umoja, *We Will Shoot Back: Armed Resistance in the Mississippi Freedom Movement* (New York: NYU Press, 2013).
128. Watkins v. Mabus, 771 F. Supp. 789 (S.D. Miss. 1991), http://legis.wisconsin.gov/senate/16/miller/files/watkins%20v.%20mabus.pdf.

CHAPTER EIGHT: WHATEVER HAPPENED TO THE ROOSEVELT REPUBLIC?

129. Nate Silver, "Donald Trump's Convention Is Flirting With Disaster," *FiveThirtyEight*, July 21, 2016, accessed February 15, 2018, http://fivethirtyeight.com/features/trumps-convention-is-flirting-with-disaster/.
130. D. D. Guttenplan, "Trouble in Ohio," *Nation*, October 31, 2016, 18–21. See also D. D. Guttenplan, "In Ohio, Trump Rallies the Deplorables," September 15, 2016, accessed February 15, 2018, https://www.thenation.com/article/in-ohio-trump-rallies-the-deplorables/.
131. Tessa Berenson, "Read Trump's Speech on Jobs and the Economy," *Time*, September 15, 2016, accessed February 15, 2018, http://time.com/4495507/donald-trump-economy-speech-transcript/.
132. Bruce Springsteen, "Youngstown," *The Ghost of Tom Joad*, lyrics in Howard Zinn and Anthony Arnove, eds., *Voices of a People's History of the United States* (New York: Seven Stories Press, 2014), 570–571.
133. Anthony J. Badger, *FDR: The First 100 Days* (New York: Hill and Wang, 2007).
134. William F. Holmes, "Colored Farmers' Alliance," Texas State Historical Association, accessed July 2, 2018, https://tshaonline.org/handbook/online/articles/aac01.
135. Arthur M. Schlesinger, *The Age of Roosevelt: The Crisis of the Old Order, 1919–1933* (London: Heinemann, 1957), 19.
136. Lawrence Goodwyn, *The Populist Moment: A Short History of the Agrarian Revolt in America* (Oxford: Oxford University Press, 1978), 167. Goodwyn's account remains essential reading for anyone wishing to understand the Populists, or Populism more generally.
137. "*Speech delivered in Portland, Maine, March 28, 1918*," Theodore Roosevelt Collection, MS Am 1834 (1085), Harvard College Library, http://www.theodorerooseveltcenter.org/Research/Digital-Library/Record.aspx?libID=o286434.
138. Goodwyn, *Populist Moment*, xvii, xix, 33.
139. Schlesinger, *Age of Roosevelt*, 130–131.

140. Matthew Josephson in League of Professional Groups for Foster and Ford, *Culture and the Crisis: An Open Letter to the Writers, Artists, Teachers, Physicians, Engineers, Scientists and Other Professional Workers of America* (New York: Workers Library Publishers, 1932), 17.
141. Norman Thomas and Paul Blanshard, *What's the Matter With New York?* (New York: Macmillan, 1932), 3.
142. Landon R. Y. Storrs, *The Second Red Scare and the Unmaking of the New Deal Left* (Princeton: Princeton University Press, 2013), 17.
143. Thomas Ferguson, "Industrial Conflict and the Coming of the New Deal: The Triumph of Multinational Liberalism in America" in Steve Fraser and Gary Gerstle, eds., *The Rise and Fall of the New Deal Order* (Princeton: Princeton University Press, 1989), 7–9.
144. Ferguson, "Industrial Conflict," 23. See also Michael J. Webber, *New Deal Fat Cats: Business, Labor, and Campaign Finance in the 1936 Presidential Election* (New York: Fordham University Press, 2006), 48–68.
145. David J. O'Brien, *American Catholics and Social Reform: The New Deal Years* (Oxford: Oxford University Press, 1968), 52.
146. "Thunder on the Left," *New York Evening Post*, November 30, 1934, 8.
147. Barry T. Hirsch and David A. Macpherson, "Union Membership and Coverage Database from the Current Population Survey: Note," *Industrial and Labor Relations Review* 56, no. 2 (January 2003), 349–354, http://www.trinity.edu/bhirsch/unionstats/UnionStats.pdf.
148. Chip Gibbons, "The Trial(s) of Harry Bridges," *Jacobin*, September 15, 2016, accessed February 15, 2018, https://www.jacobinmag.com/2016/09/harry-bridges-longshore-strike-deportation-communist-party.
149. Irving Howe, *Socialism and America* (New York: Harcourt, 1985), 60–61.
150. Meridel Le Sueur, "I Was Marching," in *Ripening: Collected Work 1927-1980* (Old Westbury: Feminist Press, 1982) pp. 158, 162.
151. Daniel Geary, "Carey McWilliams and Antifascism, 1934–1943," *Journal of American History* 90, no. 3 (2003).
152. D. D. Guttenplan, *American Radical: The Life and Times of I. F. Stone* (New York: Farrar, Straus and Giroux, 2009) 81, 119, 143.
153. Anthony Badger, *The New Deal: The Depression Years 1933–1940* (Chicago: Ivan R. Dee, 2002), 130.
154. Robert S. McElvaine, *The Great Depression: America 1929–1941* (New York: Times Books, 1984), 294.
155 Mike Davis, *Prisoners of the American Dream* (London: Verso, 1986), 60–61; Mardges Bacon, "The Federation of Architects, Engineers, Chemists and Technicians (FAECT): The Politics and Social Practice of Labor," *Journal of the Society of Architectural Historians* 76, no. 4 (December 2017), 454–463.
156. Spencer Weber Waller, *Thurman Arnold: A Biography* (New York: NYU Press, 2005), 92–94; Gary L. Reback, *Free the Market!: Why Only Government Can Keep the Marketplace Competitive* (New York: Portfolio, 2009), 22–24.
157. Joseph J. Thorndike, "New Deal Taxes: Four Things Everyone Should Know," Tax History Project, November 20, 2008, accessed February 15, 2018, http://www.taxhistory.org/thp/readings.nsf/ArtWeb/1AEBAA68B74ABB91852575oC0046BCAF?OpenDocument.
158. Anthony Badger, *The New Deal: The Depression Years 1933–1940* (Chicago: Ivan R. Dee, 2002), 132–133; Dennis C. Dickerson, *Out of the Crucible: Black Steel Workers in Western Pennsylvania, 1875–1980* (Albany: State University of New York Press, 1986), 140.
159. Maurice Isserman, *Which Side Were You On?: The American Communist Party During the Second World War* (Middletown, CT: Wesleyan University Press, 1982), 9, 14.
160. Davis, *Prisoners of the American Dream*, 60.

161. Storrs, *The Second Red Scare*, 17.
162. Michael Denning, *The Cultural Front* (London: Verso, 1997), 310–319.
163. Storrs, *The Second Red Scare*, 150–151.
164. I. F. Stone, "Blackmailer's Peace," *Nation*, October 14, 1939, 401.
165. "U.S. Federal Individual Income Tax Rates History, 1862-2013 (Nominal and Inflation-Adjusted Brackets)," Tax Foundation, October 17, 2013, accessed February 15, 2018, https://taxfoundation.org/us-federal-individual-income-tax-rates-history-1913-2013-nominal-and-inflation-adjusted-brackets/.
166. Emmanuel Saez and Gabriel Zucman, "Wealth Inequality in the United States Since 1913," October 2014, accessed March 15, 2018, http://gabriel-zucman.eu/files/SaezZucman2014Slides.pdf.
167. Nelson Lichtenstein, "From Corporatism to Collective Bargaining: Organized Labor and the Eclipse of Social Democracy in the Postwar Era" in Fraser and Gerstle, eds., *The Rise and Fall of the New Deal Order*, 125.
168. Nelson Lichtenstein, *Labor's War at Home: The CIO in World War Two* (Philadelphia: Temple University Press, 1982), 41, 84–87.
169. Guttenplan, *American Radical*, 161–164.
170. Lichtenstein, "From Corporatism to Collective Bargaining," 135.
171. Harold Preece, "The South Stirs," *Crisis* 48, no. 10 (October 1941), 317–322.
172. Lichtenstein, "From Corporatism to Collective Bargaining," 137.
173. Nell Irving Painter, *The Narrative of Hosea Hudson* (Cambridge: Harvard University Press, 1979), 339–340.
174. J. H. O'Dell, "Operation Dixie: Notes on a Promise Abandoned," *Labor Notes*, April 1, 2005. See also D. D. Guttenplan, "Who Is Jack O'Dell?," *Nation*, August 11, 2014.
175. Susan M. Hartmann, *The Home Front and Beyond: American Women in the 1940s* (Boston: Twayne, 1982), 86.
176. Dorothy Sue Cobble, *The Other Women's Movement: Workplace Justice and Social Rights in Modern America* (Princeton: Princeton University Press, 2004).
177. Sam Pizzigati, *The Rich Don't Always Win*, 56.
178. Storrs, *The Second Red Scare*, 14–15.
179. Gerald Mayer, "Union Membership Trends in the United States" (Washington, DC: Congressional Research Service, 2004); R. Alton Lee, *Truman and Taft-Hartley*, (Lexington: University of Kentucky Press, 1966), 18.
180. Alan Brinkley, "The New Deal and the Idea of the State," in Fraser and Gerstle, eds., *The Rise and Fall of the New Deal Order*, 107.
181. Lichtenstein, "From Corporatism to Collective Bargaining," 127.
182. Jane Pacht Brickman, " 'Medical McCarthyism': The Physicians Forum and the Cold War," *The Journal Of The History Of Medicine And Allied Sciences* (July 1994), pp. 380-415.
183. Lichtenstein, "From Corporatism to Collective Bargaining," 143–145.
184. Matthew N. Green, *The Speaker of the House: A Study in Leadership* (New Haven: Yale University Press, 2010), 92; Thomas Ferguson and Joel Rogers: *Right Turn: The Decline of the Democrats and the Future of American Politics* (New York: Hill and Wang, 1986), 51–60.
185. Storrs, *The Second Red Scare*, 205.
186. Benjamin Fordham, "Domestic Politics, International Pressure, and Policy Change: The Case of NSC 68," *Journal of Conflict Studies* (Spring 1997).
187. Storrs, *The Second Red Scare*, 233.
188. Robert J. Norrell, *The House I Live In: Race in the American Century* (Oxford: Oxford University Press, 2006), 146.
189. Mary L. Dudziak, *Cold War Civil Rights: Race and the Image of American Democracy* (Princeton: Princeton University Press, 2011), 9–13. For one example of what was lost, see Victor S. Navasky, *The O'Dell File* (Amazon Digital Services, 2014).

190. Dudziak, *Cold War Civil Rights*, xiv.
191. Storrs, *The Second Red Scare*, 262–264.
192. Simon Kuznets, "Economic Growth And Income Inequality," *The American Economic Review* (March 1955), 4.
193. Pizzigati, *The Rich Don't Always Win*, 2.
194. Claudia Goldin, Robert Margo, "The Great Compression: The Wage Structure in the United States at Mid-Century," *Quarterly Journal of Economics* CVII (February 1992), 1–34.
195. Saez and Zucman, "Wealth Inequality."
196. Dan Mangan, "Medicare, Medicaid Popularity High: Kaiser," CNBC, July 17, 2015, accessed March 15, 2018, https://www.cnbc.com/2015/07/16/medicare-medicaid-popularity-high-ahead-of-birthday.html.
197. Pizzigati, *The Rich Don't Always Win*, 272.
198. George Packer, *The Unwinding: An Inner History of the New America* (London: Faber & Faber, 2013), 3. For a fuller account of my differences with Packer, see D. D. Guttenplan, "New Deal to Raw Deal," *Literary Review* (September 2013).

CHAPTER NINE: ZEPHYR TEACHOUT—CORRUPTION AND ITS DISCONTENTS

199. Zephyr Teachout, "Organizing for America Will, and Should, Fail," *techPresident*, January 30, 2009, accessed April 2, 2018, http://techpresident.com/blog-entry/organizing-america-will-and-should-fail.
200. Zephyr Teachout, "Legalism and Devolution of Power in the Public Sphere: Reflections on Occupy Wall Street," *Fordham Urban Law Journal* (March 2016), 1,867–1,893.
201. Zephyr Teachout, "Bernie Sanders for President: 10 Reasons," *Huffington Post*, December 8, 2015, accessed April 2, 2018, https://www.huffingtonpost.com/zephyr-teachout/bernie-sanders-for-presid_b_8752058.html.
202. Zack Exley, "An Organizer's View of the Internet Campaign," in Zephyr Teachout and Thomas Streeter, eds., *Mousepads, Shoe Leather and Hope: Lessons from the Howard Dean Campaign* (New York: Taylor and Francis, 2008), 212–220.
203. Becky Bond and Zack Exley, *Rules for Revolutionaries: How Big Organizing Can Change Everything* (White River Junction, VT: Chelsea Green, 2016).
204. Zephyr Teachout and Lina Khan, "Market Structure and Political Law: A Taxonomy of Power," *Duke Journal of Constitutional Law and Public Policy* (2014), 37–74.
205. Dominic Rushe, "Google-Funded Thinktank Fired Scholar Over Criticism of Tech Firm," *Guardian*, August 30, 2017, accessed April 1, 2018, https://www.theguardian.com/technology/2017/aug/30/new-america-foundation-google-funding-firings.
206. Zephyr Teachout, *Corruption in America* (Cambridge: Harvard University Press, 2014), 35.
207. George Thayer, *Who Shakes the Money Tree?: American Campaign Financing Practices from 1789 to the Present* (New York: Simon and Schuster, 1974), 45–47.
208. Robert Sherrill, "Bribes," *Grand Street* 4, no. 4 (Summer 1985), 140–153.
209. Teachout, *Corruption in America*, 11, 28.
210. FEC v. NCPAC, 470 U.S. 480, 497 (1985).
211. Citizens United v. Federal Election Commission, 558 U.S. 310 (2010).
212. McCutcheon v. Federal Election Commission, 134 S. Ct. 1434 (2014).
213. McDonnell v. United States, 136 S. Ct. 2355 (2016).

INDEX

ABOUT THE AUTHOR

As the lead *Nation* election correspondent throughout the 2015–16 election season, D. D. GUTTENPLAN set the highest standard for election reporting, traveling across the country throughout the primary season, present at the major speeches and rallies of all the candidates, offering deep as well as topical coverage in dozens of articles including many that graced the *Nation* magazine's cover. Guttenplan's first book, *The Holocaust on Trial*, was praised by Ian Buruma of the *New Yorker* as "a mixture of superb reportage and serious reflection." His biography of I. F. Stone, *American Radical: The Life and Times of I .F. Stone*, won the Sperber Prize for Biography. Guttenplan wrote and presented two radio documentaries for the BBC, *Guns: An American Love Affair*, and *War, Lies and Audiotape*, about the Gulf of Tonkin incident. He also produced an acclaimed film, *Edward Said: The Last Interview*. A former editor at *Vanity Fair*, senior editor at the *Village Voice*, and media columnist at *New York Newsday*, Guttenplan's reporting on the Happy Land Social Club fire in the Bronx won a Page One Award from the New York Newspaper Guild. He was a Pulitzer Prize finalist for his investigative reporting on New York City's fire code. He lives in Vermont in the US and in London, England.

ABOUT SEVEN STORIES PRESS

SEVEN STORIES PRESS is an independent book publisher based in New York City. We publish works of the imagination by such writers as Nelson Algren, Russell Banks, Octavia E. Butler, Ani DiFranco, Assia Djebar, Ariel Dorfman, Coco Fusco, Barry Gifford, Martha Long, Luis Negrón, Peter Plate, Hwang Sok-yong, Lee Stringer, and Kurt Vonnegut, to name a few, together with political titles by voices of conscience, including Subhankar Banerjee, the Boston Women's Health Collective, Noam Chomsky, Angela Y. Davis, Human Rights Watch, Derrick Jensen, Ralph Nader, Loretta Napoleoni, Gary Null, Greg Palast, Project Censored, Barbara Seaman, Alice Walker, Gary Webb, and Howard Zinn, among many others. Seven Stories Press believes publishers have a special responsibility to defend free speech and human rights, and to celebrate the gifts of the human imagination, wherever we can. In 2012 we launched Triangle Square books for young readers with strong social justice and narrative components, telling personal stories of courage and commitment. For additional information, visit www.sevenstories.com.